THE HILL

Craig Paterson,
General Editor, Viewforth Classics

Other Viewforth Titles:
E. F. Benson, *David Blaize*. ISBN: 1453763104
E. F. Benson, *David of King's*. ISBN: 1453802819
Arnold Lunn, *The Harrovians*. ISBN: 1453809481
P. G. Wodehouse, *Tales of St Austin's*. ISBN: 1461086507

THE HILL
AN ENGLISH PUBLIC SCHOOL STORY

H. A. Vachell

1st Viewforth Classics Edition

Los Angeles, California
2011

Published by Viewforth Press, Los Angeles, California, 2011.
1st Viewforth Classics edition.
Cover, layout and notes © 2011 by Viewforth Press. All rights
reserved. Printed and distributed by createspace.com.

LCCN: 2011931031

ISBN: 1463535163
EAN-13: 9781463535162

TO

GEORGE W. E. RUSSELL

I dedicate this Romance of Friendship to you with the sincerest pleasure and affection. You were the first to suggest that I should write a book about contemporary life at Harrow; you gave me the principal idea; you have furnished me with notes innumerable; you have revised every page of the manuscript; and you are a peculiarly keen Harrovian.

In making this public declaration of my obligations to you, I take the opportunity of stating that the characters in "The Hill," whether masters or boys, are not portraits, although they may be called, truthfully enough, composite photographs; and that the episodes of Drinking and Gambling are founded on isolated incidents, not on habitual practices. Moreover, in attempting to reproduce the curious admixture of "strenuousness and sentiment—your own phrase—which animates so vitally Harrow life, I have been obliged to select the less common types of Harrovian. Only the elect are capable of such friendship as John Verney entertained for Henry Desmond; and few boys, happily, are possessed of such powers as Scaife is shown to exercise. But that there are such boys as Verney and Scaife, nobody knows better than yourself.

HORACE ANNESLEY VACHELL.

BEECHWOOD,
February 22, 1905.

Chapter One

The Manor

Five hundred faces, and all so strange!
  Life in front of me—home behind,
  I felt like a waif before the wind
Tossed on an ocean of shock and change.

Chorus:
Yet the time may come, as the years go by,
  When your heart will thrill
  At the thought of the Hill,
And the day that you came so strange and shy.

THE train slid slowly out of Harrow station.

Five minutes before, a man and a boy had been walking up and down the long platform. The boy wondered why the man, his uncle, was so strangely silent. Then, suddenly, the elder John Verney had placed his hands upon the shoulders of the younger John, looking down into eyes as grey and as steady as his own.

"You'll find plenty of fellows abusing Harrow," he said quietly; "but take it from me, that the fault lies not in Harrow, but in them. Such boys, as a rule, do not come out of the top drawer. Don't look so solemn. You're about to take a header into a big river. In it are rocks and rapids; but you know how to swim, and after the first plunge you'll enjoy it, as I did, amazingly."

"Ra—ther," said John.

In the New Forest, where John had spent most of his life at his uncle's place of Verney Boscobel, this uncle, his dead father's only brother, was worshipped as a hero. Indeed he filled so large a space in the boy's imagination, that others were cramped for room. John Verney in India, in Burmah, in Africa (he took continents in his stride), moved colossal. And when uncle and nephew met, behold, the great traveller stood not much taller than John himself! That first moment, the instant shattering of a precious delusion, held anguish. But now, as the train whirled away the silent, thin, little man, he began to expand again. John saw him scaling heights, cutting a path through impenetrable forests, wading across dismal swamps, an ever-moving figure, seeking the hitherto unknowable and irreclaimable, introducing order where chaos reigned supreme, a world-famous pioneer.

How good to think that John Verney was *his* uncle, blood of his blood, his, his, his—for all time!

And, long ago, John, senior, had come to Harrow; had felt what John, junior, felt to the core—the dull, grinding wrench of separation, the sense, not yet to be analysed by a boy, of standing alone upon the edge of a river, indeed, into which he must plunge headlong in a few minutes. Well, Uncle John had taken his "header" with a stout heart—who dared to doubt that? Surely he had not waited, shivering and hesitating, at the jumping-off place. The train was now out of sight. John slipped the uncle's tip into his purse, and walked out of the station and on to the road beyond, the road which led to the top of the Hill.

The Hill.

Presently, the boy reached some iron palings and a wicket-gate. His uncle had pointed out this gate and the steep path beyond which led to the top of the Hill, to the churchyard, to the Peachey tomb on which Byron dreamed,* to the High Street—and to the Manor. It was pleasant to remember that he was going to board at the Manor, with its traditions, its triumphs, its record. In his

---

* Byron, writing to John Murray, May 26, 1822, and giving directions for the burial of poor little Allegra's body, says—"I wish it to be buried in Harrow Church. There is a spot in the churchyard, near the footpath, on the brow of the hill looking towards Windsor, and a tomb under a large tree (bearing the name of Peachie, or Peachey), where I used to sit for hours and hours as a boy; this was ray favourite spot; but, as I wish to erect a tablet to her memory, the body had better be deposited in the church." See also "Lines written beneath an elm in the churchyard of Harrow," in *Hours of Idleness*.

uncle's day the Manor ranked first among the boarding-houses. Not a doubt disturbed John's conviction that it ranked first still.

The boy stared upward with a keen gaze. Had the mother seen her son at that moment, she might have discerned a subtle likeness between uncle and nephew, not the likeness of the flesh, but of the spirit.

September rains, followed by a day of warm sunshine, had lured from the earth a soft haze which obscured the big fields at the foot of the Hill. John could make out fences, poplars, elms, Scotch firs, and spectral houses. But, above, everything was clear. The school-buildings, such as he could see, stood out boldly against a cloudless sky, and above these soared the spire of Harrow Church, pointing an inexorable finger upwards.

Afterwards this spot became dear to John Verney, because here, where mists were chill and blinding, he had been impelled to leave the broad high-road and take a path which led into a shadowy future. In obedience to an impulse stronger than himself he had taken the short cut to what awaited him.

For a few minutes he stood outside the palings, trying to choke down an abominable lump in his throat. This was not his first visit to Harrow. At the end of the previous term, he had ascended the Hill to pass the entrance examination. A master from his preparatory school accompanied him, an Etonian, who had stared rather superciliously—so John thought—at buildings less venerable than those which Henry VI. Raised near Windsor. John, who had perceptions, was elusively conscious that his companion, too much of a gentleman to give his thoughts words, might be contrasting a yeoman's work with a king's; and when the Etonian, gazing across the plains below to where Windsor lay, a soft shadow upon the horizon, said abruptly, "I wish Eton had been built upon a hill," John replied effusively; "Oh, sir, it *is* decent of you to say that." The examination, however, distracted his attention from all things save the papers. To his delight he found these easy, and, as soon as he left the examination-room, he was popped into a cab and taken back to town. Coming down the flight of steps, he had seen a few boys hurrying up or down the road. At these the Etonian cocked a twinkling eye.

"Queer kit you Harrow boys wear," he said.

John, inordinately grateful at this recognition of himself as an Harrovian, forgave the gibe. It had struck him, also, that the shallow straw hat, the swallow-tail coat, did look queer, but he regarded them reverently as the uniform of a crack corps.

To-day, standing by the iron palings, John reviewed the events of the last hour. The view was blurred by unshed tears. His uncle and he had driven together to the Manor. Here, the explorer had exercised his peculiar personal magnetism upon the house-master, a tall, burly man of truculent aspect and speech. John realized proudly that his uncle was the bigger of the two, and that the giant acknowledged, perhaps grudgingly, the dwarf's superiority, The talk, short enough, had wandered into Darkest Africa. His uncle, as usual, said little, replying almost in monosyllables to the questions of his host; but John junior told himself exultantly that it was not necessary for Uncle John to talk; the wide world knew what he had done.

Then his house-master, Rutford, had told John where to buy his first straw hat.

"You can get one without an order at the beginning of each term," said he, in a thick, rasping voice. "But you must ask me for an order if you want a second."

Then he had shown John his room, to be shared with two other boys, and had told him the hour of lock-up. And then, after tea, came the walk down the hill, the tip, the firm grasp of the sinewy hand, and a final—"God bless you."

Coming to the end of these reflections, confronted by the inexorable future, and the necessity, no less inexorable, of stepping into it, John passed through the gate. His heart fluttered furiously, and the lump in the throat swelled inconveniently. John, however, had provided himself with a "cure-all." Plunging his hand into his pocket, he pulled out a cartridge, an unused twenty-bore gun cartridge. Looking at this, John smiled. When he smiled he became good-looking. The face, too long, plain, but full of sense and humour, rounded itself into the gracious curves of youth; the serious grey eyes sparkled; the lips, too firmly compressed, parted, revealing admirable teeth, small and squarely set; into the cheeks, brown rather than pink, flowed a warm stream of colour.

The cartridge stood for so much. Only a week before, Uncle John, on his arrival from Manchuria, had handed his nephew a small leather case and a key. The case held a double-barrelled, hammerless, ejector, twenty-bore gun, with a great name upon its polished blue barrels.

The sight of the cartridge justified John's expectations. He put it back into his pocket, and strode forward and upward.

Close to the School Chapel, John remarked a curly-headed young gentleman of wonderfully prepossessing appearance, from whom emanated an air, an atmosphere, of genial enjoyment which diffused itself. The bricks of the school-buildings seemed redder and warmer, as if they were basking in this sunny smile. The youth was smiling now, smiling—at John. For several hours John had been miserably aware that surprises awaited him, but not smiles. He knew no Harrovians; at his school, a small one, his fellows were labelled Winchester, Eton, Wellington; none, curiously enough, Harrow. And already, he had passed half a dozen boys, the first-comers, some strangers, like himself, and in each face he had read indifference. Not one had taken the trouble to say, "Hullo! Who are you?" after the rough and ready fashion of the private school.

And now this smiling, fascinating person was actually about to address him, and in the old familiar style——

"Hullo!"

"Hullo!"

"I met your governor the other day."

"Did you?" John replied. His father had died when John was seven.

Obviously, a blunder in identity had created this genial smile. John wished that his father had not died.

"Yes," pursued the smiling one, "I met him—partridge-shooting at home—and he asked me to be on the lookout for you. It's queer you should turn up at once, isn't it?"

"Yes," said John.

"Your governor looked awfully fit."

"Did he?" Then John added solemnly, "My governor died when I was a kid."

The other gasped; then he threw back his curly head and laughed.

"I say, I beg your pardon. I didn't mean to laugh. If you're not Hardacre, who are you?"

"Verney. I've just come."

"Verney? That's a great Harrow name. Are you any relation to the explorer?"

"Nephew," said John, blushing.

"Ah—you ought to have been here last Speecher.* We cheered him, I can tell you. And the song was sung: the one with his name in it."

"Yes," said John. Then he added nervously, "All the same, I don't know a soul at Harrow."

Desmond smiled. The smile assured John that his name would secure him a cordial welcome. Desmond added abruptly, "My name, Desmond, is a Harrow name. My father, my grandfather, my uncles, and three brothers were here. It does make a difference. What's your house?"

"The Manor," said John, proudly.

"Dirty Dick's!" Then, seeing consternation writ large upon John's face, he added quickly, "We call *him* Dirty Dick, you know; but the house is—er—one of the oldest and biggest—er—houses." He continued hurriedly: "I'm going into Damer's next term. Damer's is always chock-a-block, you know."

"Why is Rutford called 'Dirty Dick'?" John asked nervously. "He doesn't *look* dirty."

––––––––––––––––––––

* "Speecher"—*i.e.* Speech Day. At Harrow "er" is a favourite termination of many substantives. "Harder," for hard-ball racquets, "Footer," "Ducker," etc.

"Oh, we've licked him into a sort of shape," said Desmond. "I *believe* he toshes now—once a month, or so."

"Toshes?"

"Tubs, you know. We call a tub a 'tosh.' When Dirty Dick came here he was unclean. He told his form—oh! the cheek of it!—that in his filthy mind one bath a week was plenty," unconsciously the boy mimicked the thick, rasping tones—"two, luxury, and three—superfluity! After that he was called Dirty Dick. There's another story. They say that years ago he went to a Turkish bath, and after a rare good scraping the man who was scraping him—nasty job that!—found something which Dirty Dick recognized as a beastly flannel shirt he had lost when he was at the 'Varsity. But only the Fourth Form boys swallow *that*. Hullo! There's a pal of mine. See you again."

He ran off gaily. John walked to the shop where straw hats were sold. Here he met other new boys, who regarded him curiously, but said nothing. John put on his hat, and gave Rutford's name to the young man who waited on him. He had an absurd feeling that the young man would say, "Oh yes—Dirty Dick's!" One very nice-looking pink-cheeked boy said to another boy that he was at Damer's. John could have sworn that the hatter's assistant regarded the pink youth with increased deference.

Why had Uncle John sent him to Dirty Dick's? He hurried out of the shop, fuming. Then he remembered the hammerless gun. After all, the Manor had been *the* house once, and it might be *the* house again.

By this time the boys were arriving. Groups were forming. Snatches of chatter reached John's ears. "Yes, I shot a stag, a nine-pointer. My governor is going to have it set up for me—— What? Walked up your grouse with dogs! We drive ours—— I had some ripping cricket, made a century in one match—— By Jove! Did you really?——"

John passed on. These were "bloods," tremendous swells, grown men with a titillating flavour of the world about their distinguished persons.

A minute later he was staring disconsolately at a group of his fellows just in front of Dir—— of Rutford's side door. An impulse seized him to turn and flee. What would Uncle John say to that? So he advanced. The boys made way politely, asking no questions. As he passed through he caught a few eager words. "I was hoping that the brute had gone. It *is* a sickener, and no mistake!"

John ascended the battered, worn-out staircase, wondering who the "brute" was. Perhaps a sort of Flashman. John knew his *Tom Brown*; but some one had told him that bullying had ceased to be. Great emphasis had been laid on the "brute," whoever he might be.

Upon the second-floor passage, he found his room and one of its tenants, who nodded carelessly as John crossed the threshold.

"I'm Scaife," he said. "Are you the Lord, or the Commoner?" He laughed, indicating a large portmanteau, labelled, "Lord Esmé Kinloch."

"I'm Verney," said John.

"I've bagged the best bed," said Scaife, after a pause, "and I advise you to bag the next best one, over there. It was mine last term."

"I don't see the beds," said John, staring about him.

Scaife pointed out what appeared to be three tall, narrow wardrobes. The rest of the furniture included three much-battered washstands and chests of drawers, four Windsor chairs, and a square table, covered with innumerable inkstains and roughly-carved names.

"The beds let down," Scaife said, "and during the first school the maids make them, and shut them up again. It is considered a joke to crawl into another fellow's room at night, and shut him up. You find yourself standing upon your head in the dark, choking. It is a joke—for the other fellow."

"Did some one do that to you?" asked John.

"Yes; a big lout in the Third Fifth," Scaife smiled grimly.

"And what did you do?"

"I waited for him next day with a cricket stump. There was an awful row, because I let him have it a bit too hard; but I've not been shut up since. That bed is a beast. It collapses." He chuckled. "Young Kinloch won't find it quite as soft as the ones at White Ladies. Well, like the rest of us, he'll have to take Dirty Dick's as he finds it."

The bolt had fallen.

John asked in a quavering voice, "Then it *is* called that?"

"Called what?"

"This house. Dirty Dick's!"

Scaife smiled cynically. He looked about a year older than John, but he had the air and manners of a man of the world—so John thought. Also, he was very good-looking, handsomer than Desmond, and in striking contrast to that smiling, genial youth, being dark, almost swarthy of complexion, with strongly-marked features and rather coarse hands and feet.

"Everybody here calls it Dirty Dick's," he replied curtly.

John stared helplessly.

"But," he muttered, "I heard, I was told, that the Manor was the best house in the school."

"It used to be," Scaife answered. "To-day, it comes jolly near being the worst. The fellows in other houses are decent; they don't rub it in; but, between ourselves, the Manor has gone to pot ever since Dirty Dick took hold of it. Damer's is the swell house now."

John began to un-strap his portmanteau. Scaife puzzled him. For instance, he displayed no curiosity. He did not put the questions always asked at a Preparatory School. Without turning his thought into words, John divined that at Harrow it was bad form to ask questions. As he wanted to ask a question, a very important question, this enforced silence became exasperating.

Presently Scaife said, "I suppose you are one of the Claydon lot."

"No; my home is in the New Forest. My uncle is Verney of Verney Boscobel."

"Oh! his name is on the panels at the head of the staircase; and it's carved on a bed in the next room."

"Crikey! I must go and look at it."

"You can look at the panels, of course; but don't say 'Crikey!' and don't go into the next room. Two Fifth Form fellows have it. It would be infernal cheek."

John hoped that Scaife would offer to accompany him to the panels. Then he went alone. It being now within half an hour of lock-up, the passages were swarming with boys. Soon John would see them assembled in Hall, where their names would be called over by Rutford. Everybody—John had been told—was expected to be present at this first call-over, except a few boys who might be coming from a distance. John worked his way along the upper passage, and down the second flight of stairs till he came to the first landing. Here, close to the house notice-board, were some oak panels covered with names and dates, all carved—so John learned later—by a famous Harrow character, Sam Hoare, once "Custos" of the School. The boy glanced eagerly, ardently, up and down the panels. Ah, yes, here was his father's name, and here—his uncle's. And then out of the dull, finely-grained oak, shone other names familiar to all who love the Hill and its traditions. John's heart grew warm again with pride in the house that had held such men. The name of the great statesman and below it a mighty warrior's made him thrill and tremble. They were *Old Harrovians*, these fellows, men whom his uncle had known, men of whom his dear mother, wise soul! Had spoken a thousand times. The landing and the passages were roaring with the life of the present moment. Boys, big and small, were chaffing each other loudly. Under some circumstances, this new-comer, a stranger, ignored entirely, might have felt desolate and forlorn in the heart of such a crowd; but John was tingling with delight and pleasure.

Suddenly, the noise moderated. John, looking up, saw a big fellow slowly approaching, exchanging greetings with everybody. John turned to a boy close to him.

"Who is it?" he whispered.

The other boy answered curtly, "Lawrence, the Head of the House."

The big fellow suddenly caught John's eyes. What he read there—admiration, respect, envy—brought a slight smile to his lips.

"Your name?" he demanded.

"Verney."

Lawrence held out his hand, simply and yet with a certain dignity.

"I heard you were coming," he said, keenly examining John's face. "We can't have too many Verneys. If I can do anything for you, let me know."

He nodded, and strode on. John saw that several boys were staring with a new interest. None, however, spoke to him; and he returned to his room with a blushing face. Scaife had unpacked his clothes and put them away; he was now surveying the bare walls with undisguised contempt.

"Isn't this a beastly hole?" he remarked.

John, always interested in people rather than things, examined the room carefully. Passing down the passage he had caught glimpses of other rooms: some charmingly furnished, gay with chintz, embellished with pictures, Japanese fans, silver cups, and other trophies. Comparing these with his own apartment, John said shyly—

"It's not very beefy."

"Beefy? You smell of a private school, Verney. Now, is it worth doing up? You see, I shall be in a two-room next term. If we all chip in——" he paused.

"I've brought back two quid," said John.

Scaife's smile indicated neither approval nor the reverse. John's ingenuous confidence provoked none in return.

"We'll talk about it when Kinloch arrives. I wonder why his people sent him here."

John had studied some books, but not the Peerage. The great name of Kinloch was new to him, not new to Scaife, who, for a boy, knew his "Burke" too odiously well.

"Why shouldn't his people send him here?" he asked.

"Because," Scaife's tone was contemptuous, "because the Kinlochs—they're a great cricketing family—go to Eton. The duke must have some reason."

"The duke?"

"Hang it, surely you have heard of the Duke of Trent?"

"Yes," said John, humbly. "And this is his son?" He glanced at the label on the new portmanteau.

"Whose son should he be?" said Scaife. "Well, it's queer. Dukes and dukes' sons come to Harrow—all the Hamiltons were here, and the FitzRoys, and the St.

11

The Hill

Maurs—but the Kinlochs, as I say, have gone to Eton. It's a rum thing—very. And why the deuce hasn't he turned up?"

The clanging of a bell brought both boys to their feet.

"Lock-up, and call-over," said Scaife. "Come on!"

They pushed their way down the passage. Several boys addressed Scaife.

"Hullo, Demon!—Here's the old Demon!—Demon, I thought you were going to be sacked!"

To these and other sallies Scaife replied with his slightly ironical smile. John perceived that his companion was popular and at the same time peculiar; quite different from any boy he had yet met.

They filed into a big room—the dining-room of the house—a square, lofty hall, with three long tables in it. On the walls hung some portraits of famous Old Harrovians. As a room it was disappointing at first sight, almost commonplace. But in it, John soon found out, everything for weal or woe which concerned the Manor had taken place or had been discussed. There were two fireplaces and two large doors. The boys passed through one door; upon the threshold of the other stood the butler, holding a silver salver, with a sheet of paper on it.

"What cheek!" murmured Scaife.

"Eh?" said John.

"Dirty Dick isn't here. Just like him, the slacker! And when he does come over on our side of the House, he slimes about in carpet slippers—the beast!"

Lawrence entered as Scaife spoke. John saw that his strongly-marked eyebrows went up, when he perceived the butler. He approached, and took the sheet of paper. The butler said impressively—"Mr. Rutford is busy. Will you call over, sir?"

At any rate, the butler, Dumbleton, was worthy of the best traditions of the Manor. He had a shrewd, clean-shaven face, and the deportment of an archbishop. The Head of the House took the paper, and began to call over the names. Each boy, as his name was called, said, "Here," or, if he wished to be funny, "Here, *sir*!"

"Verney?"

The name rang out crisply.

"Here, *sir*," said John.

The Head of the House eyed him sharply.

"Kinloch?"

No answer.

"Kinloch?"

Scaife answered dryly: "Kinloch's portmanteau has come." Then Dumbleton said in his smooth, bland voice, "His lordship is in the drawing-room with Mr. Rutford."

The boys exchanged knowing glances. Scaife looked contemptuous. The next moment the last name had been called, and the boys scurried into the passages. Lawrence was the first to leave the hall. Impulsively, John rushed up to him.

"I didn't mean to be funny, I didn't really," he panted.

"Quite right. It doesn't pay," Lawrence smiled grimly, "for new boys to be funny. I saw you didn't mean it."

Lawrence spoke in a loud voice. John realized that he had so spoken purposely, trying to wipe out a new boy's first blunder.

"Thanks awfully," said John.

He reached his room to find three other boys busily engaged in abusing their house-master. They took no notice of John, who leaned against the wall.

"His lordship is in the drawing-room with Mr. Rutford."

A freckle-faced, red-headed youth, with a big elastic mouth had imitated Dumbleton admirably.

"What a snob Dick is!" drawled a very tall, very thin, aristocratic-looking boy.

"And fool," added Scaife. "This sort of thing makes him loathed."

"It *is* a sell his being here."

All three fell to talking. The question still festering in John's mind was answered within a minute. The "brute" was Rutford. Towards the end of the previous term gossip had it that the master of the Manor had been offered an appointment elsewhere. Whereat the worthier spirits in the ancient house rejoiced. Now the joy was turned into wailing and gnashing of teeth.

"Is he a beast to us?" said John.

The freckle-faced boy answered affably, "That

depends. His Imperial Highness"—he kicked the new portmanteau hard—"will not find Mr. Richard Rutford a beast. Far from it. And he's civil to the Demon, because his papa is a man of many shekels. But to mere outsiders, like myself, a beast of beasts; ay, the very king of beasts, is—Dirty Dick."

And then—oh, horrors!—the door of No. 15 opened, and Rutford appeared, followed by a seemingly young and very fashionably dressed lady. The boys jumped to their feet. All, except Scaife, looked preternaturally solemn. The house-master nodded carelessly.

"This is Scaife, Duchess," he said in his thick, rasping tones. "Scaife and Verney, let me present you to the Duchess of Trent."

He mouthed the illustrious name, as if it were a large and ripe greengage.

The duchess advanced, smiling graciously. "These"—Rutford named the other boys—"are Egerton, Lovell, and—er—Duff."

Scaife, alone of those present, appreciated the order in which his schoolfellows had been named. Egerton—known as the Caterpillar—was the son of a Guardsman; Lovell's father was a judge; Duff's father an obscure parson.

The duchess shook hands with each boy. "Your father and I are old friends," she said to Egerton; "and I have had the pleasure of meeting your uncle," she smiled at John.

Duff looked unhappy and ill at ease, because it was almost certain that his last sentence had been overheard by the house-master. The duchess asked a few questions and then took her leave. She and her son were dining with the Head Master. Rutford accompanied her.

"Did the blighter hear?" said Duff.

"How could he help it with his enormous asses' ears?" said the tall thin Egerton.

Duff, an optimist, like all red-headed, freckled boys, appealed to the others, each in turn. The verdict was unanimous.

"He hates me like poison," said Duff. "I shall catch it hot. What an unlucky beggar I am!"

"Pooh!" said Scaife. "He knows jolly well that the whole school calls him Dirty Dick."

But whatever hopes Duff may have entertained of his house-master's deafness were speedily laid in the dust. Within five minutes Rutford reappeared. He stood in the doorway, glaring.

"Just now, Duff," said he, "I happened to overhear your voice, which is singularly, I may say vulgarly, penetrating. You were speaking of me, your house-master, as 'Dick.' But you used an adjective before it. What was it?"

Duff writhed. "I don't—remember."

"Oh yes, you do. Why lie, Duff?"

John's brown face grew pale.

"The adjective you used," continued Rutford, "was 'dirty.' You spoke of me as 'Dirty Dick,' and I fancy I caught the word 'beast.' You will write out, if you please, one hundred Greek lines, accents and stops, and bring them to me, or leave them with Dumbleton, *twenty-five* lines at a time, *every* alternate half hour during the afternoon of the next half holiday. Good night to you."

"Good night, sir," said all the boys, save John and Scaife.

"Good night, Verney."

Master and pupil confronted each other. John's face looked impassive; and Rutford turned from the new boy to Scaife.

"Good night, Scaife."

Scaife drew himself up, and, in a quiet, cool voice, replied—"Good night, sir."

Duff waited till Rutford's heavy step was no longer heard; then he rushed at John.

"I say," he spluttered, "you're a good sort—ain't he, Demon? Refusing to say 'Good night' to the beast because he was ragging me. But he'll never forgive you—never!"

"Oh yes, he will," said Scaife. "It won't be difficult for Dirty Dick to forgive the future Verney of Verney Boscobel."

John stared. "Verney Boscobel?" he repeated. "Why, that belongs to my uncle. Mother and I hope he'll marry and have a lot of jolly kids of his own."

The Hill

"You hope he'll marry? Well, I'm——"

John's jaw stuck out. The emphasis on the "hope" and the upraised eyebrow smote hard.

"You don't mean to say," he began hotly, "you don't *think* that——"

"I can think what I please," said Scaife, curtly; "and so can you." He laughed derisively. "*Thinking* what they please is about the only liberty allowed to new boys. Even the Duffer learned to hold his tongue during his first term."

The Caterpillar—the tall, thin, aristocratic boy—spoke solemnly. He was a dandy, the understudy—as John soon discovered—of one of the "Bloods;" a "Junior Blood," or "Would-be," a tremendous authority on "swagger," a stickler for tradition, who had been nearly three years in the school.

"The Demon is right," said he. "A new boy can't be too careful, Verney. Your being funny in hall just now made a dev'lish bad impression."

"But I didn't mean to be funny. I told Lawrence so directly after call-over."

The Caterpillar pulled down his cuffs.

"If you didn't mean to be funny," he concluded, "you must be an ass."

Duff, however, remembered that John was nephew to an explorer.

"I say," he jogged John's elbow, "do you think you could get me your uncle's autograph?"

"Why, of course," said John.

"Thanks. I've not a bad collection," the Duffer murmured modestly.

"And the gem of it," said Scaife, "is Billington's, the hangman! The Duffer shivers whenever he looks at it."

"Yes, I do," said Duff, grinning horribly.

After supper and Prayers, John went to bed, but not to sleep for at least an hour. He lay awake, thinking over the events of this memorable day. Whenever he closed his eyes he beheld two objects: the spire of Harrow Church and the vivid laughing face of Desmond. He told himself that he liked Desmond most awfully. And Scaife too, the Demon, had been kind. But somehow John did not like

16

Scaife. Then, in a curious half-dreamy condition, not yet asleep and assuredly not quite awake, he seemed to see the figure of Scaife expanding, assuming terrific proportions, Impending over Desmond, standing between him and the spire, obscuring part of the spire at first, and then, bit by bit, overshadowing the whole.

Chapter Two

Cæsar

You come here where your brothers came,
  To the old school years ago,
A young new face, and a Harrow name,
  'Mid a crowd of strangers? No!
You may not fancy yourself alone,
  You who are memory's heir,
When even the names in the graven stone
  Will greet you with 'Who goes there—
    You?—
      Pass, Friend—All's well.'

JOHN never forgot that memorable morning when he learned for the first time what place he had taken in the school. He sat with the other new-comers, staring, open-eyed, at nearly six hundred boys, big and small, assembled together in the Speech-room. So engrossed was he that he scarcely heard the Head Master's opening prayers. John was obsessed, inebriated, with the number of Harrovians, each of whom had once felt strange and shy like himself. From his place close to the great organ, he could look up and up, seeing row after row of faces, knowing that amongst them sat his future friends and foes.

Suddenly, a neighbour nudged him. The Head Master was reading from a list in his hand the school-removes, and the names and places taken by new boys. He began at the lowest form with the name of a small urchin sitting near John. The urchin blinked and blushed as he realized that he was "lag of the school." John knew that he had answered fairly well the questions set by the examiners; he had no fear of finding himself pilloried in the Third Fourth; still, as form after form did not include his name, he grew restless and excited. Had he taken a higher place than the Middle Shell? Yes; no Verney in the Middle Shell. The Head Master began the removes of the top Shell. Now, now it must be coming. No; the clear penetrating tones slowly articulated name after name, but not his.

"Verney."

At last. Many eyes were staring at him, some enviously, a few superciliously. John had taken the Lower Remove, the highest form but one open to new boys. He was sipping the wine called Success.

Moreover, Desmond of the frank, laughing face and sparkling blue eyes, and Scaife and Egerton were also in the Lower Remove.

After this, John sat in a blissful dream, hardly conscious of his surroundings, seeing his mother's face, hearing her sigh of pleasure when she learned that already her son was halfway up the school.

You may be sure those first forty-eight hours were brim-full of excitements. First, John bought his books, stout leather-tipped, leather-backed volumes, on which his name will be duly stamped on fly-leaf and across the edges of the pages. And he bought also, from "Judy" Stephens,* a "squash" racquet, "squash" balls, and a yard ball. From the school Custos—"Titchy"—a noble supply of stationery was procured. Moreover, young Kinloch announced that his mother had given him three pounds to spend upon the decoration of No. 15, so Scaife declared his intention of spending a similar sum, and in consequence No. 15 became a gorgeous apartment, the cynosure of every eye that passed. The characters of the three boys were revealed plainly enough by their simple furnishings. Scaife bought sporting prints, a couple of Detaille's lithographs, and an easy-chair, known to dwellers upon the Hill as a "frowst;" Kinloch hung upon his side of the wall four pretty reproductions of French engravings, and with the help of three yards of velveteen and some cheap lace he made a very passable imitation of

---

* The racquet Professional.

the mantel-cover in his mother's London boudoir; John scorned velveteen, lace, "frowsts," and French engravings. He put his money into a pair of red curtains, and one excellent photogravure of Landseer's "Children of the Mist." Having a few shillings to spare, he bought half a dozen ferns, which were placed in a box by the window, and watered so diligently that they died prematurely.

Secondly, John played in a house-game at football, and learned the difference between a scrimmage at a small preparatory school and the genuine thing at Harrow. Lawrence insisted that all new boys should play, and the Caterpillar informed him that he would have to learn the rules of Harrow "footer" by heart, and pass a stiff examination in them before the House Eleven, with the penalty of being forced to sing them in Hall if he failed to satisfy his examiners. The Duffer lent him a House shirt of green and white stripes, and a pair of white duck shorts, and with what pride John put them on, thinking of the far distant day when he would wear a "fez"* instead of the commonplace house-cap! Lawrence said a few words.

"You'll have to play the compulsory games, Verney, which begin after the Goose Match,† but I want to see you playing as hard as ever you can in the house-games. You'll be knocked about a bit; but a Verney won't mind that—eh?"

"Rather not," said John, feeling very valiant.

Thirdly, there was the first Sunday, and the first sermon of the Head Master, with its plain teaching about the opportunities and perils of Public School life. John found himself mightily affected by the singing, and the absence of shrill treble voices. The booming basses and baritones of the big fellows made him shiver with a curious bitter-sweet sensation never experienced before.

Lastly, the pleasant discovery that his Form treated

---

* The cap of honour worn by the House Football Eleven.
† The Goose Match, the last cricket-match of the year, played on the nearest Saturday to Michaelmas Day.

him with courtesy and kindness. Desmond, in particular, welcomed him quite warmly. And then and there John's heart was filled with a wild and unreasonable yearning for this boy's friendship. But Desmond—he was called "Cæsar," because his Christian names were Henry Julius—seemed to be very popular, a bright particular star, far beyond John's reach although for ever in his sight. Cæsar never offered to walk with him: and he refused John's timid invitation to have food at the "Tudor Creameries."* Was it possible that a boy about to enter Damer's would not be seen walking and talking with a fellow out of Dirty Dick's? This possibility festered, till one morning John saw his idol walking up and down the School Yard with Scaife. That evening he said to Scaife—

"Do you like Desmond?"

"Yes," Scaife replied decisively. "I like him better than any fellow at Harrow. You know that his father is Charles Desmond—the Cabinet Minister and a Governor of the school?"

"I didn't know it. I suppose Cæsar Desmond likes you—*awfully.*"

"Do you? I doubt it."

No more was said. John told himself that Cæsar—he liked to think of Desmond as Cæsar—could pick and choose a pal out of at least three hundred boys, half the school. How extremely unlikely that he, John, would be chosen! But every night he lay awake for half an hour longer than he ought to have done, wondering how, by hook or crook, he could do a service to Cæsar which must challenge interest and provoke, ultimately, friendship.

Meantime, he was slowly initiated by the Caterpillar into Harrow ways and customs. Fagging, which began after the first fortnight, he found a not unpleasant duty. After first and fourth schools the other fags and he would stand not far from the pantry, and yell out "Breakfast," or "Tea," as it might be, "for Number So-and-So." Perhaps

---

* A fashionable "tuck" shop.

one had to nip up to the Creameries to get a slice of salmon, or cutlets, or sausages. Fagging at Harrow—which varies slightly in different houses—is hard or easy according to the taste and fancy of the fag's master. Some of the Sixth Form at the Manor made their fags unlace their dirty football boots. Kinloch, who since he left the nursery had been waited upon by powdered footmen six feet high, now found, to his disgust, that he had to varnish Trieve's patent-leathers for Sunday. Trieve was second in command, and had been known as "Miss" Trieve. John would have gladly done this and more for Lawrence, his fag-master; but Lawrence, a manly youth, scorned sybaritic services. The Caterpillar taught John to carry his umbrella unfolded, to wear his "straw" straight (a slight list to port was allowed to "Bloods" only), not to walk in the middle of the road, and so forth. How he used to envy the members of the Elevens as they rolled arm-in arm down the High Street! How often he wondered if the day would ever dawn when Cæsar and he, outwardly and inwardly linked together, would stroll up and down the middle-walk below the Chapel Terrace: that sunny walk, whence, on a fair day, you can see the insatiable monster, London, filling the horizon and stretching red, reeking hands into the sweet country—the middle-walk, from which all but Bloods were rigidly excluded.

Much to his annoyance—an annoyance, be it said, which he managed to hide—John seemed to attract young Kinloch almost as magnetically as he himself was attracted to Cæsar. John had not the heart to shake off the frail delicate child, who was christened "Fluff" after his first appearance in public. Fluff had taken the First Fourth and ingenuously confessed to any one who cared to listen that he ought to have gone to Eton. A beast of a doctor prescribed the Hill. And even the almighty duke failed to get him into Damer's, another grievance. He had been entered since birth at the crack house at Eton; and now to be pitchforked into Dirty Dick's at Harrow——! The Duffer kicked him, feeling an unspeakable cad when poor Fluff burst into tears.

"Sorry," said the Duffer. "Only you mustn't slang Harrow. And you'd better get it into your silly head that it's the best school in this or any other world—isn't it, Demon?"

"I'm sure the Verneys, and the Egertons, and the Duffs have always thought so."

"But it isn't really," whimpered poor Fluff. "You fellows know that everybody talks of Eton and Harrow. Who ever heard of Harrow and Eton? People say—I've heard my eldest brother, Strathpeffer, say it again and again—'Eton and Harrow,' just as they say 'Gentlemen and Players.' "

"Oh," said the Caterpillar. "The Etonians are the gentlemen—eh? Well, Fluff, after their performance at Lord's last year, you couldn't expect us to admit that they're—players."

The Duffer chuckled.

"I say, Caterpillar, that was a good 'un."

"Not mine," said the Caterpillar, solemnly, "My governor's, you know."

The Duffer continued: "Now, Fluff, I won't touch your body, because you might tumble to pieces, but if I hear you slanging the school or our house, I'll pull out handfuls of fluff. D'ye hear?"

"Yes," said Fluff, meekly.

"Say '*Floreat Herga*' on your bended knees!"

Fluff obeyed.

"And remember," said the Duffer, impressively, "that we've had a king here, haven't we, Caterpillar?"

"Yes," said the Caterpillar.

"I never believed it," said Scaife.

"He was a Spaniard,* or an Italian, you know," the Duffer explained. "The duke of something or t'other; and an ambassador came down and offered the beggar the Spanish crown, when he was in the First Fourth, and of course he gobbled it—who wouldn't? And then Victor Emmanuel interfered. That's all true, you can take your

---

* H.R.H. Prince Thomas of Savoy, Duke of Genoa, was elected King by the Cortes of Spain, October 3, 1869, while he was a boy at Harrow. The crown was finally declined January 1, 1870. The Prince was nick-named "King Tom."

Bible oath, because my governor told me so, and he—well, he's a parson."

"Then it *must* be true," said Scaife. "Now, young Fluff, don't forget that Harrow is a school fit for a king and nearer to Heaven than Eton by at least six hundred feet."

So saying, the Demon marched out of the room, followed by Fluff, slightly limping.

"Sorry I turfed* that little ass so hard," said the Duffer to John. "I say, Verney, the Demon is rather a rum 'un, ain't he? Sometimes I can't quite make him out. He's frightfully clever and all that, but I had a sort of beastly feeling just now that he didn't—eh?—quite mean what he said. Was he laughin' at *us*, pullin' our legs—what?"

John's brain worked slowly, as he had found out to his cost under a form-master who maintained that it was no use having a fact stored in the head unless it slipped readily out of the mouth. The Duffer, who never thought, because speaking was so much easier, grew impatient at John's silence.

"Well, you needn't look like an owl, Verney. You know that Scaife's grandfather was a navvy."

"I don't know," John replied.

"And I don't care," said the Duffer. "Let's go and have some food at the Creameries."

Looking back afterwards, John often wondered whether, unconsciously, the Duffer had sown a grain of mustard-seed destined to grow into a large tree. Or had the intuition that Scaife was other than what he seemed furnished the fertile soil into which the seed fell? In any case, from the end of this first week began to increase the suspicion, which eventually became conviction, that the Demon, keen at games, popular in his house, clever at work—clever, indeed! Inasmuch as he never achieved more or less than was necessary—generous with his money, handsome and well-mannered, blessed, in fine,

---

* To "turf," *i.e.* to kick.

with so many gifts of the gods, yet lacked a soul.

This, of course, is putting into words the vague speculations and reasonings of a boy not yet fourteen. If an Olympian—one of the masters, for instance, or the Head of the House—had said, "Verney, has the Demon a soul?" John would have answered promptly, "Ra—ther! He's been awfully decent to Fluff and me. We'd have had a hot time if it hadn't been for him," and so forth. ... And, indeed, to doubt Scaife's sincerity and goodness seemed at times gross disloyalty, because he stood, firm as a rock, between the two urchins in his room and the turbulent crowd outside. This defence of the weak, this guarding of green fruit from the maw of Lower School boys, afforded Scaife an opportunity of exercising power. He had the instincts of the potter, inherited, no doubt; and he moulded the clay ready to his hand with the delight of a master-workman. Nobody else knew what the man of millions had said to his boy when he despatched him to Harrow; but the Demon remembered every word. He had reason to respect and fear his sire.

"I'm sending you to Harrow to study, not books nor games, but boys, who will be men when you are a man. And, above all, study their weaknesses. Look for the flaws. Teach yourself to recognize at a glance the liar, the humbug, the fool, the egotist, and the mule. Make friends with as many as are likely to help you in after life, and don't forget that one enemy may inflict a greater injury than twenty friends can repair. Spend money freely; dress well; swim with the tide, not against it."

A year at Harrow confirmed Scaife's confidence in his father's worldly wisdom. Big for his age, strong, with his grandsire's muscles, tough as hickory, he had become the leader of the Lower School boys at the Manor. The Fifth were civil to him, recognizing, perhaps, the expediency of leaving him alone ever since the incident of the cricket stump. The Sixth found him the quickest of the fags and uncommonly obliging. His house-master signed reports which neither praised nor blamed. To Dirty Dick the boy was the son of a man who could write a cheque for a million.

The Hill

Two things worthy of record happened within a month; the one of lesser importance can be set down first. Charles Desmond, Cæsar's father, came down to Harrow and gave a luncheon at the King's Head. From time immemorial the Desmonds had been educated on the Hill. The family had produced some famous soldiers, a Lord Chancellor, and a Prime Minister. In the Fourth Form Room the stranger may read their names carved in oak, and they are carved also in the hearts of all ardent Harrovians. Mr. Desmond, though a Cabinet Minister, found time to visit Harrow once at least in each term. He always chose a whole holiday, and after attending eleven-o'clock Bill* in the Yard, would carry off his son and his son's friends. The School knew him and loved him. To the thoughtful he stood for the illustrious past, the epitome of what John Lyon's† boys had fought for and accomplished. Four sons had he—Harrovians all. Of these Cæsar was youngest and last. Each had distinguished himself on the Hill either in work or play, or in both.

Charles Desmond stood upon the step just above the master who was calling Bill.

"That's Cæsar's father," said Scaife. "I'm going to lunch with him. Isn't he a topper?"

John's eyes were popping out of his face. He had never seen any man like this resplendent, stately personage, smiling and nodding to the biggest fellows in the school.

"And my governor says," Scaife added, "that he's not a rich man, nothing much to speak of in the way of income over and above his screw as a Cabinet Minister."

Scaife moved away, and John could hear him say to another boy, in an easy, friendly tone, "Mr. Desmond told Cæsar that he wanted to meet *me*—very civil of him—eh?"

Presently John was in line waiting to pass by the steps.

"Verney?"

---

* Calling over.
† John Lyon founded Harrow School, 1571.

26

"Here, sir."

He was hurrying by, with a backward glance at the great man. Suddenly Cæsar's father beckoned, nodding cheerily. John ascended the steps, to feel the grasp of a strong hand, to hear a ringing voice.

"You're John Verney's nephew. Just so. I think I should have spotted you, even if Harry had not told me you were in his form. You must lunch with us. Cut along, now."

So John was dismissed, brimful of happiness, which almost overflowed when Cæsar met him with an eager— "I'm so glad, Verney. I say, the governor's a nailer at picking out the old names, isn't he?"

So John ate his luncheon in distinguished company, and felt himself for the first time to be somebody. As the youngest guest present, to him was accorded the place of honour, next the most charming host in Christendom, who put him at ease in a jiffy. How good the cutlets and the pheasant tasted! And how the talk warmed the cockles of his heart! The brand of the Crossed Arrows shone upon all topics. Who could expect, or desire, aught else? Cæsar's governor seemed to know what every Harrovian had done worth the doing. Easily, fluently, he discoursed of triumphs won at home, abroad. In the camp, on the hustings, at the bar, in the pulpit. And his anecdotes, which illustrated every phase of life, how pat to the moment they were! One boy complained ruefully of having spent three terms under a form-master who had "ragged" him. Charles Desmond sympathized—

"Bless my soul," said he, "don't I remember being three terms in the Third Fifth when that tartar old Heriot had it? I dare swear I got no more than my deserts. I was an idle vagabond, but Heriot made my life such a burden to me that I entreated my people to take me away from Harrow, And then my governor urged me to put my back into the work and get a remove. And I did. And would you believe it, upon the first day of the next term I wired to my people, 'You must take me away. I've got my remove all right—and so has Heriot.'"

How gaily the speaker led the laugh which followed this recital! And the chaff! Was it possible that Cæsar dared to chaff a man who was supposed to have the peace of Europe in his keeping? And, by Jove! Cæsar could hold his own.

So the minutes flew. But John noticed, with surprise, that the Demon didn't score. In fact, John and he were the only guests that contributed nothing to the feast save hearty appetites. It was strange that the Demon, the wit of his house and form, never opened his mouth except to fill it with food. He answered, it is true, and very modestly, the questions addressed to him by his host; but then, as John reflected, any silly fool in the Fourth Form could do that.

After luncheon, the boys were dismissed, each with a hearty word of encouragement and half a sovereign. John was passing the plate-glass splendours of the Creameries, when the Demon overtook him, and they walked down the winding High Street together. Scaife had never walked with John before.

"That was worth while," Scaife said quietly. John could not interpret this speech, save in its obvious meaning.

"Rather," he replied.

"Why?" said Scaife, very sharply.

"Eh?"

"Why was it worth while?"

John stammered out something about good food and jolly talk.

"Pooh!" said Scaife, contemptuously. "I thought you had brains, Verney." He glanced at him keenly. "Now, speak out. What's in that head of yours? You can be cheeky, if you like."

John wondered bow Scaife had divined that he wished to be cheeky. His mentor had said so much to Fluff and him about the propriety of not putting on "lift" or "side" in the presence of an older boy, that he had choked back a retort which occurred to him.

"You're thinking," continued the Demon, in his clear voice, "that I didn't use my brains just now, but, my blooming innocent, I can assure you I did. Very much so. I played possum. Put that into your little pipe and smoke it."

28

At four-o'clock Bill, John noticed Cæsar's absence: a fact accounted for by the presence of a mail-phaeton, which, he knew, belonged to Mr. Desmond, drawn up— oddly enough—opposite the Manor. What a joke to think that Cæsar was drinking tea with Dirty Dick!

After Bill, having nothing better to do, John and Fluff went for a walk on the Sudbury road. They had played football before Bill, and each had realized his own awkwardness and insignificance. Poor Fluff, almost reduced to tears, with a big black bruise upon his white forehead, confessed that he preferred peaceful games— like croquet, and intended to apply for a doctor's certificate of exemption. Demanding sympathy, he received a slating.

"I play nearly as rotten a game as you do, Fluff," John said; "but Scaife expects us to be Torpids,* so we jolly well have to buck up. That bruise over your eye has taken off your painted-doll look. Now, if you're going to blub, you'd better get behind that hedge."

Fluff exploded.

"This is a beastly hole," he cried. "And I loathe it. I'm going to write to my father and beg him to take me away."

"You ought to be at a girls' school."

"I hate everything and everybody. I thought you were my friend, the only friend I had."

John was somewhat mollified.

"I am your friend, but not when you talk rot."

"Verney, look here, if you'll be decent to me, I will try to stick it out. I wish I was like you; I do indeed. I wish I was like Scaife. Why, I'd sooner be the Duffer, freckles and all, than myself."

John looked down upon the delicately-tinted face, the small, regular, girlish features, the red, quivering mouth. Suddenly he grasped that this was an appeal from

---

* Boys who have not been more than two years in the school are eligible as "Torpids"; out of each house a Torpid football Eleven is chosen.

weakness to strength, and that he, no older and but a little bigger than Fluff, had strength to spare, strength to shoulder burdens other than his own.

"All right," he said stiffly; "don't make such a fuss!"

"You'll have me for a friend, Verney?"

"Yes; but I ain't going to kiss your forehead to make it well, you know."

"May I call you John, when we're alone? And I wish you'd call me Esmé, instead of that horrid 'Fluff.'"

John pondered deeply.

"Look here," he said. "You can call me John, and I'll call you Esmé, when we're Torpids. And now, you'd better cut back to the house. I must think this all out, and I can't think straight when I look at you."

"May I call you John once?"

"You are the silliest idiot I ever met, bar none. Call me 'John,' or 'Tom Fool,' or anything; but hook it afterwards!"

"Yes, John, I will. You're the only boy I ever met whom I really wanted for a friend." He displayed a radiant face, turned suddenly, and ran off. John watched him, frowning, because Fluff was a good little chap, and yet, at times, such a bore!

He walked on alone, chewing the cud of a delightful experience; trying, not unsuccessfully, to recall some of Mr. Desmond's anecdotes. How proud Cæsar was of his father! And the father, obviously, was just as proud of his son. What a pair! And if only Cæsar were his friend! By Jove! It was rather a rum go, but John was as mad keen to call Cæsar friend as poor Fluff to call John friend. Serious food for thought, this. "But I would never bother him," said John to himself, "as Fluff has bothered me, never!"

"Hullo, Verney!"

"Hullo!" said John.

Coincidence had thrust Cæsar out of his thoughts and on to the narrow path in front of him.

"I'm not a ghost," said Cæsar.

John hesitated.

"I was thinking of you," he confessed; "and then I heard your voice and saw you. It gave me a start. I say, it *was* good of your governor to ask me."

"Hang my governor! He's the——"

Cæsar closed his lips firmly, as if he feared that terrible adjectives might burst from them. John missed the sparkling smile, the gay glance of the eyes.

"What's up?" he demanded.

Cæsar hesitated; looked at John, read, perhaps, the sympathy, the honest interest, possibly the affection, in the grey orbs which met his own so steadily.

"What's up?" he repeated. "Why, I'm not going into Damer's, after all."

"Oh!" said John.

"My governor has just told me. I came down here to curse and swear."

"Not going into Damer's? What rot—for you!"

"It is sickening. Look here, Verney; I feel like telling you about it. I know you won't go bleating all over the shop. No. I said to myself, 'Mum's the word,' but——"

John's heart beat, his body glowed, his grey eyes sparkled.

"It's like this," continued Cæsar, after a slight pause. "Damer told the governor that two fellows he had expected to leave at the end of this term were staying on. The governor hinted that Damer added something about straining a point, and letting me in ahead of three other fellows; but the governor wouldn't listen to that——"

"Jolly decent of him," said John.

"Was it? In my opinion he ought to have thought of me first. All my brothers have been at Damer's. And he knew I'd set my heart on going there. Look how civil the fellows are to me. I've been in and out of the house like a tame cat. Confound it! if Damer did want to strain a point, why shouldn't he? The governor played his own game, not mine. What right has he to be so precious unselfish at my expense? I argued with him; but he can put his foot down. Let's cut all that. Of course, I don't want to stop in a beastly Small House for ever, and, if Damer's is closed to me, I should like Brown's, but Brown's is full too. And there are other good houses. But where—where do you think I *am* going?"

"Reed's?"

"I don't call Reed's so bad. No; I'm going to Dirty

Dick's. I'm coming to you."

"Oh, I say."

"Why, dash it all, you're grinning. I don't want to be a cad—Dirty Dick's is *your* house—but—after Damer's! O Lord!"

The grin faded out of John's face. Cæsar's loss outweighed his own gain.

"Your governor was a Manorite," he said slowly.

"Yes, in its best days; and he's always had a sneaking liking for it; but he knows, he knows, I say, that now it's rotten, and yet he sends me there. Why?"

"Ask another," said John.

"I asked him another, and what do you think he said, in that peculiar voice of his which always dries me up? 'Harry,' said he, 'when you're a little older and a good deal wiser, you'll be able to answer that question yourself.'"

John's face brightened. A glimmering of the truth shone out of the darkness. He tried to advance nearer to it, gropingly.

"I dare say——"

"Well, go on!"

"Your governor may feel that we want a fellow like you."

John was blushing because he remembered what the Head of the House had said about the Verneys. Desmond glanced at him keenly. He detested flattery laid on too thick. But this was a genuine tribute. For the first time he smiled.

"Thank you, Verney," he said, more genially. "What you say is utter rot; but it was decent of you to say it, and I'm glad that you and I are going to be in the same house."

For his life John could not help adding, "And Scaife, you forget Scaife?" Jealousy pierced him as Scaife's name slipped out.

"Yes, there's the Demon. I always liked him."

"And he likes you."

"Does he? Good old Demon! I like to be liked. That's the Irish in me. I'm half Irish, you know. I want fellows to be friendly to me. I'd forgotten Scaife. That's rum too, because he's not the sort one forgets, is he? No. I wonder if I could get into the Demon's room next term?"

"I'm to his room. It's a three-room."

"A two-room is much jollier."

"Our room is not bad."

Cæsar was hardly listening. John caught a murmur: "The old Demon and I would get along capitally."

Chapter Three

Kraipalē[*]

Life is mostly froth and bubble;
Two things stand like stone—
Kindness in another's trouble,
Courage in your own.

SOME five years afterwards John Verney learned what had passed between Cabinet Minister and Head Master upon that eventful day which sent Cæsar to curse and swear upon the Sudbury road. The Head Master was not an Harrovian, and on that account was the better able to perceive time-honoured abuses. At Harrow the dominant chord among masters and boys is a harmony of strenuousness and sentiment. Inevitably, the sentiment becomes, at times, sentimental; and then strenuousness pushes it into a corner. When honoured veterans are wearing out, loyalty, gratitude for past service, reluctance to inflict pain, keep them in positions of responsibility which mentally and physically they are unfit to administer. It is almost as difficult to turn an Eton or Harrow master out of his house, as to turn a parson of the Church of England out of his pulpit. More, in selecting a house-master as in selecting a parson, a man's claims to preferment are too often determined by scholarship, by length of former service, by interest with authority, rather than by ability to govern a body of boys made up of widely different parts. A capable form-master may prove an incapable house-master. Richard Rutford, to give a concrete example, came to Harrow knowing nothing about Public Schools, and caring as little for the

---

[*] κραιπάλη is translated by Liddell and Scott as "the result of a debauch."

The Hill

traditions of the Hill, but with the prestige of being a Senior Classic. Nobody questioned his ability to teach Greek. In his own line, and not an inch beyond, the Governors were assured that Rutford was a success. In due time he accepted a Small House, so small that its autocrat's incapacity as an administrator escaped notice. Rutford waited patiently for a big morsel. He wrote a couple of text-books; he married a wife with money and influence; he entertained handsomely. It is true he became popular neither with masters nor boys, but his wine was as sound as his scholarship, and his wife had a peer for a second cousin. Eventually he accepted the Manor. Within a month, those in authority suspected that a blunder had been made; within a year they knew it. The house began to go down. Leaven lay in the lump, but not enough to make it rise, because the baker refused to stir the dough. First and last, Rutford disliked boys, misunderstood them, insulted them, ignored those who lacked influential connections, toadied and pampered the "swells."

Just before John Verney came to Harrow, the Manor was showing unmistakable signs of decay. A new Head Master, recognizing "dry-rot," realizing the necessity of cutting it out, was confronted with that bristling obstacle—Tradition. He possessed enough moral courage to have told Rutford to resign, because in a thousand indescribable ways the man had neglected his duty; but, so said the Tones, such a step might provoke a public scandal, and if Rutford refused to go—what then? Nothing definite could be proved against the man. His sins had been of omission. Dismayed, not defeated, the Head Master considered other methods of regenerating the Manor. Very quietly he made his appeal to the Old Harrovians, many of whom were sending their sons and nephews to other houses. He invited co-operation. John Verney, the Rev. Septimus Duff, Colonel Egerton—half a dozen enthusiastic Manorites—stepped forward. Lastly, for Charles Desmond the Head Master baited his hook.

"The reform which we have at heart," said he, "must come from within and from below. The house wants a Desmond in it. I was not allowed to wield the axe; but, after all, there are more modern methods of decapitation. And, believe me, I am not asking any man more than I am prepared to do myself. My own nephew goes to the Manor after next holidays."

"Um!" said Mr. Desmond, stroking his chin.

"Lawrence, the Head of the House, is a tower of strength, like all the Lawrences."

"How did you beguile the Duke of Trent?"

"Fortune gave me that weapon. The duke"—he laughed genially——

"Yes?"

"Will turn scales which my heaviest arguments won't budge. A bit of luck! The duke wanted to send his son, a delicate lad, to Harrow, and I did mention to him that Rutford had a vacancy."

"O Ulysses! And Scaife? How did you handle that large bale of bank-notes?"

"Rutford captured Scaife."

"Handsome boy—his son. Lunched with us this morning. Well, well, you have persuaded me. But what an unpleasant quarter of an hour I shall have with Harry!"

As a new boy, John slaved at "footer," and displayed a curious inaptitude for squash racquets. At all games Cæsar and Scaife were precociously proficient. John's clumsiness annoyed them. Often the Caterpillar joined him and Fluff, giving them to understand that this must be regarded as an act of grace and condescension which might be suitably acknowledged at the Tudor Creameries.

The Caterpillar mightily impressed the two small boys. He had acquired his nick-name from the very leisurely pace at which he advanced up the school. He wore "Charity tails," as they were called, the swallow-tail coat of the Upper School mercifully given to boys of the Lower School who are too tall to wear with decency the short Eton jacket; he possessed a trouser-press; and his "bags" were perfectly creased and quite spotless. From tip to toe, at all seasons and in all weathers, he looked conspicuously spick and span. Chaff provoked the solemn retort: "One should be well groomed." He spoke impersonally, considering it bad form to use the first person singular. Amongst the small boys he ranked as the Petronius of the Lower School.

One day the Caterpillar said grandiloquently, "You kids will oblige me by not shouting and yelling when you speak to me. I've a bit of a head."

"What's wrong with it?" said Fluff.

"It looks splendid *outside*," said John, in his serious voice.

The Caterpillar, detecting no cheek, answered gravely—

"Some of us had a wet night of it, last night."

"Wet?" exclaimed the innocent Fluff. "Why, all the stars were shining."

"Your brothers at Eton know what a 'wet night' means," said the Caterpillar, "I was talking with one of the Fifth, when a fellow came in with a flask. A gentleman ought to be able to carry a few glasses of wine, but one is not accustomed to spirits."

"Spirits?"

"Whisky, not prussic acid, you know."

"But where do they get the whisky?" demanded John.

"Comparing it with my father's old Scotch, I should say at the grocer's," replied the Caterpillar. "There's some drinking going on in our house, and—and other things. One mentions it to you kids as a warning."

"Thanks," said John.

"Not at all; you're rather decent little beggars. They" (the Fifth Form was indicated), "they've let you alone so far, but you may have trouble next term, so look out! And if you want advice, come to me."

Beneath his absurd pompous manner beat a kindly heart, and the small boys divined this and were grateful. None the less the word "spirits" frightened them. Next day John happened to find himself alone with Cæsar. Very nervously he asked the question—

"I say, do any of the big fellows at Damer's drink?"

"Drink? Drink—what?"

"Well, spirits."

Cæsar snorted an indignant denial. The fellows at Damer's were above that sort of thing. The house prided itself upon its tone. Tone constituted Damer's glory, and was the secret of its success. John nodded, but two days afterwards the Demon took him by the arm, twisted it sharply, and said—

"What the deuce did you mean by telling Cæsar that the Manorites drink?"

"Oh, Scaife—I didn't."

"You gave us away."

"*Us?*" John's eyes opened. "*You* don't drink with 'em?" he faltered.

"Don't bother your head about what I do, or don't do," Scaife answered roughly; "and because you took the Lower Remove don't think for an instant that you are on a par with Cæsar and me, or even the old Caterpillar—for you ain't."

"I know that," said John, humbly.

"Don't forget it, or there may be ructions."

"I shan't forget it."

"That's right. And, by the way, you're getting into the habit of hanging about Cæsar, which bores him to death. Stop it."

But to this John made no reply. He read dislike in Scaife's bold eyes, detected it in his clear peremptory voice, felt it in the cruel twist of the arm. And he had brains enough to know that Scaife was not the boy to dislike any one without reason. John crawled to the conclusion that Scaife had become jealous of his increasing intimacy with Desmond.

However, when the three boys were preparing their Greek for First School, Scaife seemed his old self, friendly, amusing, and cool as a cucumber. Long ago he had initiated John into Manorite methods of work.

"Our object is," he explained to the new boy, "to get through the 'swat' with as little squandering of valuable time as possible. It doesn't pay to be skewed. We must mug up our 'cons' well enough to scrape along without 'puns' and extra school."

The three co-operated. Out of forty lines of Vergil, Scaife would do fifteen, John fifteen, and the Caterpillar ten; *ten*, because, as he pointed out, he had been nearly three years in the school. Then each fellow in turn construed his lines for the benefit of the others. A difficult passage was taken by Scaife to a clever friend in the Fifth. Sometimes Scaife would be absent twenty minutes, returning flushed of face, and slightly excited. John wondered if he had been drinking, and wondered also what Cæsar would say if he knew. About this time fear possessed his soul that Cæsar would come into the Manor and be taught by Scaife to drink. An occasional nightmare took the form of a desperate struggle between himself and Scaife, in which Scaife, by virtue of superior strength and skill, had the mastery, dragging off the beloved Cæsar, to plunge with him into fathomless pools of Scotch whisky. Somehow in these horrid dreams, Cæsar played an impressive part. Scaife and John fought for his body, while he looked on, an absurd state of affairs, never—as John reflected in his waking hours—likely to happen in real life. Of all boys Cæsar seemed to be the best equipped to fight his own battles, and to take, as he would have put it, "jolly good care of himself."

After the first of the football house-matches, Scaife got his "fez" from Lawrence, the captain of the House Eleven, and the only member of the School Eleven in Dirty Dick's. Some of the big fellows in the Fifth seized this opportunity to "celebrate," as they called it. Scaife was popular with the Fifth because—as John discovered later—he cheerfully lent money to some of them and never pressed for repayment.

And Scaife's getting his "fez" before he was fifteen might be reckoned an achievement. Cæsar, in particular, could talk of nothing else. He predicted that the Demon would be Captain of both Elevens, school racquet-player, and bloom into a second C. B. Fry.

John, upon this eventful evening, soon became aware of a shindy. It happened that Rutford was giving a dinner-party, and extremely unlikely to leave the private side of the house. John heard snatches of song, howls, and cheers. Ordinarily Lawrence (in whose passage the shindy was taking place) would have stopped this hullabaloo; but Lawrence was dining with his house-master, and Trieve, an undersized, weakly stripling, lacked the moral courage to interfere. John was getting a "con" from Trieve when an unusually piercing howl penetrated the august seclusion.

"What are they doing?" asked Trieve, irritably.

John hesitated. "It's the Fifth," he blurted out. "They've got Scaife in there, you know."

"Oh, indeed! Scaife is an excuse, is he, for this fiendish row? Go and tell Scaife I want to see him."

John looked rather frightened. He felt like a spaniel about to retrieve a lion. And scurrying along the passage he ran headlong into the Duffer, to whom he explained his errand.

"Phew-w-w!" said that young gentleman. "I'd sooner it was you than me, Verney. They're pretty well ginned-up, I can tell you."

John tapped timidly at the door of the room whence the songs and laughter proceeded. Then he tapped again, and again. Finally, summoning his courage, he rapped hard. Instantly there was silence, and then a furtive rustling of papers, followed by a constrained "Come in!"

John entered.

Most of the boys—there were about six of them—gazed at him in stupefaction. Scaife, very red in the face, burst into shrill shouts of laughter. Somehow the laughter disconcerted John. He forgot to deliver his message, but stood staring at Scaife, quaking with a young boy's terror of the unknown. Upon the table were some siphons, syrups, and the remains of a "spread."

"What the blazes do you want?" said Lovell, the owner of the room.

"I want Scaife," said John. "I mean that Trieve wants Scaife."

"Oh, Miss Trieve wants Master Scaife, does she? Well, young 'un, you tell Trieve, with my compliments, that Scaife can't come. See? Now—hook it!"

But John still stared at Scaife. The boy's dishevelled appearance, his wild eyes, his shrill laughter, revealed another Scaife.

"You'd better come, Scaife," he faltered.

"Not I," said Scaife. He spoke in a curiously high pitched voice, quite unlike his usual cool quiet tone. "Wait a mo'—I'm not Trieve's fag. I'm nobody's fag now, am I?"

He appealed to the crowd. It was an unwritten rule at

The Hill

the Manor, that members of the House cricket—or football—Elevens were exempt from fagging. But the common law of fagging at Harrow holds that any lower boy is bound to obey the Monitors, provided such obedience is not contrary to the rules of the school. In practice, however, no boy is fagged outside his own house, except for cricket-fagging in the summer term.

"Fag? Not you! Tell Miss Trieve to mind her own business."

John departed, feeling that an older and wiser boy might have tact to cope with this situation. For him, no course of action presented itself except delivering what amounted to a declaration of war.

"Won't come? Is he mad?"

"'Can't come,' they said."

"Oh, can't come? Has he hurt himself—sprained anything?"

John was truthful (more of a habit than some people believe). He told the truth, just as some boys quibble and prevaricate, simply and naturally. But now, he hesitated. If he hinted—a hint would suffice—that Scaife had hurt himself—and what more likely after the furious bit of playing which had secured his "fez"?—Trieve, probably, would do nothing. John felt in his bones that Trieve would be glad of an excuse to do—nothing.

"No; he hasn't sprained himself."

"Then why don't he come?"

"I—I——" Then he burst into excited speech. "He looks as if he *was* a little mad. Oh, Trieve, won't you leave him alone? Please do!

They must stop before prayers, and then Lawrence will be here."

O unhappy John—thou art not a diplomatist! Why lug in Lawrence, who has inspired mordant jealousy and envy in the heart of his second in command?

"Tell Scaife to come here at once," said Trieve, eying a couple of canes in the corner. "And if he should happen to ask what I want him for, say that I mean to whop him."

John fled.

"Whop him?"

The Fifth howled rage and remonstrance. Scaife

fiercely announced his intention of not taking a whopping from Trieve. None the less, the announcement had a sobering effect upon the elder boys. The consequence of a refusal must prove serious. Sooner or later Scaife would be whopped, probably by Lawrence, no ha'penny matter that!

"You'd better go, Demon," said Lovell. "Trieve can't hurt you. I'd speak to the idiot, only he hates me so poisonously, just as I hate him."

"I'll go," said the Caterpillar.

John had not noticed the Caterpillar before. He stood up, spick and span, carefully adjusting his coat, pulling down his immaculate cuffs.

"Good old Caterpillar," said somebody. "By Jove, he really thinks that Trieve will listen to—him!"

"Any one who has been nearly three years in this house," said the Caterpillar, "has the right to tell Miss Trieve that she is—er—not behaving like a lady."

"And he'll tell you you're screwed, you old fool."

"I am not screwed," replied the Caterpillar, solemnly. "Whisky and potass does not agree with everybody; but I am not screwed, not at all." So speaking he sat down rather suddenly.

Lovell shrugged his shoulders, glanced at the Caterpillar and Scaife, and left the room. Within two minutes he returned, chapfallen and frowning.

"I knew it would be useless. Look here, Demon, you must grin and bear it."

"No," said Scaife, "not from Miss Trieve."

He laughed as before. The Fifth exchanged glances. Then Scaife said thickly, "Give me another drink, I want a drink; so does young Verney. Look at him!"

John was white about the gills and trembling, but not for himself.

"Do go, Scaife!" he entreated.

The Fifth formed a group; holding a council of war, engrossed in trying to find a way out of a wood which of a sudden had turned into a tangled thicket. And so what each would have strenuously prevented came to pass. Scaife pulled a bottle from under a sofa-cushion, and put it to his lips—John, standing at the door, could not see what was taking place.

When the bottle was torn from Scaife's hands, the mischief had been done. The boy had swallowed a quantity of raw spirit. Till now the whisky had been much diluted with mineral water.

"I'm going to him," yelled Scaife, struggling with his friends. "And I'm going to take a cricket stump with me. Le'me go—le'me go!"

The Caterpillar surveyed him with disgust. After a brief struggle Scaife succumbed, helpless and senseless.

"One is reminded sometimes," said the Caterpillar, solemnly, "that the poor Demon is the son of a Liverpool merchant, bred in or about the Docks."

Nobody, however, paid any attention to Egerton, who, to do him justice, was the only boy present absolutely unmindful of his own peril.

Expulsion loomed imminent. The window was flung wide open, eau de Cologne liberally applied. Scaife lay like a log.

And then, in the middle of the confusion, Trieve walked in.

"Scaife has had a sort of fit," explained an accomplished liar. "You know what his temper is, Trieve? And when he heard that you meant to 'whop' him, he went stark staring mad."

This explanation was so near the truth that Trieve accepted it, probably with mental reservations.

"You had better send for Mrs. Puttick," he replied coldly.

The Caterpillar was despatched for the matron; but before that worthy woman panted upstairs, Scaife had been carried to his own room, hastily undressed and put into bed, where he lay breathing stertorously. The matron, good easy soul, accepted the boys' story unhesitatingly. A fit, of course, poor dear child! Mr. Rutford must be summoned.

With the optimism of youth, those present began to hope that dust might be thrown into the eyes of Dirty Dick. And, with a little discreet delay, the Demon might recover, when he could be relied upon to play his part with adroitness and ability. Accordingly, the matron was

44

urged to try her ministering hand first, amid the chaff, which, even in emergencies, slips so easily out of boys' mouths.

"Mrs. Puttick, you're better than any doctor—Scaife is all right, *really*. We knew that he was subject to fits— Rather! Some one was telling me that one of his aunts died in a fit.—Shut up, you silly fool," this in a whisper, emphasized by a kick; "do you want to send her out of this with a hornets' nest tied to her back hair?—That's a lie, Mrs. Puttick. He's humbugging you. Scaife told me that his fits were nothing. Yes; he had a slight sunstroke when he was a kid, you know, and the least bit of excitement affects him."

"Perhaps I'd better fetch a drop of brandy," said Mrs. Puttick, staring anxiously at Scaife. "He looks very bad."

"Yes, please do, Mrs. Puttick."

She bustled away.

"Now we *must* bring him to," said the Fifth Form.

Everything was tried, even to the expedient of flicking Scaife's body with a wet towel; but the boy lay motionless, his face horribly red against the white pillow, his heavy breathing growing more laboured and louder. And despite the perfume of the eau de Cologne which had drenched pillow and pyjamas, the smell of whisky spread terror to the crowd. If Rutford came in, he would swoop on the truth.

"We'll souse the brandy all over him," said the Caterpillar; "and then no one can guess."

"How about burnt feathers?" suggested Lovell. He had seen a fainting housemaid treated with this family restorative.

Mrs. Puttick appeared with the brandy, which Lovell administered externally. Still, Scaife remained unconscious. Then a pillow was ripped open, and enough feathers burned to restore—as the Caterpillar put it afterwards—a ruined cathedral. The stench filled the passage and brought to No. 15 a chattering crowd of Lower Boys. And then the conviction seized everybody that Scaife was going to die.

"Make way, make way, please!"

It was Rutford, who, followed by Lawrence, strode

down the passage into No. 15, and up to the bed.

"If you please, sir," said Lovell, "Scaife has had a fit."

"It looks like a fit," said Rutford, gravely. "I have telephoned for the doctor. You've tried," he sniffed the air, "all the wrong remedies, of course. Feathers—phaugh!—perfume—brandy! The boy must be propped up and the blood drawn from his head by applying hot water to his feet."

The Fifth exchanged glances. Why had this not occurred to them? What a fool Mrs. Puttick was!

"A rush of blood to the head!" Rutford like to hold forth, and he had been told that he was a capital after-dinner speaker. He had just risen from an excellent dinner; he was not much alarmed; and his audience listened with flattering attention. Scaife was lifted into a chair; ice was applied to his head; his feet were thrust into a "tosh" filled with steaming water.

"Note the effect," said Rutford. Already a slight change might be perceived; the breathing became easier, the face less red. Rutford continued in his best manner: "Mark the *vis medicatrix naturae*. Nature, assisted by hot water, gently accomplishes her task. Very simple, and not one of you had the wit to think of a remedy close at hand, and so easy to administer. The breathing is becoming normal. In a few minutes I predict that we shall have the satisfaction of seeing the poor dear fellow open his eyes, and he will tell us that he is but little the worse. Yes, yes, a rush of blood to the head producing cerebral disturbance."

He smiled blandly, receiving the homage of the Fifth.

"And now, Lovell, what do you know about this? Did this fit take place here?"

"In my room, sir."

"In your room—eh? What was Scaife, a Lower Boy, doing in your room?"

"Lawrence gave him his 'fez' to-day, sir."

Lawrence nodded.

"Ah! And Scaife was excited, perhaps unduly excited—eh?"

The Fifth joined in a chorus of, "Yes, sir.—Oh, yes, sir—Awfully excited, sir.—Never saw a boy so excited, sir."

"That will do. Now, Lovell, go on!"

"We had some siphons in our room, sir." A stroke of genius this—for the siphons were still on the table and the syrups, and the *débris* of cakes and meringues. Rutford would be sure to examine the scene of the catastrophe; and the whisky bottle was carefully hidden "We were having a spread, sir, and we asked Scaife to join us. His play to-day made him one of us."

The other boys gazed admiringly at Lovell. What a cool, knowing hand!

"Yes, yes, I see nothing objectionable about that."

"Well, sir—we were rather noisy——"

"Go on."

"To speak the exact truth, sir, I fear we were *very* noisy; and Trieve, it seems, heard us. Instead of sending for me, sir, he sent Verney for Scaife—"

"Ah!"

Lovell's hesitation at this point was really worthy of Coquelin *cadet*.

"Of course you know, sir, that Scaife's getting his 'fez' releases him from house-fagging. We thought Trieve had forgotten that, sir; and that it would be rather fun—I'm not excusing myself, sir—we thought it would be a harmless joke if we persuaded Scaife not to go."

"Um!"

"We were very foolish, sir. And then Trieve sent another message saying that Scaife was to go to his room at once to be—whopped."

"To be whopped. Um! Rather drastic that, very drastic under the circumstances."

"So we thought, sir; and I went to represent the facts to Trieve——"

"Well?"

"I'm not much of a peacemaker, I fear, sir. Trieve refused to listen to me. He insisted upon whopping Scaife for what he called disobedience and impudence. Upon my honour, sir, I tried, we all tried, to persuade Scaife to take his whopping quietly, but he seemed to go quite mad. He has a violent temper, sir——"

"Yes, yes."

"A very violent temper. He—he——"

"Frothed at the mouth," put in a bystander. "I particularly noticed that."

"Really, really——"

"Yes," said Lovell, nodding his head reflectively. "He frothed at the mouth, and then——"

"Grew quite black in the face," interpolated a third boy, who was determined that Lovell should not carry off all the honours.

"I should say—purple," amended Lovell. "And then he gave——"

"A beastly gurgle——"

"A sort of snort, and fell flat on his face. I'm not sure that he didn't strike the edge of the table as he fell."

"He did," said one of the boys. "I saw that."

At this moment Scaife moved in his chair, drawing all eyes to his face.

John, peering from behind the circle of big boys, could see the first signs of returning consciousness, a flicker of the eyelids, a convulsive tremor of the limbs. Rutford bent down.

"Well, my dear Scaife, how are you? We've been a little anxious, all of us, but, I ventured to predict, without cause. Tell us, my poor boy, how do you feel?"

Scaife opened his eyes. Then he groaned dismally. Rutford was standing to the right of the chair and footbath. The fifth were facing Scaife. He met their anxious, admonishing glances, unable to interpret them.

Lovell senior repeated the house-master's question— "How are you, old chap?"

But, in his anxiety to convey a warning, he came too near, obscuring Rutford's massive figure. Scaife groaned again, putting his hand to his head.

"How am I?" he repeated thickly. "Why, why, I'm jolly well screwed, Lovell; that's how I am! Jolly well screwed—hay? Ugh! how screwed I am. Ugh!"

The groans fell on a terrifying silence. Rutford glanced keenly from face to face. Then he said slowly—"The wretched boy is--drunk!"

At the sound of his house-master's voice, Scaife relapsed into an insensibility which no one at the moment cared to pronounce counterfeit or genuine. Rutford glared at Lovell.

"Who was in your room, Lovell?"

Without waiting for Lovell to answer, the other boys, each in turn, said, "I, sir," or "Me, sir." John came last.

"Anybody else, Lovell?"

A discreet master would not have asked this question, but Dirty Dick was the last man to waive an advantage. Now, the Caterpillar had quietly left No. 15, as soon as Rutford entered it. Not from any cowardly motive, but—as he put it afterwards—" because one makes a point of retiring whenever a rank outsider appears. One ought to be particular about the company one keeps." It says something for the boy's character, that this statement was accepted by the house as unvarnished truth. Lovell glanced at the other Fifth Form boys, as Rutford repeated the question.

"Anybody else, Lovell? Be careful how you answer me!"

"Nobody else," said Lovell.

"On your honour, sir?"

"On my honour, sir."

And, later, all Manorites declared that Lovell had lied like a gentleman. Rutford and he stared at each other, the boy pale, but self-possessed, the big burly man flushed and ill at ease.

"You will all go to my study. A word with you, Lawrence."

The boys filed quietly out. Rutford looked at John and Fluff. Large fat tears were trickling down Fluff's cheeks. Somehow he felt convinced that John was involved in a frightful row.

"Run away, Kinloch," said his house-master. "I wish to speak with Lawrence and Verney."

He turned to Lawrence as he spoke. John glanced at Scaife. His eyes were open. Silently, Scaife placed a trembling finger upon his lips. The action, the expression in the eyes, were unmistakable. John understood, as plainly as if Scaife had spoken, that silence, where expulsion impended, was not only expedient but imperative. Kinloch crept out of the room. Rutford examined Scaife, who feigned insensibility. Then he addressed Lawrence.

The Hill

"Go to Lovell's room, Lawrence, and institute a thorough search. If you find wine or spirits, let me know at once."

Lawrence left the room.

"Now, Verney, I am going to ask you a few questions." He assumed his rasping truculent tone. "And don't you dare to tell me lies, sir!"

John was about to repudiate warmly his housemaster's brutal injunction, when the habit of thinking before he spoke closed his half-opened lips. Immediately, his face assumed the obstinate, expressionless look which made those who searched no deeper than the surface pronounce him a dull boy. Rutford, for instance, interpreted this stolidity as unintelligence and lack of perception. John, meantime, was struggling with a thought which shaped itself slowly into a plan of action. He had just heard Lovell lie to save the Caterpillar. John knew well enough that he might be called upon to lie also, to save not himself, but Scaife. If he held his tongue and refused to answer questions, Rutford would assume, and with reason, that Scaife had been made drunk by the Fifth Form fellows.

Then John said quietly, "I am not a liar, sir."

"Certainly, I have never detected you in a lie," said Rutford.

"All the same," continued John, in a hesitating manner, "I would lie, if I thought a lie might save a friend's life."

Rutford was so unprepared for this deliberate statement, that he could only reply—

"Oh, you would, would you?"

"Yes," said John; then he added, "Any decent boy or man would."

"Oh! Oh, indeed! This is very interesting. Go on, Verney."

"Scaife said he *felt* as if he was jolly well screwed, sir; but he isn't. I'm quite sure he isn't. He may feel like it; but he isn't."

John could see Scaife's eyes, slightly blood-shot, but sparkling with a sort of diabolical sobriety. At that moment, one thing alone seemed certain, Scaife had regained full possession of his faculties. Rutford stared at John, frowning.

"You dare to look me in the face and tell me that Scaife is not drunk?"

Very seriously, John answered, "I'm sure he's not drunk, sir."

Rutford eyed the boy keenly.

"Have you ever seen anybody drunk?" he demanded.

"I live in the New Forest," said John, as gravely as before, "and on Whit-Monday——" He was aware that he had made an impression upon this big, truculent man.

"Don't try to be funny with me, Verney."

"Oh no, sir, as if I should dare!"

"Well, well, we are wasting time. Trieve sent you to Lovell's room to fetch Scaife?"

"Yes, sir."

"And what was Scaife doing when you went into the room? Be very careful!"

John considered. "He was laughing, sir."

"Laughing, was he?"

"But he stopped laughing when I gave him Trieve's message, and then he said what Lovell told you, sir."

"Never mind what Lovell told me. Give me your version of the story."

"Scaife asked the other fellows if Trieve had any right to fag him, now that he had got his 'fez.' If he had been drunk, sir, he wouldn't have thought of that, would he?"

"Um," said Rutford, slightly shaken. John described his return to Trieve's room, and Trieve's threat.

"Lovell and you tell the same story."

"Why, yes, sir." John made no deliberate attempt to look simple; but his face, to the master studying it, seemed quite guileless.

Just then, Dumbleton ushered in the doctor. To him Rutford recited what he knew and what he suspected. He had hardly finished speaking, when Scaife opened his eyes for the second time. By a curious coincidence, the doctor used the words of the house-master.

"Well, sir, how do you feel?" And then Scaife answered, in the same dazed fashion as before—

"I feel as if I was jolly well screwed, sir."

The Hill

Rutford nodded portentously.

"I feel," continued Scaife, "as I did once long ago, when I was a kid and got hold of some curacoa at one of my father's parties."

"Just so," said the doctor.

"Same buzzing in the head, same beastly feeling, same—same old—same old—giddiness." He closed his eyes, and his head fell heavily upon his chest.

"It looks like concussion," said the doctor, doubtfully. "You say he fell?" He turned to John.

"I was just outside the door," said John.

"We'll put him into the sick-room, Mr. Rutford. And in a day or two he'll be himself again."

"Are you sure that what I—er—feared—er——?"

The doctor frowned. "The boy has had brandy, of course."

"Mrs. Puttick and Lovell gave him plenty of that," John interpolated.

"I believe you can exonerate the boy entirely," said the doctor.

John saw that Rutford seemed relieved.

"I have ordered Lovell's room to be searched. If no wine or spirits are found, I shall be glad to believe that I have made a very pardonable mistake."

While Scaife was being removed, Lawrence came in with his report.

Nothing alcoholic had been discovered in Lovell's room. After prayers, which were late that night, Dirty Dick made a short speech.

"I had reason to suspect," said he, "that a gross breach of the rules of the school had been made to-night by certain boys in this house. It appears I was mistaken. No more will be said on the subject by me; and I think that the less said by you, big and small, the better. Good night."

He strode away into the private side.

Two days later, Scaife came back to No. 15. John wondered why he stared at him so hard upon the first occasion when they happened to be alone. Then Scaife said—

"Well, young Verney. I sha'n't forget that, if it hadn't

been for you, I should have been sacked. And I sha'n't forget either that you're not half such a fool as you look."

John exhibited surprise.

"The way you handled the beast," continued Scaife, "was masterly. I heard every word, though my head was bursting. I shall tell Lovell that you saved us. Oh, Lord—didn't I give the show away?"

He never tried to read the perplexity upon the other's face, but went away laughing. He came back with the Caterpillar half an hour later, and the three boys sat down as usual to prepare some Livy. John was sensible that his companions treated him not only as an equal—a new and agreeable experience—but as a friend. In the course of the first ten minutes Scaife said to the Caterpillar—

"He told Dick to his face that he would lie to save a pal."

And the Caterpillar replied seriously, "Good kid, very good kid. Lovell says he's going to give a tea in his honour."

"No he isn't. It's my turn."

Accordingly, upon the next half holiday, Scaife gave a tea at the Creameries. Of all the strange things that had happened during the past fortnight, this to our simple John seemed the strangest. He was not conscious of having done or said anything to justify the esteem and consideration in which Scaife, the Caterpillar, and Lovell seemed to hold him.

"You've forgotten Desmond," he said to Scaife, when the latter mentioned the names of his guests.

"Cæsar isn't coming. By the way, Verney, you've not been talking to Cæsar about the row in our house?"

"No," said John. "Lawrence came round and said that I must keep my mouth shut."

"And naturally you did what you were told to do?"

The half-mocking tone disappeared in a burst of laughter as John answered—

"Yes, of course."

"And I suppose it never entered your head that Lawrence would not have been so particular about shutting your mouth without good reason."

"Perhaps," said John, after a pause, "Lawrence was in a funk lest, lest——"

"Go on!"

"Lest the thing would be exaggerated."

"Exactly. Lots of fellows would go about saying that I was dead drunk—eh?"

"They might."

"And that would be coming dangerously near the truth."

"Oh, Scaife! Then you really were——"

Scaife laughed again. "Yes, I really was, my Moses in the bulrushes!

Don't look so miserable. I guessed all along that you weren't *quite* in the know. Well, I'm every bit as grateful. You stood up to Dick like a hero. And my tea is in your honour."

"Oh, Scaife—you—you won't do it again?"

"Get screwed?" said Scaife, gravely. "I shall not. It isn't good enough. We've chucked the stuff away."

"If they'd found it——"

"Ah—if! The old Caterpillar attended to that. He's a downy bird, I can tell you. When Dick came into our room, he slipped back to Lovell's room, carried off the whisky, hid it, washed the glasses, and then dirtied them with siphon and syrup. The Caterpillar and you showed great head. We shall drink your healths to-morrow—in tea and chocolate."

John wondered what Scaife had said to the Fifth. At any rate, they asked John no questions, and treated him, with distinguished courtesy and favour; but that evening, when John was fagging in Lawrence's room, the great man said abruptly—

"I saw you walking with Lovell senior this afternoon."

John explained. Lawrence frowned.

"Oh, you've been celebrating, have you? Thanksgiving service at the Creameries. Now, look here, Verney, I've met your uncle, and he asked me to keep an eye on you. Because of that I made you my fag—you, a green hand, when I had the pick of the House."

"It was awfully good of you," said John, warmly.

"We'll sink that. I'm five years older than you, and I

know every blessed—and *cursed*"—he spoke with great emphasis—" thing that goes on in this house. I know, for instance, that dust was thrown, and very cleverly thrown, into Rutford's eyes, and you helped to throw it.

Don't speak! You didn't quite know what you were up to. Well, it's lucky for Lovell and Co. that one innocent kid was mixed up in that affair. But it's been rather unlucky for you. I'd sooner see you kicked about a bit by those fellows than petted. I'm sorry—sorry, do you hear?—the whole lot were not sacked. And now you can hook it. I've said enough, perhaps too much, but I believe I can trust you."

After this John showed his gratitude by painstaking attention to fagging. Lawrence became aware of faithful service: that his toast was always done to a turn, that his daily paper was warmed, as John had seen the butler at home warm the *Times*, that his pens were changed, his blotting-paper renewed, and so forth. In John's eyes, Lawrence occupied a position near the apex of the world's pyramid of great men.

Chapter Four

Torpids

Again we rush across the slush,
 A pack of breathless faces,
And charge and fall, and see the ball
 Go whizzing through the bases.

THE remainder of the term slipped away without further accident or incident. Apart from the preparation of work, John saw little of Scaife or Egerton. The Fifth nodded to him in a friendly fashion when he passed them in the street, and, greater kindness on their part, left him alone. Possibly, Lawrence had said a word to Lovell. Such leisure as John enjoyed (a new boy at Harrow has not much) he spent with the devoted Fluff. Desmond and Scaife walked together on Sunday afternoons. But the fact that Desmond seemed to be vanishing out of his horizon made no difference to John's ever-increasing affection for him. Very humbly he worshipped at a distance. On clear, dry days Fluff and he would climb to the top of the wall of the squash racquet-courts to see Scaife and Desmond play a single. They were extraordinarily well-matched in strength, activity, and skill. John noticed, however, that the Demon lost his temper when he lost a game, whereas Cæsar only laughed. Somehow John divined that the Demon was making the effort of his life to secure Desmond's friendship. And Cæsar had ideals, standards to which the Demon pretended to attain.

Good simple John made sure that Cæsar would elevate the Demon to his plane, that evil would be exorcised by good. Only in his dreams did the Demon have the advantage.

Just before the end of the term, Cæsar said to him—

"After all, I'm jolly glad I'm coming into your House,

because the old Demon is such a ripper; and he and I have been talking things over. He's as mad keen as I am about games, and although the Manorites have not played in a cock-house match at cricket or footer for years, still there is a chance for us at Torpids next term. You'll play, Verney. You've improved a lot, so the Demon says, and he'll be captain. Then there are the sports. If only Dirty Dick could be knocked on the head, the Manor might jump to the front again."

"It will," said John.

When the School reassembled after Christmas, Desmond entered the Manor, and found himself with Scaife in a two-room. A civil note from the man of millions had arranged this. To John was given a two-room, also, with the Duffer as stable companion. Fluff remained in No. 15. The Duffer had got his remove from the Top Shell into John's form. Scaife and Desmond were elevated into the Upper Remove. It followed, therefore, that Scaife and Desmond prepared work in their own room, the Caterpillar joining the Duffer and John. Thus it will be seen that, although Desmond had become a Manorite, he was, practically speaking, out of John's orbit.

The Caterpillar had now been three years in the school, and he governed himself accordingly. He put on a "barmaid"* collar and spent much time on the top step of the boys' entrance to the Manor. No mere two-year-old presumed to occupy this sacred spot. Had he dared to do so, the Caterpillar would have made things very sultry for him. Also, he informed the Duffer and John that, by virtue of his position, he proposed to prepare no work at all. Each "con" was divided into two equal parts: the Duffer "mugged" up one; John the other. Then the Caterpillar would be summoned, and glean the harvest. The Duffer had a crib or two, but the Caterpillar forbade their use.

---

* "Barmaid" collar is the double collar, at that time just coming into fashion.

"You kids," said he, "ought not to use 'Bohns.' Besides, it's dangerous."

The Caterpillar's deportment and coolness filled John and the Duffer with respect and admiration. The master in charge of the Lower Remove happened to be short-sighted. The Caterpillar took shameful advantage of this. At repetitions, for instance, he would read Horace's odes off a torn-out page concealed in the palm of his hand, or—if practicable—pin the page on to the master's desk.

He had genius for extricating himself (and others) out of what boys call tight places. One anecdote, well known to the Lower School and repeated as proof of the Caterpillar's masterly methods, may serve to illustrate the sort of influence Egerton wielded. When he was in the Fourth, his form met in the Old Schools in a room not far from that august chamber used by the Head Master and Upper Sixth. One day, the master in charge of the form happened to be late. The small boys in the passage celebrated his absence with dance and song. When the belated man arrived, a monitor awaited him. The Head Master presented his compliments to Mr. A—— and wished to learn the names of the boys who had created such a scandalous disturbance. Mr. A—— invited the roysterers to give up their names under penalties of extra school. Hateful necessity! Silence succeeded. A—— grew irate. The monitor tried to conceal a smile.

"Any boy who was making any noise at all—stand up."

The Caterpillar rose slowly, long and thin, spick and span.

"If you please, sir," said he, "I was *whispering!*"

A——'s sense of humour was tickled.

"My compliments to the Head Master," said he, "and please tell him that I find, on careful inquiry, that Egerton was—whispering."

A shout of laughter from Olympus proclaimed that the message had been delivered. The Caterpillar had saved the situation.

John became a disciple of this accomplished young gentleman and tried to imitate him. For Egerton represented, faithfully enough, traditions to which John bowed the knee. Upon any point of schoolboy honour his authority ruled supreme. He told the truth among his peers; he loathed obscenity; he disliked and condemned bad language.

"The best men don't swear much," he would say. "It's doosid bad form. I allow myself a 'damn' or two, nothing more. My great-grandfather, who was one of the Regency lot, was known as Cursing Egerton, but nowadays we leave that sort of thing to bargees."

Quite unconsciously, John assimilated the Caterpillar's axioms.

"We're not sent here at enormous expense to learn only Latin and Greek. At Harrow and Eton one is licked into shape for the big things: diplomacy, politics, the Services. One is taught manners, what? I'm not a marrying sort of man, but if I do have sons I shall send 'em here, even if I have to pinch a bit."

This was the side of Egerton which appealed so strongly to John. The Caterpillar was an Harrovian to the core, like the Duffer and Cæsar Desmond. He deplored the increasing predominance of sons of very rich men. And he anathematized Harrovian fathers who were persuaded by Etonian wives to send their sons to the Plain instead of to the Hill. That some of the famous Harrow families, who owed so much to the School, should forsake it, seemed to Egerton the unpardonable sin.

During this term, regretfully must it be recorded that John scamped his "prep" and "ragged" in form whenever a suitable chance presented itself. The Duffer and he bribed a "Chaw"* to throw gravel against the windows of the room where the boys were supposed to be mastering the problems of Euclid and algebra. The "tique"† master had been Third Wrangler, but he couldn't tackle his Division properly. Upon this occasion the "chaw" created such a disturbance that (on audacious demand) leave was granted to the Duffer and John to capture the

---

* "Chaw," short for Chawbacon.
† "Tique," *ab.* for arithmetic. "Tique-beaks" are mathematical masters.

offender. The young rascals pursued the "chaw" as far as the Metropolitan Station, and presented that conscientious youth with another sixpence. Then it occurred to John that it might be expedient to capture some bogus prisoner; so by means of talk, sugared with chocolates, they persuaded a little girl to impersonate the thrower of gravel. The little girl, carefully coached in her part, was led to the Wrangler, but stage-fright made her burst into tears at the critical moment. Somehow or other the truth leaked out; the Duffer and John were sent up to the Head Master and "swished." Each collected a few twigs of the birch, carefully preserved to this day.

Meantime, the Torpid house-matches were coming on, and the School agreed, wonderingly, that Dirty Dick's had a chance of being cock-house. The fact that the Manor had lost caste brought about this possibility. Boys just under fifteen found room at the Manor when other houses were full. All the Manorites in the Shell and Removes were fellows who had come to Harrow rather over than under fourteen years of age.

And when the list of the Torpid Eleven was posted, didn't John's heart boil with pride when he read his own name at the bottom of it?

The Manor won the first and the second of the matches. Then came the semi-finals with Damer's. When the teams met in the playing-fields the difference in the size of the players was remarked. Damer's Torpids were small boys, not much bigger than John or the Duffer. But they had behind them that stupendous force which is fashioned out of pride, *esprit de corps,* self-confidence begotten of long-continued success, and, strongest of all, the conviction that every man-Jack would fight till he dropped for the honour and glory of the crack house at Harrow. Not a boy in Damer's team was Scaife's equal as a player, but in Scaife's strength lay the weakness of the Manorites. They relied upon one player; Damer's pinned faith to eleven.

As it happened to be a fine day, the School turned out in force to witness the match. Most of the masters were present, and some ladies. Rutford, however, had business elsewhere. The School commented upon his absence with sly smiles and shrugs of the shoulder. Some of the Manorites were indifferent; the better sort raged. The Caterpillar appeared upon the ground in a faultless overcoat, carrying a large bag of lemons. His straw hat was cocked at a slight angle.

"One is really uncommonly obliged to Dirty Dick for staying away," he told everybody. "Speaking personally, the mere sight of him is very upsetting to me. Keen as one feels about this match, one can't deny that there is not room in a footer field for Dirty Dick and a self-respecting person."

None the less, the absence of their house-master had a bad effect upon the Torpids. Damer, you may be sure, had come down, prepared to cheer louder than any boy in his house; Damer, it was whispered, had been known to shed tears when his house suffered defeat; Damer, in fine, inspired ardours—a passion of endeavour.

Scaife won the toss and kicked off.

For the first five minutes nothing of interest happened. Damer's played collectively; the Manorites rather waited upon the individual. When Scaife's chance came, so it was predicted, he would go through the Damer's centre as irresistibly as a Russian battleship cuts through a fleet of fishing-smacks.

Rutford being absent, Dumbleton, the butler, stood well to the fore. He never missed a house match, and no one could guess, looking at his wooden countenance, how the game was going; for he accepted either defeat or victory with dignified self-restraint. A smart bit of work provoked a bland, "Well played, sir, *very well* played, sir!" uttered in the same respectful tone in which he requested Lovell, let us say, to go to Mr. Rutford's study after prayers. The fags believed that "Dumber," who had begun his career as boot-boy at the Manor in the glorious days of old, had given notice to leave when he learned that Dirty Dick was about to assume command; but had been prevailed upon to stay by the promise of an enormous salary. Nothing disturbed his equanimity. On the previous Saturday evening, John had heated the wrong end of the poker in No. 15, knowing that Dumber's duty constrained him to march round the House after "lights out," to rake out any fires that might be still burning. Snug under his counterpane, the practical joker awaited, chuckling, a choleric word from the impassive and impeccable butler. How did Dumber divine that the poker was unduly hot and black with soot underneath? Who can answer that question? The fact remains that he seized John's best Sunday trousers which were laid out on a chair, and holding the poker with these, accomplished his task without remark or smile. The trousers had to be sent to the tailor's to be cleaned.

Not far from Dumber stood a group of small boys, including the unhappy Fluff—unhappy because he was not playing, despite arduous training (entirely to please John) and systematic coaching. His failure meant further separation from John, whom, it will be remembered, he would have been allowed to call by his Christian name, had he been included amongst the Torpids. Of late, Fluff had not seen much of John, and in his dark hours he allowed his thoughts to linger, not unpleasantly sometimes, upon premature death and John's subsequent remorse.

Meantime, Scaife and Desmond were playing a furious game which must have proved successful had it not been for the admirable steadiness of the enemy. Lawrence watched their efforts with compressed lips and frowning brows. He knew—who better?—that his cracks were tearing themselves to tatters; but his protests were drowned by the shrill cheers of the fags.

"Rutfords—Rutfor-r-r-r-ds! Go it, old Demon!—Jolly well played, Cæsar!—Sky* him!—Well skied, sir!—Ah-h-h-h! Well given—well taken!"

The last, long-drawn-out exclamation proclaimed that "Yards"† had been given to Scaife right in front of Damer's

---

* To "sky," i.e. to charge and overthrow.
† In the Harrow game a boy may turn and kick the ball into the hands of one of his own side. The boy who catches it calls "Yards!" and, the opposite side withdrawing three yards, the catcher is allowed a free kick.

base. Damer's retreated; Scaife, with heaving chest, balanced the big ball between the tips of his fingers.

"Oh-h-h-h-h!"

Scaife had missed an easy shot. Lawrence could see that the boy was trembling with disappointment and mortification. Barbed arrows from Damer's small boys pierced Manorite hearts.

"Jolly well boshed, Scaife!—Good, kind, old Demon!—Thank you, Scaife!—" and like derisive approbation rolled from lip to lip.

The Caterpillar turned to Lovell. "Showing temper, ain't he?"

"Yes," said Lovell.

"Clever chap," said the Caterpillar, reflectively; "but one is reminded that a stream can't rise higher than its source. Not mine that—the governor's! Cæsar is facing the chaff with a grin."

The game began again. But soon it became evident that Scaife had lost, not only his temper, but his head. He rushed here and there with so little judgment that the odds amongst the sporting fellows went to six to four against the Manor. At the beginning of the game they were six to four the other way. And, inevitably, Scaife's wild and furious efforts unbalanced Desmond's play. Both boys were out of their proper places to the confusion of the rest of the team. Within half an hour Damer's had scored two bases to nothing.

The Caterpillar distributed halves of lemons. Lawrence went up to Scaife. The captain of the Torpids was standing apart, not far from Desmond, who was sucking a lemon with a puzzled expression. Gallant, sweet-tempered, and always hopeful, Cæsar could not understand his friend's passion of rage and resentment. With the tact of his race, however, he held aloof, smiling feebly, because he had sworn to himself not to frown. Had he looked to his right, he would have seen John, also sucking a lemon, but understudying his idol's nonchalant attitude and smile. John was sensible of an overpowering desire to fling himself upon the ground and howl. Instead he sucked his lemon, stared at Desmond, and smiled—valiantly.

"Scaife," said Lawrence, gravely, "you're not playing the game."

Scaife scowled. "I only know I've half killed myself," he muttered.

Lawrence continued in the same steady voice, "Yes; because you missed an easy base which has happened to me and every other player scores of times. Come here, Desmond."

Desmond joined them. Lawrence's face brightened when he saw hopeful eyes and a gallant smile.

"You don't despair?"

"We'll knock 'em into smithereens yet."

"That's the Harrow spirit, but temper your determination to win with a little common sense. You've overdone it, both of you. Take my tip: they'll play up like blazes. Defend your own base; and then when they're spent, trample on 'em."

"Thank you," said Desmond.

Scaife nodded sulkily.

None the less he had too great respect for Lawrence's ability and experience as a captain to disregard his advice. After the kick-off, Damer's *did* play up, and the Manor had to defend its base against sustained and fierce attack. Again and again a third base was almost kicked, again and again superior weight prevailed in the scrimmages.

Within ten minutes Damer's were gasping and weary. And then, the ball was forced out of the scrimmage and kicked to the top side, Desmond's place in the field. Comparatively fresh, seeing the glorious opportunity, grasping it, hugging it, Cæsar swooped on the ball. He had the heels of any boy on the opposite side. Down the field he sped, faster and faster, amid the roars of the School, roars which came to his ears like the deep booming of breakers upon a lee shore. To many of those watching him, the sight of that graceful figure, that shining ardent face, revealing the promise which youth and beauty always offer to a delighted world, became an ineffaceable memory. Damer turned to the Head of his house.

"And Desmond ought to be one of *us*," he groaned.

The Hill

And now Cæsar had passed all forwards. If he keep his wits a base is certain. The full back alone lies between him and triumph. But this is the moment, the psychological moment, when one tiny mistake will prove irrevocable. The Head of Damer's whispers as much to Damer, who smiles sadly.

"His father's son will not blunder now," he replies. Nor does he. The mistake—for mistake there must be on one side or t'other—is made by Damer's back. As the ball rolls halfway between them, the back hesitates and falters.

One base to two—and eighteen minutes to play!

The second base was kicked by Scaife five minutes later.

By this time the School knew that they were looking on at a cock-house match, not a semi-final. It was the wealth of Dives against the widow's mite that the winner of this match would defeat easily either of the two remaining houses. And not a man or boy on the ground could name with any conviction the better eleven. The betting languished at evens.

Moreover, both sides were playing "canny," risking nothing, nursing their energies for the last furious five minutes. Damer began to fidget; then he dropped out of the front rank of spectators. He couldn't stand still to see his boys win—or lose. He paced up and down behind the fags, who winked at each other.

"Damer's got the needle," they whispered.

Dumbleton, however, stood still; a graven image of High Life below Stairs.

"What do you think, Dumber?" asked Fluff.

"I think, my lord," replied Dumber, solemnly, "that every minute improves our chance, but if it goes on much longer," he added phlegmatically, "I shall fall down dead. My 'eart's weak, my lord."

This was an ancient joke delivered by Dumber as if it were brand-new, and received by the fags in a like spirit.

"Bless you, you've got no heart, Dumber. It's turned into tummy long ago," or, in scathing accents, "It's not your heart that's out of whack, Dumber, but your blithering old headpiece. What a pity you can't buy a new one!" and so on and so forth.

Very soon, however, this chaff ceased. Excitement began to shake the spectators. They felt it up and down their spinal columns; it formed itself into lumps in their throats; it gave one or two cramp in the calves of their legs; It reddened many cheeks and whitened as many more. The Caterpillar pulled out his watch.

"Three and a half minutes," he announced in a voice which fell like the crack of doom upon the silent crowd. If they could have cheered or chaffed! But the absolute equality of the last desperate struggle prevented any demonstration. The ball was worried through a scrimmage, escaped to the right, slid out to the left, only to be returned whence it came. It seemed as if both sides were unable to kick it, and when kicked it seemed to refuse to move as if weighted by the ever-increasing burden of suspense.

"Now—now's your chance!" yelled the Manorites.

To their flaming senses the ball appeared to be lying, a huge blurred sphere, upon the muddy grass; and the Elevens were stupidly staring at it. The Saints be praised! Some fellow can move. Who is it? The players, big and little, are so daubed with mud from head to foot as to be unrecognizable. Ah-h-h! It's young Verney.

"Good kid! Well played—I say, well played, well pla-a-a-a-yed!"

Our John has, it seems, distinguished himself. He has charged valiantly into the captain of Damer's at the moment when that illustrious chief is about to kick the ball to a trusted lieutenant on the left. He succeeds in kicking the ball into John's face. John goes over backwards; but the ball falls just in front of the Duffer.

"Kick it, Duffer—kick it, you old ass!"

The Duffer kicks it most accurately, kicks it well out to the top side. Now, can Desmond repeat his amazing performance? Yes—No—he can't. The conditions are no longer the same. Half a dozen fellows are between him and the Damer base.

Alas! The Manor is about to receive a second object-lesson upon the fatuity of trusting to individuals. Confident in Cæsar's ability to take the ball at least within kicking distance of the base, they have rushed forward, leaving unguarded their own citadel. Cæsar, going too fast, misjudges the distance between himself and the back. A second later the ball is well on its way to the Manor's base. The back awaits it, coolly enough; knowing that Damer's forwards are offside. Then he kicks the sodden, slippery ball—hard. An exclamation of horror bursts from the Manorites. Their back has kicked the ball straight into the hands of the Damerite captain, the steadiest player on the ground.

"*Yards!*"

The chief collects himself for a decisive effort, and then despatches the ball straight and true for the target. It passed between the posts within forty-five seconds of time.

Chapter Five

Fellowship

"Fellowship is Heaven, and the lack of it is Hell."

JOHN was squelching through the mud, wondering whether his nose was broken or not, when Lawrence touched his shoulder.

"Never mind, Verney," he said cheerily; "the Manor will be cock-house at Torpids next year, and I venture to prophesy that you'll be Captain."

"Oh, thanks, Lawrence," said John.

But, much as he appreciated this tribute from the great man, and much as it served to mitigate the pangs of defeat, a yet happier stroke of fortune was about to befall him. Desmond, who always walked up from the football field with Scaife, conferred upon John the honour of his company.

"Where's Scaife?" said John.

"The Demon is demoniac," said Desmond. "He's lost his hair, and he blames me. Well, I did my best, and so did he, and there's no more to be said. It's a bore that we shall be too old to play next year. I told the Demon that if we had to be beaten, I would sooner take a licking from Damer's than any other house; and he told me that he believed I wanted 'em to win. When a fellow's in that sort of blind rage, I call him dotty, don't you?"

"Yes," said John.

"You played jolly well, Verney; I expect Lawrence told you so."

"He did say something decent," John replied.

The Caterpillar joined them as they were passing through the stile.

"We should have won," he said deliberately, "if the Demon hadn't behaved like a rank out-rider."

"Scaife is my pal," said Desmond, hotly.

The Hill

The Caterpillar shrugged his shoulders, and held high his well-cut aquiline nose, as he murmured—"One doesn't pretend to be a Christian, but as a gentleman one accepts a bit of bad luck without gnashing one's teeth. What? That Spartan boy with the fox was a well bred 'un, you take my word for it. Scaife isn't."

The Caterpillar joined another pair of boys before Desmond could reply. John looked uncomfortable. Then Desmond burst out with Irish vehemence—"Egerton is always jawing about breeding. It's rather snobbish. I don't think the worse of Scaife because his grandfather carried a hod.

The Egertons have been living at Mount Egerton ever since they left Mount Ararat, but what have they done? And he ought to make allowances for the old Demon. He was simply mad keen to win this match, and he has a temper. You like him, Verney, don't you?"

John hesitated, realizing that to speak the truth would offend the one fellow in the school whom he wished to please and conciliate. Then he blurted out—

"No--I don't."

"You don't?" Desmond's frank blue eyes, Irish eyes, deeply blue, with black lashes encircling them, betrayed amazement and curiosity—so John thought—rather than anger. "You don't?" he continued. "Why not? The old Demon likes you; he says you got him out of a tight place. Why don't you like him, Verney?"

John's mind had to speculate vaguely whether or not Desmond knew the nature of the tight place—*tight* was such a very descriptive adjective—out of which he had pulled Scaife. Then he said nervously—"I don't like him because—because he likes—you."

"Likes me? What a rum 'un you are, Verney! Why shouldn't he like me?"

"Because," said John, boldly meeting the emergency with the conviction that he had burnt his ships, and must advance without fear, "because he's not half good enough for you."

Desmond burst out laughing; the clear ringing laugh of his father, which had often allayed an incipient mutiny below the gangway, and charmed aside the impending disaster of a snatch-division. And it is on *one's own side* in the House of Commons that good temper tells preeminently.

"Not good enough for me!" he repeated. "Thanks awfully. Evidently you have a high opinion of—*me.*"

"Yes," said John.

The quiet monosyllable, so soberly, so seriously uttered, challenged Desmond's attention. He stared for a moment at John's face—not an attractive object. Blood and mud disfigured it. But the grey eyes met the blue unwaveringly. Desmond flushed.

"You've stuck me on a sort of pedestal." His tone was as serious as John's.

"Yes," said John.

They were opposite the Music Schools. The other Manorites had run on. For the moment they stood alone, ten thousand leagues from Harrow, alone in those sublimated spaces where soul meets soul unfettered by flesh. Afterwards, not then, John knew that this was so. He met the real Desmond for the first time, and Desmond met the real John in a thoroughfare other than that which leads to the Manor, other than that which leads to any house built by human hands, upon the shining highway of Heaven.

Shall we try to set down Desmond's feelings at this crisis? Till now, his life had run gaily through fragrant gardens, so to speak: pleasances full of flowers, of sweet smelling herbs, of stately trees, a paradise indeed from which the ugly, the crude, the harmful had been rigorously excluded. Happy the boy who has such a home as was allotted to Harry Desmond! And from it, ever since he could remember, he had received tender love, absolute trust, the traditions of a great family whose name was part of English history, an exquisite refinement, and, with these, the gratification of all reasonable desires. And this magnificent upbringing shone out of his radiant face, the inexpressible charm of youth unspotted—white. Scaife's upbringing, of which you shall know more presently, had been far different, and yet he, the cynic and the unclean, recognized the God in Harry Desmond. He had not, for instance, told Desmond of the nature of that "tight" place;

The Hill

he had kept a guard over his tongue; he had interposed his own strong will between his friend and such attention as a boy of Desmond's attractiveness might provoke from Lovell senior and the like. It is true that Scaife was well aware that without these precautions he would have lost his friend; none the less, above and beyond this consciousness hovered the higher, more subtle intuition that the good in Desmond was something not lightly to be tampered with, something awe-inspiring; the more so because, poor fellow! he had never encountered it before.

Desmond stood still, with his eyes upon John's discoloured face. Not the least of Cæsar's charms was his lack of self-consciousness. Now, for the first time, he tried to see himself as John saw him—on a pedestal. And so strong was John's ideal that in a sense Desmond did catch a glimpse of himself as John saw him. And then followed a rapid comparison, first between the real and the ideal, and secondly between himself and Scaife. His face broke into a smile.

"Why, Verney," he exclaimed, "you mustn't turn me into a sort of Golden Calf. And as for Scaife not being good enough for me, why, he's miles ahead of me in everything. He's cleverer, better at games, ten thousand times better looking, and one day he'll be a big power, and I shall always be a poor man. Why, I—I don't mind telling you that I used to keep out of Scaife's way, although he was always awfully civil to me, because he has so much and I so little."

"He's not half good enough for you," repeated John, with the Verney obstinacy. Unwittingly he slightly emphasized the "good."

"Good? Do you mean 'pi'? He's not *that*, thank the Lord!"

This made John laugh, and Desmond joined in. Now they were Harrow boys again, within measurable distance of the Yard, although still in the shadow of the Spire. The Demon described as "pi" tickled their ribs.

"You must learn to like the Demon," Desmond continued, as they moved on. Then, as John said nothing, he added quickly, "He and I have made up our minds not to try for a remove this term. You see, next term is the jolliest term of the year—cricket and 'Ducker'* and Lord's. And we shall know the form's swat thoroughly, and have time to enjoy ourselves. You'll be with us. Your remove is a 'cert'—eh?"

John beamed. He had made certain that Cæsar would be in the Third Fifth next term and hopelessly out of reach.

"Oh yes, I shall get my remove. So will the Caterpillar."

"Hang the Caterpillar," said Desmond.

"He'd ask for a silken rope, as Lord Ferrers did," said John, with one of his unexpected touches of humour. Again Desmond bent his head in the gesture John knew so well, and laughed.

"I say, Verney, you *are* a joker. Well, the old Caterpillar's a good sort, but he's not fair to Scaife. Here we are!"

They ran upstairs to "tosh" and change. John found the Duffer just slipping out of his ducks. He looked at John with a rueful grin.

"Are you going to chuck me?" he asked.

"Chuck you?"

"Fluff says you've chucked him. He was in here a moment ago to ask if your nose was squashed. I believe the silly little ass thinks you the greatest thing on earth."

"I don't chuck anybody," said John, indignantly. And he made a point of asking Fluff to walk with him on Sunday.

After the Torpid matches the school settled down to train (more or less) for the athletic sports. John came to grief several times at Kenton brook, essaying to jump it at places obviously—as the Duffer pointed out—beyond his stride. The Duffer and he put their names down for the house-handicaps, and curtailed their visits to the Creameries. After this self-denial it is humiliating to record that neither boy succeeded in winning anything. Cæsar won the house mile handicap; Scaife won the

---

* "Duck-Puddle," is the school bathing-place.

The Hill

under sixteen high jump—a triumph for the Manor; and Fluff, the despised Fluff, actually secured an immense tankard, which one of the Sixth offered as a prize because he was quite convinced that his own particular pal would win it. The distance happened to be half a mile. Fluff was allowed an enormous start, and won in a canter.

The term came to an end soon after these achievements, and John spent a week of the holidays at White Ladies, the Duke of Trent's Shropshire place. Here, for the first time, he saw that august and solemn personage, a Groom of the Chambers, with carefully trimmed whiskers, a white tie, a silky voice, and the appearance of an arch-deacon. This visit is recorded because it made a profound impression upon a plastic mind. John had never sat in the seats of the mighty. Verney Boscobel was a delightful old house, but it might have been put, stables and all, into White Ladies, and never found again. Fluff showed John the famous Reynolds and Gainsborough portraits, the Van Dycks and Lelys, the Romneys and Richmonds. Fair women and brave men smiled or frowned at our hero wherever he turned his wondering eyes. After the first tour of the great galleries, he turned to his companion.

"I say," he whispered solemnly, "some of 'em look as if they didn't like my calling you—Fluff."

"I wish you'd call me Esmé."

"All right," said John, "I will; and—er—although you didn't get into the Torpids, you can call me—John."

"Oh, John, thanks awfully."

Ponies were provided for the boys to ride, and they shot rabbits in the Chase. Also, they appeared at dinner, a tremendous function, and were encouraged by some of the younger guests to spar (verbally, of course) with the duke's Etonian sons. Fluff looked so much stronger and happier that his parents, delighted with their experiment, were inclined to cry up the Hill, much to the exasperation of the dwellers in the Plain.

When he left White Ladies John had learned one valuable lesson. His sense of that hackneyed phrase, *noblesse oblige*, the sense which remains nonsense with so many boys (old and young), had been quickened. Little more than a child in many ways, he realized, as a man does, the true significance of rank and wealth. The Duke of Trent had married a pleasure-loving dame; White Ladies was essentially a pleasure-house, to which came gladly enough the wit and beauty of the kingdom. And yet the duke, not clever as compared to his guests, not even good-looking as compared to the splendid gentlemen whom Van Dyck and Lely had painted, *undistinguished*, in fine, in everything save rank and wealth, worked, early and late, harder than any labourer upon his vast domain. And when John said to Fluff, "I say, Esmé, why does the duke work so beastly hard?" Fluff replied with emphasis, "Why, because he has to, you know. It's no joke to be born a duke, and I'm jolly glad that I'm a younger son. Father says that he has no amusements, but plenty of occupation. Mother says he's the unpaid land-agent of the Trent property."

John went back to Verney Boscobel, and repeated what Fluff had said, as his own.

"It was simply splendid, mum, like a sort of castle in fairyland and all that, but I *am* glad I'm not a duke. And I expect that even an earl has a lot of beastly jobs to do which never bother *us*."

"Oh, you've found that out, have you, John? Well, I hesitated when the invitation came; but I'm glad now that you went."

"Yes; and it's ripping to be home again."

The summer term began in glorious sunshine; and John forgot that he owned an umbrella. The Caterpillar and he had achieved their remove, but the unhappy Duffer was left behind alone with the hideous necessity of doing his form's work by himself. The boys occupied the same rooms, but John prepared his Greek and Latin with Scaife, Cæsar, and the Caterpillar; whom he was now privileged to call by their nick-names. They began to call him John, hearing young Kinloch do so; and then one day, Scaife, looking up with his derisive smile, said—"I'm going to call you Jonathan."

"Good," said Desmond. "All the same, we can't call either the Duffer or Fluff—David, can we?"

The Hill

"I was not thinking of Kinloch or Duff," said Scaife, staring hard at John. And John alone knew that Scaife read him like a book, in which he was contemptuously amused—nothing more. After that, as if Scaife's will were law, the others called John—Jonathan.

Very soon, the sun was obscured by ever-thickening clouds, John happened to provoke the antipathy of a lout in his form known as Lubber Sprott. Sprott began to persecute him with a series of petty insults and injuries. He accused him of "sucking up" to a lord, of putting on "lift" because he was the youngest boy in the Upper Remove, of kow-towing to the masters—and so forth. Then, finding these repeated gibes growing stale, he resorted to meaner methods. He upset ink on John's books, or kicked them from under his arm as he was going up to the New Schools. He put a "dringer"* into the pocket of John's "bluer."† He pinched him unmercifully if he found himself next to John in form, knowing that John would not betray him. When occasion offered he kicked John. In short, he was successful in taking all the fun and sparkle out of the merrie month of May.

Finally, Cæsar got an inkling of what was going on.

"Is Sprott ragging you?" he asked point-blank.

"Ye-es," said John, blushing. "It's n-nothing," he added nervously. "He'll get tired of it, I expect."

"I saw him kick you," said Desmond, frowning. "Now, look here, Jonathan, you kick him; kick him as hard as ever you can where, where he kicks you—eh? And do it to-morrow in the Yard, at nine Bill, when everybody is looking on. You can dodge into the crowd; but if I were

---

* A "Dringer" is composed of the following ingredients: a layer of strawberries is secreted in sugar and cream at the bottom of a clean jam-pot; and this receives a decent covering of strawberry ice, which brings the surface of the dringer and the top edge of the jam-pot into the same plane. The whole may be bought for sixpence.

† A "Bluer" is the blue-flannel jacket worn in the playing fields. It must be worn *buttoned* by boys who have been less than two years in the school.

you I'd kick him at the very moment he gets into line, and then he can't pursue. And if he does pursue—which I'll bet you a bob he don't, he'll have to tackle you and me."

"I'll do it," said John.

Next day, a whole holiday, at nine Bill, both Cæsar and John were standing close to the window of Custos' den, waiting for Lubber Sprott to appear. While waiting, an incident occurred which must be duly chronicled inasmuch as it has direct bearing upon this story. Only the week before Rutford had come up to the Yard late for Bill, he being the master whose turn it was to call over. Such tardiness, which happens seldom, is reckoned as an unpardonable sin by Harrow boys. Briefly it means that six hundred suffer from the unpunctuality of one. Therefore, when Rutford appeared, slightly flushed of countenance and visibly annoyed, the School emphasized their displeasure by derisive cheers. Rutford, ever tactless where boys were concerned, was unwise enough to make a speech from the steps condemning, in his usual bombastic style, a demonstration which he ought to have known he was quite powerless to punish or to prevent. When he had finished, the School cheered more derisively than before. After Bill, he left the Yard, purple with rage and humiliation.

Upon this particular morning, one of the younger masters, Basil Warde, was calling Bill. The School knew little of Warde, save that he was an Old Harrovian in charge of a Small House, and that his form reported him—queer. He had instituted a queer system of punishments, he made queer remarks, he looked queer: in fine, he was generally regarded as a radical, and therefore a person to be watched with suspicion by boys who, as a body, are intensely conservative. He was of a clear red complexion with lapis-lazuli blue eyes, that peculiar blue which is the colour of the sea on a bright stormy day. The Upper School knew that, as a member of the Alpine Club, Warde had conquered half a dozen hitherto unconquerable peaks.

Into the Yard and into this book Warde comes late. As he hurried to his place, the School greeted him as they had greeted Rutford only the week before. If anything, the

The Hill

demonstration was slightly more hostile. That Bill should be delayed twice within ten days was unheard-of and outrageous. When the hoots and cheers subsided, Warde held up his hand. He smiled, and his chin stuck out, and his nose stuck up at an angle familiar to those who had scaled peaks in his company. In silence, the School awaited what he had to say, hoping that he might slate them, which would afford an excuse for more ragging. Warde, guessing, perhaps, the wish of the crowd, smiled more genially than before. Then, in a loud clear voice, he said—"I beg pardon for being late. And I thank you for cheering me. I haven't been cheered in the Yard since the afternoon when I got my Flannels."

A deafening roar of applause broke from the boys. Warde might be queer, but he was a good sort, a gentleman, and, henceforward, popular with Harrovians.

He began to call over as Lubber Sprott neared the place where Desmond and John awaited him. The Lubber took up his position near the boys, turning a broad back to them. He stood with his hands in his pockets, talking to another boy as big and as stupid as himself. The Lubber, it may be added, ought to have worn "Charity" tails, but he had not applied for permission to do so. He was fat and gross rather than tall, and certainly too large for his clothes.

"Now," said Cæsar.

John measured the distance with his eye, as Cæsar thoughtfully nudged other members of the Upper Remove. John had room for a very short run. The Lubber was swaying backwards and forwards. John timed his kick, which for a small boy he delivered with surprising force, so accurately that the Lubber fell on his face. The boys looking on screamed with laughter. The Lubber, picking himself up (John dodged into the crowd, who received him joyfully) and glaring round, encountered the contemptuous face of Desmond.

"Let me have a shot," said Cæsar.

The Lubber advanced, spluttering with rage.

"Where is he—where is he, that infernal young Verney?"

By this time fifty boys at least were interested

spectators of the scene. Desmond stood square in the Lubber's path.

"You like to kick small boys," said Cæsar, in a very loud voice. "I'm small, half your size, why don't you kick me?"

The Lubber could have crushed the speaker by mere weight; but he hesitated, and the harder he stared at Desmond the less he fancied the job of kicking him. Quality confronted quantity.

"Kick me," said Desmond, "if—if you dare, you big, hulking coward and cad!"

"Come on, Lubber, get into line!" shouted some boy.

Sprott turned slowly, glancing over his vast, fat shoulder to guard against further assault. Then he took his place in the line, and passed slowly out of the Yard and out of these pages. He never persecuted John again.*

Not yet, however, was the sun to shine in John's firmament. As the days lengthened, as June touched all hearts with her magic fingers, insensibly relaxing the tissues and warming the senses, John became more and more miserably aware that, in the fight between Scaife and himself for the possession of Desmond, the odds were stupendously against him. Truly the Demon had the subtlety of the serpent, for he used the failings which he was unable to hide as cords wherewith to bind his friend more closely to him. When the facts, for instance, of what had taken place in Lovell's room came to Desmond's ears, he denied fiercely the possibility of Scaife, his pal, making a "beast" of himself. The laughter which greeted his passionate protest sent him hot-foot to Scaife himself.

"They say," panted Cæsar, "that last winter you were dead drunk in Lovell's room. I told the beasts they lied."

Scaife's handsome face softened. Was he touched by Cæsar's loyalty? Who can tell? Always he subordinated emotion to intelligence: head commanded heart.

---

* Small boys are not advised to copy John's tactics. The victory is not always to the weak.

The Hill

"Perhaps they did," he answered steadily; "and perhaps they didn't. I deny nothing; I admit nothing. But"—his fine eyes, so dark and piercing, flamed—" Cæsar, if I was dead drunk at your feet now, would you turn away from me, would you chuck me?"

Desmond winced. Scaife pursued his advantage.

"If you *are* that sort of a fellow—the Pharisee"— Desmond winced again—"the saint who is too pure, too holy, to associate with a sinner, say so, and let us part here—and now. For I *am* a—sinner. You are not a sinner. Hold hard! let me have my say. I've always known that this moment was coming. Yes, I am a sinner. And my governor is a sinner, a hardened sinner. His father made our pile by what you would call robbery. The whole world knows it, and condones it, because we are so rich. Even my mother——"

He paused, trembling, white to the lips.

"Don't," said Desmond. "Please don't."

"You're right. I won't. But I'm handicapped on both sides. It's only fair that you should know what sort of a fellow you've chosen for a pal. And it's not too late to chuck me. Rutford will put Verney in here, if I ask him. And, by God! I'm in the mood to ask him *now*.

Shall I go to him, Desmond, or shall I stay?"

He had never raised his voice, but it fell upon the sensitive soul of the boy facing him as if it were a clarion-call to battle.

Desmond sprang forward, ardent, eager, afire with generous self-surrender.

"Forgive me," he cried. "Oh, forgive me, because I can't forgive myself!"

After this breaking of barriers, Scaife took less pains to disguise a nature which turned as instinctively to darkness as Desmond's to light. A score of times protest died when Scaife murmured, "There I go again, forgetting the gulf between us;" and always Desmond swore stoutly that the gulf, if a gulf did yawn between them, should be bridged by friendship and hope. But, insensibly, Cæsar's ideals became tainted by Scaife's materialism. Scaife, for instance, spent money lavishly upon "food" and clothes. So far as a Public Schoolboy is able, he never denied his splendid young body anything it coveted. Desmond, too proud to receive favours without returning them, tried to vie with this reckless spendthrift, and found himself in debt. In other ways a keen eye and ear would have marked deterioration. John noticed that Cæsar laughed, although he never sneered, at things he used to hold sacred; that he condemned, as Scaife did, whatever that clever young reprobate was pleased to stigmatize as narrow minded or intolerant.

Cricket, however, kept them fairly straight. Each was certain to get his "cap,"* if, as Lawrence told them, they stuck to the rigour of the game. This was Lawrence's last term. He had stayed on to play at Lord's, and when he left Trieve would become the Head of the House—a prospect very pleasing to the turbulent Fifth.

About the middle of June John suffered a parlous blow. He was never so happy as when he was sitting in Scaife's room, cheek by jowl with Desmond, sharing, perhaps, a "dringer," poring over the same dictionary. This delightful intimacy came to a sudden end in this wise. The form-master of the Upper Remove happened to be a precision in English. A sure road to his favour was the right use of a word. The Demon, appreciating this, bought a dictionary of synonyms, and made a point of discarding the commonplace and obvious, substituting a phrase likely to elicit praise and marks. Desmond and John joined in this hunt of the right word with enthusiasm.

One evening the four boys encountered the simple sentence—"*majoris pretii quam quod æstimari possit.*"

" 'Priceless' 'll cover that," said Cæsar.

"Or 'inest*ee*mable,' " said the Demon.

The three other boys stared at the Demon, and then at each other. The Caterpillar, something of a purist in his way, drawled out—"One pronounces that 'inestimable.' "

"My father doesn't," said Scaife, hotly. "I've heard him

---

* The house-cap, only given to members of the house Cricket Eleven,

say 'inesteemable.' "

"No doubt," said Egerton, coldly. "How does *your* father pronounce it, Cæsar?"

Desmond said hurriedly, "Oh, 'inestimable;' but what does it matter?"

The Demon sprang up, furious. "It matters this," he cried. "I'm d——d if I'll have Egerton sitting in my room sneering at my governor. After this he'll do his work in his own room, or I'll do mine in the passage."

Before Desmond could speak, Scaife had whirled out of the room, slamming the door. John looked stupefied with dismay.

The Caterpillar shrugged his shoulders. Then he said slowly—"Scaife's father pronounces 'connoisseur' 'connoysure,' and so does Scaife."

Desmond stood up, flushed and distressed, but emphatic.

"Scaife is right about one thing," ha said. "He won't sit here like a cad and listen to Egerton sneering at his father. I'm very sorry, but after this we'd better split up. Verney and you, Egerton; and Scaife and I."

"Certainly," said the Caterpillar, rising in his turn.

Poor John cast a distracted and imploring glance at Desmond, which flashed by unheeded. Then he got up, and followed the Caterpillar out of the room. The passage was empty.

The Caterpillar sniffed as if the atmosphere in Scaife's room had been polluted.

"One has nothing to regret," he remarked. "Scaife has good points, and—er—bad. You've noticed his hands—eh? *Very* unfinished! And his foot—short, but broad." The Caterpillar surveyed his long, slender feet with infinite satisfaction; then he added, with an accent of finality, "Scaife talks about going into the Grenadiers; but they'll give him a hot time there, a very hot time. One is really sorry for the poor fellow, because, of course, he can't help being a bounder. What does puzzle me is, why did Cæsar want such a fellow for his pal?"

"But he didn't," said John.

"Eh?—what?"

"Scaife wanted Cæsar," John explained. "And I've

noticed, Caterpillar, that whatever Scaife wants he gets."

"He wants breeding, Jonathan, but he'll never get that—never."

After this, John saw but little of Desmond; and Scaife hardly spoke to him. Accordingly, much of our hero's time was spent in the company of the Duffer and Fluff. The three passed many delightful hours together at "Ducker." Armed with buns and chocolate, they would rush down the hill, bathe, lie about on the grass, eat the buns, and chaff the kids who were learning to swim.

> "Long, long, in the misty hereafter
>   Shall echo, in ears far away,
> The lilt of that innocent laughter,
>   The splash of the spray."

During the School matches they spent the afternoons on the Sixth Form ground, carefully criticizing every stroke. The theory of the game lay pat to the tongue, but in practice John was a shocking bungler. At his small preparatory school in the New Forest, he had not been taught the elementary principles of either racquets or cricket; but he had a good eye, played a capital game of golf, rode and shot well for a small boy. Fluff, although still delicate, gave promise of being a cricketer as good, possibly, as his brothers, when he became stronger.

Upon Speech Day John's mother and uncle came down to Harrow, and you may be sure that John escorted them in triumph to the Manor. Mrs. Verney has since confessed that John's expression as she greeted him surprised and distressed her. He looked quite unhappy. And the dear woman, thinking that he must be in debt, seriously considered the propriety of tipping him handsomely *in advance*. A moment later, as she slipped out of an old and shabby dust-cloak, revealing the splendours of a dress fresh from Paris, she divined from John's now radiant face what had troubled him.

"John," she said, "you didn't really think that I was going to shame you by wearing this dreadful cloak—did you?"

"I wasn't quite sure," John answered; then he burst

out, "Mum, you look simply lovely. All the fellows will take you for my sister."

And after the great function in Speech-room came the cheering. How John's heart throbbed when the Head of the School, standing just outside the door, proclaimed the illustrious name—

"Three cheers for Mr. John Verney."

And how the boys in the road below cheered, as the little man descended the steps, hat in hand, bowing and blushing! Everybody knew that he was on the eve of departure for further explorations in Manchuria. He would be absent, so the papers said, three years at least. The School cheered the louder, because each boy knew that they might never see that gallant face again.

Later in the afternoon a selection of Harrow songs was given in the Speech-room. "Five Hundred Faces," as usual, was sung by a new boy, who is answered, in chorus, by the whole School. How John recalled his own feelings, less than a year ago, as he stood shivering upon the bank of the river, funking the first plunge! And his uncle, now sitting beside him, had said that he would soon enjoy himself amazingly—and so he had! The new boy began the second verse. His voice, not a strong one, quavered shrilly—

"A quarter to seven! There goes the bell!
The sleet is driving against the pane;
But woe to the sluggard who turns again
And sleeps, not wisely, but all too well!"

In reply to the weak, timid notes came the glad roar of the School—

"Yet the time may come, as the years go by,
When your heart will thrill
At the thought of the Hill,
And the pitiless bell, with its piercing cry!"

Ah, that pitiless bell! And yet because of it one wallowed in Sunday and whole-holiday "frowsts."* John, you see, had the makings of a philosopher. And now the Eleven were grunting "Willow the King." And when the last echo of the chorus died away in the great room, Uncle John whispered to his nephew that he had heard Harrow songs in every corner of the earth, and that convincing proof of merit shone out of the fact that their charm waxed rather than waned with the years; they improved, like wine, with age.

Cæsar's father came down with the Duke of Trent. The duke tipped John magnificently and asked him to spend his *exeat* at Trent House, and to witness the Eton and Harrow match at Lord's from the Trent coach. John accepted gratefully enough; but his heart was sore because, just before the row over that infernal word "inestimable," Cæsar had asked John if he would like to occupy an attic in Eaton Square. After the row nothing more was said about the attic; but John would have preferred bare boards in Eaton Square to a tapestried chamber in Park Lane.

Now, during the whole of this summer term there was much animated discussion in regard to the rival claims of lines or spots upon the white waistcoat worn by all self respecting Harrovians at Lord's. Upon this important subject John had betrayed scandalous indifference. Accordingly, just before the match, the Caterpillar took him aside and spoke a solemn word.

"Look here," he said; "one doesn't as a rule make personal remarks, but it's rather too obvious that you buy your clothes in Lyndhurst. I was sorry to see that the Duke of Trent was the worst-dressed man at Speecher; but a duke can look like a tinker, and nobody cares."

---

* Lying in bed in the morning when there is no First School is a "frowst." By a subtle law of association, an armchair is also a "frowst."

The Hill

"I'd be awfully obliged if you'd tell me what's wrong," said John, humbly.

"Everything's wrong," said the Caterpillar, decisively. He looked critically at John's boots. "Your boots, for instance—most excellent boots for wading through the swamps in the New Forest, but quite impossible in town. And the 'topper' you wear on Sunday! Southampton, you say? Ah, I thought it was a Verney heirloom. Now, it wouldn't surprise me to hear that your mother, who dresses herself quite charmingly, bought your kit."

"She did," John confessed.

"Just so. One need say no more. Now, you come along with me."

They marched down the High Street to the most fashionable of the School tailors, where John was measured for an Eton jacket of the best, white waistcoat with blue spots, light bags; while the Caterpillar selected a new "topper," an umbrella, a pair of gloves, and a tie.

"Be very careful about the bags," said the Caterpillar. "They are cutting 'em in town a trifle tighter about the lower leg, but loose above. You understand?"

"Perfectly, Mr. Egerton," replied the obsequious snip. "What we call the 'tighto-looso' style, sir."

"I don't think they call it that in Savile Row," said the Caterpillar; "but be careful."

The tailor was assured that he would receive an order properly signed by Mr. Rutford. And then John was led to the bootmaker's, and there measured for his first pair of patent-leathers. The Caterpillar was so exhausted by these labours that a protracted visit to the Creameries became imperative.

"You've always looked like a gentleman," said the Caterpillar, after his "dringer," "and it's a comfort to me to think that now you'll be dressed like one."

So John went up to town looking very smart indeed; and Fluff (who had ordered a similar kit) whispered to John at luncheon that his brothers, the Etonians, had expressed surprise at the change for the better in their general appearance.

This luncheon was eaten on the top of the duke's coach, and it happened that the next coach but one belonged to Scaife's father. John could just see Scaife's handsome head, and Cæsar sitting beside him. The boys nodded to each other, and the Etonians asked questions. At the name of Scaife, however, the young Kinlochs curled contemptuous lips.

"Unspeakable bounder, old Scaife, isn't he?" they asked; and the duchess replied—

"My dears, his cheques are honoured to any amount, even if he isn't."

Her laughter tinkled delightfully; but John reflected that Desmond was eating the Scaife food and drinking the Scaife wine—all bought with ill-gotten gold.

Later in the afternoon it became evident that the Scaife champagne was flowing freely. To John's dismay, the Harrovians (including Cæsar) on the top of the Scaife coach became noisy. The Caterpillar and his father, Colonel Egerton, sauntered up, and were invited by the duke to rest and refresh themselves. John was amused to note that the colonel was even a greater buck than his son. He quite cut out the poor old Caterpillar, challenging and monopolizing the attention of all who beheld him.

"Those boys are makin' the devil of a row," said the colonel, fixing his eyeglass. "Ah, the Scaifes! A man I know dined with them last week. He reported everything overdone, except the food. Their *chef* is Marcobruno, you know."

Presently, to John's relief, Desmond left the Scaifes and joined the Trent party, upon whom his gay, radiant face and charming manners made a most favourable impression. He laughed at the duchess's stories, and made love to her quite unaffectedly. The Etonians looked rather glum, because their wickets were falling faster than had been expected. Desmond told the duke, in answer to a question, that his father was in his seat in the pavilion, with his eyes glued to the pitch.

"He's awfully keen," said Cæsar.

"You boys are not so keen as we were," said the duke, nodding reflectively.

"Oh, but we are, sir—indeed we are," said Cæsar. "Aren't we, Caterpillar?"

The Caterpillar replied, thoughtfully. "One bottles up

that sort of thing, I suppose."

"Ah," said the duke, kindly, "if it is the right sort of thing, it's none the worse for being bottled up."

The boys went to the play that night and enjoyed themselves hugely. Next day, however, the match ended in a draw. John was standing on the top of the coach, very disconsolate, when he saw Desmond beckoning to him from below. The expression on Cæsar's face puzzled him.

"How can you pal up with those Etonians?" whispered Cæsar, after John had descended. "Every Eton face I see now I want to hit." Then he added, with a smile and a chuckle, "I say, there's going to be a ruction in front of the Pavvy. Come on."

A minute later John was in the thick of a very pretty scrimmage between the Hill and the Plain. Hats were bashed in; cornflowers torn from buttonholes; pale-blue tassels were captured; umbrellas broken. Finally, the police interfered.

"Short, but very, very sweet," said Cæsar, panting.

John and he were lamentable objects for fond parents to behold, but the sense of depression had vanished. And then Cæsar said suddenly—

"By Jove! I *have* got a bit of news. It quite takes the sting out of this draw."

"What's happened?"

"My governor has been talking with Warde. Rutford is leaving Harrow."

John gasped. "That is ripping."

"Isn't it? But who do you think is coming to us? Why, Warde himself.

He was at the Manor when it was *the* house, and the governor says that Warde will make it *the* house again. He's got his work cut out for him—eh?"

"You bet your life," said John.

Chapter Six

A Revelation

Forty years on, when afar and asunder
　Parted are those who are singing to-day,
When you look back, and forgetfully wonder
　What you were like in your work and your play;
Then, it may be, there will often come o'er you
　Glimpses of notes like the catch of a song,—
Visions of boyhood shall float them before you,
　Echoes of dreamland shall bear them along.

BEFORE the end of the summer term, both Desmond and Scaife received their "caps" and a word of advice from Lawrence.

"There are going to be changes here," said he; "and I wish I could see 'em, and help to bring 'em about. Now, I'm not given to buttering fellows up, but I see plainly that the rebuilding of this house depends a lot upon you two. It's not likely that you're able to measure your influence; if you could, there wouldn't be much to measure. But take it from me, not a word, not an action of yours is without weight with the lower boys. Everything helps or hinders. Next term there will be war—to the knife—between Warde and some fellows I needn't name, and Warde will win. Remember I said so. I hope you," he looked hard at Desmond, "will fight on the right side."

The boys returned to their room, jubilant because the house-cap was theirs, but uneasy because of the words given with it. As soon as they were alone, Scaife said sullenly—

"Does Lawrence expect us to stand in with Warde against Lovell and his pals? If he does, he's jolly well mistaken, as far as I'm concerned."

Desmond flushed. He had spent nearly five terms at Harrow, but only two at the Manor. Of what had been done or left undone by certain fellows in the Fifth he was still in twilight ignorance. He discerned shadows, nothing more, and, boylike, he ran from shadows into the sunlight. Desmond knew that there were beasts at the Manor. Had you forced from him an expression approaching, let us say, definiteness, he would have admitted that beasts lurked in every house, in every school in the kingdom. You must keep out of their way (and ways)—that was all. And he knew also that too many beasts wreck a house, as they wreck a regiment or a nation.

But once or twice within the past few months he had suspected that his cut-and-dried views on good and evil were not shared by Scaife. Scaife confessed to Desmond that the Old Adam was strong in him. He liked, craved for, the excitement of breaking the law. Hitherto, this breaking of the law had been confined to such offences as smoking or drinking a glass of beer at a "pub,"* or using cribs, or, generally speaking, setting at naught authority. That Scaife had escaped severe punishment was due to his keen wits.

Now, when Scaife gave Desmond the unexpurgated history of the row which so nearly resulted in the expulsion of six boys, Desmond had asked a question—

"Do you *like* whisky? I loathe it."

Scaife laughed before he answered. Doubtless one reason why he exacted interest and admiration from Desmond lay in a rare (rare at fifteen) ability to analyse his own and others' actions.

"I loathe it too," he admitted. "Really, you know, we drank precious little, because it is such beastly stuff. But I liked, we all liked, to believe that we were doing the correct thing—eh? And it warmed us up. Just a taste made the Caterpillar awfully funny."

"I see."

"Do you see? I doubt it, Cæsar. Perhaps I shall horrify

---

* All "public houses" are out of bounds.

you when I tell you that vice interests me. I used to buy the *Police News* when I was a kid, and simply wallow in it. I told a woman that last Easter, and she laughed—she was as clever as they make 'em—and said that I suffered from what the French call *la nostalgie de la boue*; that means, you know, the homesickness for the gutter. Rather personal, but dev'lish sharp, wasn't it?"

"I think she was a beast."

"Not she, she's a sort of cousin; she came from the same old place herself, that's why she understood. You don't want to know what goes on in the slums, but I do. Why? Because my grand-dad was born in 'em."

"He pulled himself out by brains and muscles."

"But he went back—sometimes. Oh yes, he did. And the governor—I'm up to some of *his* little games. I could tell you——"

"Oh—shut up!" said Cæsar, the colour flooding his cheeks.

Upon the last Saturday of the term the School Concert took place. Few of the boys in the Manor, and none out of it, knew that John Verney had been chosen to sing the treble solo; always an attractive number of the programme. John, indeed, was painfully shy in regard to his singing, so shy that he never told Desmond that he had a voice. And the music-master, enchanted by its quality, impressed upon his pupil the expediency of silence. He wished to surprise the School.

The concerts at Harrow take place in the great Speech-room. Their characteristic note is the singing of Harrow songs. To any boy with an ear for music and a heart susceptible of emotion these songs must appeal profoundly, because both words and music seem to enshrine all that is noble and uplifting in life. And, sung by the whole School (as are most of the choruses), their message becomes curiously emphatic. The spirit of the Hill is acclaimed, gladly, triumphantly, unmistakably, by Harrovians repeating the creed of their fathers, knowing that creed will be so repeated by their sons and sons' sons. Was it happy chance or a happier sagacity which decreed that certain verses should be sung by the School "Twelve," who have struggled through form after form and

The Hill

know (and have not yet had time to forget) the difficulties and temptations which beset all boys? They, to whom their fellows unanimously accord respect at least, and often—as in the case of a Captain of the Cricket Eleven enthusiastic admiration and fealty; these, the gods, in a word, deliver their injunction, transmit, in turn, what has been transmitted to them, and invite their successors to receive it. To many how poignant must be the reflection that the trust they are about to resign might have been better administered! But to many there must come upon the wings of those mighty, rushing choruses the assurance that the Power which has upheld them in the past will continue to uphold them in the future. In many—would one could say in all—is quickened, for the first time, perhaps, a sense of what they owe to the Hill, the overwhelming debt which never can be discharged.

Desmond sat beside Scaife. Scaife boasted that he could not tell "God save the Queen" from "The Dead March in Saul." He confessed that the concert bored him. Desmond, on the other hand, was always touched by music, or, indeed, by anything appealing to an imagination which gilded all things and persons. He was Scaife's friend, not only (as John discovered) because Scaife had a will strong enough to desire and secure that friendship, but because—a subtler reason—he had never yet seen Scaife as he was, but always as he might have been.

Desmond told Scaife that he could not understand why John had bottled up the fact that he was chosen to sing upon such an occasion. Scaife smiled contemptuously.

"You never bottle up anything, Cæsar," said he.

"Why should I? And why should he?"

"I expect he'll make an awful ass of himself."

"Oh no, he won't," Desmond replied. "He's a clever fellow is Jonathan."

As he gave John his nickname, Desmond's charming voice softened. A boy of less quick perceptions than Scaife would have divined that the speaker liked John, liked him, perhaps, better than he knew. Scaife frowned.

"There are several Old Harrovians," he said, indicating

the seats reserved for them. "It's queer to me that they come down for this caterwauling."

Desmond glanced at him sharply, with a wrinkle between his eyebrows. For the moment he looked as if he were short-sighted, as if he were trying to define an image somewhat blurred, conscious that the image itself was clear enough, that the fault lay in the obscurity of his own vision.

"They come down because they're keen," he replied. "My governor can't leave his office, or he'd be here. I like to see 'em, don't you, Demon?"

"I could worry along without 'em," the Demon replied, half-smiling. "You see," he added, with the blend of irony and pathos which always captivated his friend, "you see, my dear old chap, I'm the first of my family at Harrow, and the sight of all your brothers and uncles and fathers makes me feel like Mark Twain's good man, rather lonesome."

At once Desmond responded, clutching Scaife's arm.

"You're going to be Captain of the cricket and footer Elevens, and School racquet-player, and a monitor; and after you leave you'll come down here, and you'll see that Harrow hasn't forgotten you, and then you'll know why these fellows cut engagements. My governor says that an hour at a School Concert is the finest tonic in the world for an Old Harrovian."

"Oh, shut up!" said Scaife; "you make me feel more of an outsider than good old Snowball." He glanced at a youth sitting close to them. Snowball was as black as a coal: the son of the Sultan of the Sahara. "Yes, Cæsar, you can't get away from it, I *am* an 'alien.'"

"You're a silly old ass! I say, who's the guest of honour?"

Next to the Head Master was sitting a thin man upon whose face were fixed hundreds of eyes. The School had not been told that a famous Field Marshal, the hero of a hundred fights, was coming to the concert. And, indeed, he had accepted an invitation given at the last moment—accepted it, moreover, on the understanding that his visit was to be informal. None the less, his face was familiar to all readers of illustrated papers. And, suddenly, conviction seized the boys that a conqueror was among them, an Old Etonian, making, possibly, his first visit to the Hill. Scaife whispered his name to Desmond. "Why, of course," Desmond replied eagerly. "How splendid!"

He leaned forward, devouring the hero with his eyes, trying to pierce the bronzed skin, to read the record. From his seat upon the stage John, also, stared at the illustrious guest. John was frightfully nervous, but looking at the veteran he forgot the fear of the recruit. Both Desmond and he were wondering what "it felt like" to have done so much. And—they compared notes afterwards—each boy deplored the fact that the great man was not an Old Harrovian. There he sat, cool, calm, slightly impassive. John thought he must be rather tired, as a man ought to be tired after a life of strenuous endeavour and achievement.

He had done—so John reflected—an awful lot. Even now, he remained the active, untiring servant of Queen and country. And he had taken time to come down to Harrow to hear the boys sing. And, dash it all! he, John, was going to sing to him.

At that moment Desmond was whispering to Scaife—

"I say, Demon; I'm jolly glad that I've not got to sing before *him*. I bet Jonathan is in a funk."

"A big bit of luck," replied Scaife, reflectively. Then, seeing the surprise on Desmond's face, he added, "If Jonathan can sing—and I suppose he can, or he wouldn't be chosen—this is a chance——"

"Of what?"

"Cæsar, sometimes I think you've no brains. Why, a chance of attracting the notice of a tremendous swell—a man, they say, who never forgets—never! Jonathan may want a commission in the Guards, as I do; and if he pleases the great man, he may get it."

"Jonathan's not thinking of that," said Desmond. "Shush-h-h!"

The singers stood up. They faced the Field Marshal, and he faced them. He looked hardest at Lawrence, pointed out to him by the Head Master. Perhaps he was thinking of India; and the name of Lawrence indelibly cut upon the memories of all who fought in the Mutiny. And

Lawrence, you may be sure, met his glance steadily, being fortified by it. The good fellow felt terribly distressed, because he was leaving the Hill; and, being a humble gentleman, the old songs served to remind him, not of what he had done, but of what he had left undone—the words unspoken, the actions never now to be performed. The chief caught his eye, smiled, and nodded, as if to say, "I claim your father's son as a friend."

When the song came to an end, John was seized, with an almost irresistible impulse to bolt. His turn had come. He must stand up to sing before nearly six hundred boys, who would stare down with gravely critical and courteously amused eyes. And already his legs trembled as If he were seized of a palsy. John knew that he could sing. His mother, who sang gloriously, had trained him. From her he had inherited his vocal chords, and from her he drew the knowledge how to use them.

When he stood up, pale and trembling, the silence fell upon his sensibilities as if it were a dense, yellow fog. This silence, as John knew, was an unwritten law. The small boy selected to sing to the School, as the representative of the School, must have every chance. Let his voice be heard! The master playing the accompaniment paused and glanced at his pupil. John, however, was not looking at him; he was looking within at a John he despised—a poltroon, a deserter about to run from his first engagement. He knew that the introduction to the song was being played a second time, and he saw the Head Master whispering to his guest. Paralysed with terror, John's intuition told him that the Head Master was murmuring, "That's the nephew of John Verney. Of course you know him?" And the Field Marshal nodded. And then he looked at John, as John had seen him look at Lawrence, with the same flare of recognition in the steel-grey eyes. Out of the confused welter of faces shone that pair of eyes—twin beacons flashing their message of encouragement and salvation to a fellow-creature in peril—at least, so John interpreted that piercing glance. It seemed to say, far plainer than words, "I have stood alone as you stand; I have felt my knees as wax; I have wished to run away. But—*I didn't.*

Nor must you. Open your mouth and sing!"

So John opened his mouth and sang. The first verse of the lyric went haltingly.

Scaife growled to Desmond, "He *is* going to make an ass of himself."

And Desmond, meeting Scaife's eyes, half thought that the speaker wished that John would fail—that he grudged him a triumph. None the less, the first verse, sung feebly, with wrong phrasing and imperfect articulation, revealed the quality of the boy's voice; and this quality Desmond recognized, as he would have recognized a fine painting or a bit of perfect porcelain. All his short life his father had trained him to look for and acclaim quality, whether in things animate or inanimate. He caught hold of Scaife's arm.

"Make an ass of himself!" he whispered back. "Not he. But he may make an ass of me."

Even as he spoke he was aware that tears were horribly near his eyes. Some catch in John's voice, some subtle inflection, had smitten his heart, even as the prophet smote the rock.

"Rot!" said Scaife, angrily.

He was angry, furiously angry, because he saw that Cæsar was beyond his reach, whirled innumerable leagues away by the sound of another's voice. John had begun the second verse. He stared, as if hypnotized, straight into the face of the great soldier, who in turn stared as steadily at John; and John was singing like a lark, with a lark's spontaneous delight in singing, with an ease and self-abandonment which charmed eye almost as much as ear. Higher and higher rose the clear, sexless notes, till two of them met and mingled in a triumphant trill.

To Desmond, that trill was the answer to the quavering, troubled cadences of the first verse; the vindication of the spirit soaring upwards unfettered by the flesh—the pure spirit, not released from the pitiful human clay without a fierce struggle. At that moment Desmond loved the singer—the singer who called to him out of heaven, who summoned his friend to join him, to see what he saw—"the vision splendid."

John began the third and last verse. The famous soldier covered his face with his hand, releasing John's eyes, which ascended, like his voice, till they met joyfully the eyes of Desmond. At last he was singing to his friend—*and his friend knew it.* John saw Desmond's radiant smile, and across that ocean of faces he smiled back. Then, knowing that he was nearer to his friend than he had ever been before, he gathered together his energies for the last line of the song—a line to be repeated three times, loudly at first, then more softly, diminishing to the merest whisper of sound, the voice celestial melting away in the ear of earth-bound mortals. The master knew well the supreme difficulty of producing properly this last attenuated note, but he knew also that John's lungs were strong, that the vocal chords had never been strained. Still, if the boy's breath failed; if anything—a smile, a frown, a cough—distracted his attention, the end would be—weakness, failure. He wondered why John was staring so fixedly in one direction.

Now—now!

The piano crashed out the last line; but far above it, dominating it, floated John's flute-like notes. The master played the same bars for the second time. He was still able to sustain, if it were necessary, a quavering, imperfect phrase. But John delivered the second repetition without a mistake, singing easily from the chest. The master put his foot upon the soft pedal. Nobody was watching him. Had any one done so, he would have seen the perspiration break upon the musician's forehead. The piano purred its accompaniment. Then, in the middle of the phrase, the master lifted his hands and held them poised above the instrument. John had to sing three notes unsupported. He was smiling and staring at Desmond. The first note came like a question from the heart of a child; the second, higher up, might have been interpreted as an echo to the innocent interrogation of the first, the head no wiser than the heart; but the third and last note had nothing in it of interrogation: it was an answer, all-satisfying--sublime. Nor did it seem to come from John at all, but from above, falling like a snowflake out of the sky.

The Hill

And then, for one immeasurable moment—*silence.*

John slipped back to his seat, crimson with bashfulness, while the School thundered applause. The Field Marshal shouted "Encore," as loudly as any fag; but the Head Master whispered—"We don't encourage *encores.* A small boy's head is easily turned."

"Not his," the hero replied.

Two numbers followed, and then the School stood up, and with them all Old Harrovians, to sing the famous National Anthem of Harrow, "Forty Years on." Only the guests and the masters remained seated.

> Forty years on, growing older and older,
> Shorter in wind, as in memory long,
> Feeble of foot and rheumatic of shoulder,
> What will it help you that once you were strong?
> God give us bases to guard or beleaguer,
> Games to play out, whether earnest or fun;
> Fights for the fearless, and goals for the eager,
> Twenty, and thirty, and forty years on!
> Follow up! Follow up! Follow up! Follow up!
> Till the field ring again and again,
> With the tramp of the twenty-two men.
> Follow—up!"

As the hundreds of voices, past and present indissolubly linked together, imposed the mandate, "*Follow up!*" the Head Master glanced at his guest, but left unsaid the words about to be uttered. Tears were trickling down the cheeks of the man who, forty years before, had won his Sovereign's Cross—For Valour.

After the concert, but before he left the Speech-room, the Field Marshal asked the Head Master to introduce Lawrence and John, and, of course, the Head of the School. When John came up, there was a twinkle in the veteran's eye.

"Ha—ha!" said he; "you were in a precious funk, John Verney."

"I was, sir," said John.

"Gad! Don't I know the feeling? Well, well," he

chuckled, smiling at John, "you climbed up higher than I've ever been in my life. What was it—hey? 'F' in 'alt'?"

"'G,' sir."

"You sang delightfully. Tell your uncle to bring you to see me next time you are in town. You must consider me a friend," he chuckled again—" an old friend. And look ye here," his pleasant voice sank to a whisper, "I daren't tip these tremendous swells, but I feel that I can take such a liberty with you. Shush-h-h! Good-bye."

John scurried away, bursting with pride, feeling to the core the strong grip of the strong man, hearing the thrill of his voice, the thrill which had vibrated in thousands of soldier-hearts. Outside, Fluff was awaiting him.

"Oh, Jonathan, you can sing, and no mistake."

"Five—six—seven mistakes," John answered.

The boys laughed.

John told Fluff what the hero had said to him, and showed the piece of gold.

"What ho! The Creameries! Come on, Esmé."

At the Creameries several boys congratulated John, and the Caterpillar said—

"You astonished us, Jonathan; 'pon my soul you did. Have a 'dringer' with me? And Fluff too? By the way, be sure to keep your hair dipped close. These singing fellows with manes may be lions in their own estimation, but the world looks upon 'em as asses."

"That's not bad for you, Caterpillar," said a boy in the Fifth.

"Not my own," said the Caterpillar, solemnly—" my father's. I take from him all the good things I can get hold of."

John polished off his "dringer," listening to the chaff, but his thoughts were with Desmond. He had an intuition that Desmond would have something to say to him. As soon as possible he returned to the Manor.

There he found his room empty. John shut the door and sat down, looking about him half-absently. The Duffer had not contributed much to the mural decoration, saying, loftily, that he preferred bare walls to rubbishy engravings and Japanese fans. But, with curious inconsistency (for he was the least vain of mortals), he had bought at a "leaving auction" a three-sided mirror—once the property of a great buck in the Sixth. The Duffer had got it cheap, but he never used it. The lower boys remarked to each other that Duff didn't dare to look in it, because what he would see must not only break his heart but shatter the glass. Generally, it hung, folded up, close to the window, and the Duffer said that it would come in handy when he took to shaving.

John's eye rested on this mirror, vacantly at first, then with gathering intensity. Presently he got up, crossed the room, opened the two folding panels, and examined himself attentively, pursing up his lips and frowning. He could see John Verney full face, three-quarter face, and half face. And he could see the back of his head, where an obstinate lock of hair stuck out like a drake's tail. John was so occupied in taking stock of his personal disadvantages that a ringing laugh quite startled him.

"Why, Jonathan! Giving yourself a treat—eh?"

John turned a solemn face to Desmond. "I think my head is hideous," he said ruefully.

"What do you mean?"

"It's too long," John explained. "I like a nice round head like yours, Cæsar. I wish I wasn't so ugly."

Desmond laughed. John always amused him. Cæsar was easily amused, saw the funny side of things, and contrasts tickled his fancy agreeably. But he stopped laughing when he realized that John was hurt. Then, quickly, impulsively, he said—

"Your head is all right, old Jonathan. And your voice is simply beautiful." He spoke seriously, staring at John as he had stared in the Speech-room when John began to sing. "I came here to tell you that. I felt odd when you were singing—quite weepsy, you know. You like me, old Jonathan, don't you?"

"Awfully," said John.

"Why did you look at me when you sang that last verse? Did you know that you were looking at me?"

"Yes."

"You looked at me because—well, because—bar chaff—you—liked—me?"

"Yes."

"You—you like me better than any other fellow in the school?"

"Yes; better than any other fellow In the world."

"Is it possible?"

"I have always felt that way since—yes—since the very first minute I saw you."

"How rum! I've forgotten just where we did meet—for the first time."

"I shall never forget," said John, in the same slow, deliberate fashion, never taking his eyes from Desmond's face. Ever since he had sung, he had known that this moment was coming. "I shall never forget it," he repeated—"never. You were standing near the Chapel. I was poking about alone, trying to find the shop where we buy our straws. And I was feeling as all new boys feel, only more so, because I didn't know a soul."

"Yes," said Desmond, gravely; "you told me that. I remember now; I mistook you for young Hardacre."

"You smiled at me, Cæsar. It warmed me through and through. I suppose that when a fellow is starving he never forgets the first meal after it."

"I say. Go on; this is awfully interesting."

"I can remember what you wore. One of your boot laces had burst——"

"Well; I'm——"

"I had a wild sort of wish to run off, and buy you a new lace——"

"Of all the rum starts I——"

"Afterwards," John continued, "I tried to suck-up. I asked you to come and have some 'food.' Do you remember?"

"I'll bet I came, Jonathan."

"No; you didn't. You said 'No.'"

"Dash it all! I certainly said, 'No, thanks.'"

"I dare say; but the 'No' hurt awfully because I did feel that it was cheek asking you."

"Jonathan, you funny old buster, I'll never say 'No' again. 'Pon my word, I won't. So I said 'No.' That's odd, because it's not easy for me to say 'No.' The governor pointed that out last hols. Somehow, I can't say 'No,' particularly if there's any excitement in saying 'Yes.' And my beastly 'No' hurt, did it? Well, I'm very, *very* sorry."

He held out his hand, which John took. Then, for a moment, there was a pause before Desmond continued awkwardly—

"You know, Jonathan, that the Demon is my pal. You like him better than you did, don't you?"

John had the tact not to speak; but he shook his head dolefully.

"And I couldn't chuck him, even if I wanted to, which I don't—which I don't," he repeated, with an air of satisfying himself rather than John. And John divined that Scaife's hold upon Desmond's affections was not so strong as he had deemed it to be. Desmond continued. "But I want you, too, old Jonathan, and if—if——"

"All right," said John, nobly. He perceived that Desmond's loyalty to Scaife made him hesitate and flush. "I understand, Cæsar, and if I can't be first, let me be second; only, remember, with me you're first, rain or shine."

Desmond looked uneasy. "Isn't that a case of 'heads I win, tails you lose'?"

John considered; then he smiled cheerfully, "You know you are a winner, Cæsar. You're cut out for a winner; you can win whatever you want to win."

"Oh, that's all rot," said Desmond. He looked very grave, and in his eyes lay shadows which John had never seen before.

And so ended John's first year at Harrow.

Chapter Seven

Reform

"It must be a gran' thing to be a colledge profissor."
"Not much to do," said Mr. Hennessy.
"But a gr—reat deal to say," said Mr. Dooley.

WHEN John returned to the Hill at the beginning of the winter term the great change had taken place. Rutford had assumed the duties of Professor of Greek at a Scotch University; Warde was in possession of the Manor; Scaife and Desmond and John—but not the Caterpillar—had got their remove. They were Fifth Form boys—and in tails! John, it is true, although tougher and broader, was still short for his years and juvenile of appearance, but Scaife and Desmond were quite big fellows, and their new coats became them mightily. Trieve was Head of the House; Lovell, Captain of the House football Eleven and in the Lower Sixth.

"Lovell will have to behave himself now," the Duffer remarked to Scaife, who laughed derisively, as he answered—

"He couldn't, even if he tried."

Warde welcomed the House at lock-up, and introduced the boys to his wife and daughter. Mrs. Warde had a plain, pleasant face. Miss Warde, however, was a beauty, and she knew it, the coquette, and had known it from the hour she could peep into a mirror. The Caterpillar pronounced her "fetching." Being only fifteen, she wore her hair in a plait tied by a huge bow, and the hem of her skirt barely touched the neatest ankle on Harrow Hill. Give her a saucy, pink-and-white face, pop a pert tip-tilted nose into the middle of it just above a pouting red mouth, and just below her father's lapis-lazuli eyes, and you will see Iris Warde. Her hair was reddish, not red—call it a warm chestnut; and she had a dimple.

The Hill

After the introductions, mother and daughter left the hall. Warde stood up, inviting the House to sit down. Warde was about half the width of the late Rutford, but somehow he seemed to take up more room.

He had spent the summer holidays in Switzerland, climbing terrific peaks. Snow and sun had coloured his clear complexion. John, who saw beneath tanned skins, reflected that Warde seemed to be saturated with fresh air and all the sweet clean things which one associates with mountains. "He loves hills," thought John, "and he loves our Hill." Warde began to speak in his jerky, confidential tones. Dirty Dick had always been insufferably dull, pompous, and didactic.

"I don't like speechmaking," said Warde, "but I want to put one thing to you as strongly as a man may. I have always wished to be master of the Manor. Some men may think mine a small ambition. Master of a house at Harrow? Nothing big about that. Perhaps not. But I think it big. And it is big—for me. Understand that I'm in love with my job—head over heels. I'd sooner be master of the Manor than Prime Minister. I couldn't tackle his work. Enough of that. Now, forget for a moment that I'm a Master. Let me talk as an Old Harrovian, an old Manorite who remembers everything, ay—everything, good and bad. Some lucky fellows remember the good only; we call them optimists. Others remember the bad. Pessimists those. Put me between the two. The other day I had an eye, *one* eye, fixed on the top of a certain peak—by Jove! how I longed to reach that peak!—but the other eye was on a *crevasse* at my feet. Had I kept both eyes on the peak, I should be lying now at the bottom of that *crevasse*. You take me? Well, twenty years ago I sat here, in hall, my last night in the old house, and I hoped that one day I might come back. Why? This is between ourselves, a confidence. I came to the Manor from a beastly school, such schools are hardly to be found nowadays—a hardened young sinner at thirteen. The Manor licked me into shape. Speaking generally, I suppose the tone of the house insensibly communicated itself to me. The Manor was cock-house at games and work. I began by shirking both. But the spirit of the Hill was too much for me. I couldn't shirk that. Some jolly old boys, we all know them and like them, are always saying that their early school-days were the happiest of their life. They're fond of telling this big lie just as they're settling down to their claret. I really believe that they believe what they say, but it is a lie. The smallest boy here knows it's a lie. Let's hark back a bit. I said I was licked into shape— and I mean *licked.* I had a lot of really hard fagging— much harder than any of you boys know—I was sent up and swished, I had whoppings innumerable, and it wasn't pleasant. My mother had pinched herself to send me here, because my father had been here before me; and I wondered why she did it. At that time I couldn't see why cheaper schools shouldn't be not only as good as Harrow, but perhaps better. Not till I was in the Fifth did I get a glimmering of what my mother and the Manor were doing for me. When I got into the Sixth and into the Eleven, I knew. And my last year here made up, and more too, for the previous four. I enjoyed that year thoroughly. I had ceased to be a slacker. I tell you, all of you, that happiness, like liberty, must be earned before we can enjoy it. And you are sent here to earn it. I'm not going to keep you much longer. I have come to the marrow of the matter. I owe the Manor a debt which I hope to pay to— you. Just as you, in turn, will pay back to boys not yet born the money your people have gladly spent on you, and other greater things beside. I want to see this house at the top of the tree again: cock-house at cricket, cock-house at footer, with a Balliol Scholar in it, and a school racquet-player. And now Dumbleton is going to bring in a little champagne. We'll drink high health and fellowship to the Manor and the Hill!"

His face broke into the smile his form knew so well; he sat down, as the house roared its welcome to a friend.

As soon as the champagne was drunk ("Dumber" was careful to put more froth than wine into the glasses of the kids), the boys filed out of the Hall. The Duffer, Desmond, John, and the Caterpillar assembled in John's room. Desmond, you may be sure, was afire with resolution. Warde was the right sort, a clinker, a first flighter. And he meant to stick by him through thick and thin. John said nothing. The Caterpillar drawled out—

"Warde didn't surprise me—much. I've found out that he's one of the Wardes of Warde-Pomeroy, the real old stuff. Our families intermarried in Elizabeth's reign."

"Chance to do it again, Caterpillar," said the Duffer. "Warde's daughter is an uncommonly pretty girl."

Then the Caterpillar used the epithet "fetching."

"She's fetching, very fetching," he said. "It's a pleasure to remember that we're of kin. One must be civil to Warde. He's a well bred 'un."

"You think too much of family," said Desmond.

"*One can't,*" replied the Caterpillar, solemnly. "One knows that family is not everything, but, other things being equal, it means refinement. The first of the Howards was a swineherd, I dare say, but generations of education, of association with the best, have turned them from swineherds into gentlemen, and it takes generations to do it."

"Good old Caterpillar!" said the Duffer.

"Not my own," said the Caterpillar; adding, as usual, "My governor's, you know."

"Warde hasn't a soft job ahead of him," said Desmond. "Soft or hard, he'll handle it his own way."

Desmond went out, wondering what had become of Scaife. Scaife was in his room, talking to Lovell senior, who had spent a fortnight with Scaife's people in Scotland, fishing and grousing. Desmond had been asked also, but his father, rather to Cæsar's disgust (for the Scaife moor was famous), had refused to let him go. Lovell and Scaife were arguing about something which Desmond could not understand.

"I left it to my partner," said Scaife, "and the fool went no trumps holding two missing suits. The enemy doubled, my partner redoubled, and the others redoubled again: that made it ninety-six a trick. The fellow on the left held my partner's missing suits; he made the Little Slam, and scored nearly six hundred below the line. It gave 'em the rubber, too, and I had to fork out a couple of quid."

"What are you jawing about, Demon?" said Desmond.

"Bridge. It's the new game. It's going to be the rage. Do you play bridge, Cæsar?"

"No. I want to learn it."

"All right, I must teach you."

"We could get up a four in this house," said Lovell. "We three and the Caterpillar. He plays, I know. The Colonel is one of the cracks at the Turf. It would be an awful lark. A mild gamble: small points—eh?

A bob a hundred. What do you say, Cæsar?"

Desmond hesitated. Bridge had not yet reached its delirious stage. But Desmond had seen it played, had heart his father praise it as the most fascinating of card-games, and had determined to learn it at the first convenient opportunity. None the less Warde's words still echoed in his ear.

"I think we ought to give Warde a chance," he said.

"You don't mean to say you were taken in by him?" said Lovell, contemptuously.

Desmond burst into enthusiastic praise of Warde and his methods. Lovell shrugged his shoulders and walked out of the room, nodding to Scaife, but ignoring Desmond.

"You must go canny with Lovell," said Scaife. "He's the fellow who ought to give you your 'fez' after the first house-game."

"Never mind that. You won't play bridge, Demon, will you?"

"Why not?" said Scaife. "Where's the harm? Your governor plays——"

"Yes; but——"

"You're afraid of getting sacked?"

"I'm not."

"All right; I'll take that back. You're not a funk, Cæsar, but you're so easily humbugged. Warde caught you with his 'pi jaw' and a glass of gooseberry."

"The champagne was all right, wasn't it?"

"Oh, ho! So you do mean to stand in with Warde against Lovell and me?

Thanks for being so candid. Now I'll be candid with you. I like Lovell. There's no nonsense about him. He don't put on frills because he's in the Sixth, and he don't mean to take to their sneaking, spying ways. He's just as anxious as Warde to see the Manor cock-house at footer and cricket, and I'm as keen as he is; but we stop there. The Balliol Scholarship may go hang. And as for sympathy and fellowship and pulling together between masters and boys, I never did believe in it, and never shall. My hand is against the masters, so long as they interfere with anything I want to do. I like bridge, and I mean to play it. And I'll take jolly good care that I'm not nailed. That's part of the fun, as the drinking used to be. I chucked that because it wasn't good enough; but bridge is ripping, and, take my word for it, you'll be keener than I when you begin."

"Perhaps. But I'm not going to begin here."

"Right—oh!"

Scaife turned aside, whistling, but out of the corner of his shrewd eye he marked the expression of Desmond's face, the colour ebbing and flowing in the round boyish cheeks, the perplexity on the brow. Then he spoke in a different voice.

"Don't worry, old chap. You've stuck to me through thick and thin, and I'm grateful, really and truly. You're right, and I'm wrong; I always am wrong. I was looking forward to larks. If you count 'em purple sins, I don't blame you for letting me go to the devil by myself."

"I never said bridge was a purple sin."

"Warde thinks it is. If you're going to look at life here with his eyes, you'll have to rename things. Babies play Beggar my Neighbour for chocolates; why shouldn't we play bridge for a bob a hundred? The game is splendid for the brain; ten thousand times better than translating Greek choruses."

"But it is—gambling, Demon; you can't get away from that."

"Pooh! It's gambling if I bet you a 'dringer' that you won't make ten runs in a house-match; it's gambling if I raffle a picture and you take a sixpenny ticket. Are you going to give up that sort of gambling?"

"No; but——"

"What would Warde say to our co-operative system of work—eh? You're not prepared to go the whole hog? You want to pick and choose. Good! But give me the same right, that's all. Play bridge with your old pals, or don't play, just as you please."

No more was said. Scaife's manner rather than his matter confounded the younger and less experienced boy. Scaife, too, tackled problems which many men prefer to leave alone. Here heredity cropped up. Scaife's sire and grandsire were earning their bread before they were sixteen. Of necessity they faced and overcame obstacles which the ordinary Public School-boy never meets till he leaves the University.

For some time after this bridge was not mentioned. Lovell, acting, possibly, under advice from Scaife, treated Desmond courteously, and gave him his "fez" after the first house-game. Both boys now were members of the Manor cricket and football Elevens, and, as such, persons of distinction in their small world. Scaife, moreover, began to play football with such extraordinary dash and brilliancy, that it seemed to be quite on the cards that he might get his School Flannels. This possibility, and the Greek in the Fifth, absorbed his energies for the first six weeks of the winter quarter. John had come back to Scaife's room to prepare work. Desmond felt that Scaife had been generous in proposing that John should join them, because in many small ways it had become evident that the Demon disliked John, although he still spoke of the tight place out of which John had hauled him. Through Scaife John received his "fez"; and when John wore it for the first time, Scaife came up and said, smiling—

"I'm nearly even with you, Verney."

"What do you mean?" said John.

"You know well enough what I mean," said Scaife, winking his eye maliciously.

John flushed, because in his heart he did know. But when he told Egerton what Scaife had said, that experienced man of the world turned up his nose.

"Just like him," he said. "He wants you to feel that he has wiped out his debt."

"Do you think my 'fez' ought to have been given to young Lovell?"

The Caterpillar, who played back for the Manor, considered the question.

The Hill

"I don't know," he said. "You are pretty nearly equal; but it's a fact that the Demon turned the scale. He pointed out to Lovell that if he gave a 'fez' to his young brother, the house might accuse him of favouritism. That did the trick."

This made John uneasy and unhappy for a week or two; but the consciousness that another might be better entitled to the coveted "fez" made him play up with such energy that he succeeded in proving to all critics that he had honestly earned what luck had bestowed on him.

During the last week of October, John began those long walks with Desmond which, afterwards, he came to regard as perhaps the most delightful hours spent at Harrow. Scaife detested walking. He had his father's power of focusing attention and energy upon a single object. For the moment he was mad about football. Talk about books, scenery, people, bored him, and he said so with his usual frankness and impatience of restraint. Desmond, on the other hand, was also like his father, inasmuch as his tastes were catholic. He was a bit of a naturalist, learned in the lore of woods and fields, and he liked to talk about books, and he liked to talk about his home. Simple John would sooner hear Cæsar talk than listen to the heavenly choir. So it came to pass that once a week at least the boys would stroll down the avenue at Orley Farm (where Anthony Trollope's sad boyhood was passed), or take the Northwick Walk, which winds through meadows to the Bridge, or visit John Lyon's farm at Preston, or, getting signed for Bill, attempt a longer ramble to Ruislip Reservoir, or Oxhey Wood, or Headstone with its moated grange, or Horsington Hill with its long-stretching view across the Uxbridge plain.

Very soon it became the natural thing for Cæsar to give John a glimpse, at least, of whatever floated in and out of his mind. John, being himself a creature of reserves, could not quite understand this unlocking of doors, but he appreciated his privileges. Cæsar's ingenuousness, sympathy, and impulsiveness, seemed the more enchanting because John himself was of the look-before-you-leap, think-before-you-speak, sort. One Sunday evening they were hurrying back to Chapel, when

110

they passed a woman carrying a heavy child. The poor creature appeared to be almost fainting with fatigue and possibly hunger. Her pinched face, her bent figure, her thin garments, bespoke a passionate protest against conditions which obviously she was powerless to avert or control. The boys glanced at her with pitying eyes as they passed. Then Desmond said quickly—

"I say, Jonathan, she looks as if she was going to fall down."

John, seeing what was in his friend's mind, said—

"We must hurry up, or we shall miss Chapel."

They offered the woman sixpences, and blushes, because through the tattered shawl might be seen a shrunken bosom.

The woman stared, stammered, and burst into tears.

"We shall miss Chapel," John repeated.

"Hang Chapel," said Desmond.

He was looking at the child. When the woman took the silver, she let the child slip to the ground, where it lay inert.

"What's the matter with it?" said Desmond.

Half sobbing, the woman explained that the child had sprained its ankle.

"I'm just about done," she gasped; "an' the sight o' you two young gen'lemen runnin' up the 'ill finished me. I ain't the leaky sort," she added fiercely, still gasping and trembling.

Then she bent down and tried to lift the heavy child, which moaned feebly.

"You run on, Jonathan," said Desmond.

"Why?"

"I'm going to carry this kid up the hill."

"I'll help."

"No—hook it, you ass."

"I won't hook it."

Between them they carried the child as far as the Speech-room, where a policeman accepted a shilling, and gave in return a positive assurance that he would see woman and child to their destination. When the boys were alone, John said—

"Cæsar——"

"Well?"

"What a fellow you are! I wouldn't have thought of that. It was splendid."

"Oh, shut up." There was a slight pause, then Cæsar said defiantly, "I thought of carrying that kid; but I wouldn't have done it, unless I'd known that every boy was safe in Chapel. I couldn't have faced the chaff. And—you could."

They were punished for cutting Chapel, because Cæsar refused to give the reason which would have saved them.

"I'd have told the truth," he admitted to John, "if I could have shouldered that kid with the Manorites looking on."

John agreed that this was an excellent and a Cæsarean (he coined the adjective on this occasion) reason.

Among the Fifth Form boys of the Manor was a big coarse-looking youth of the name of Beaumont-Greene. Everybody called him Beaumont-Greene in full, because upon his first appearance at Bill he had stopped the line of boys by refusing to answer to the name of Greene.

"My name," said he, in a shrill pipe, "is Beaumont-Greene, and we spell the Greene with a final 'e'."

Beaumont-Greene was a type of boy, unhappily, too common at all Public Schools. He had no feeling whatever for Harrow, save that it was a place where it behoved a boy to escape punishment if he could, and to run, hot foot, towards anything which would yield pleasure to his body.

He was known to the Manorites as a funk at footer, and a prodigious consumer of "food" at the Creameries. His father, having accumulated a large fortune in manufacturing what was advertised in most of the public prints as the "Imperishable, Seamless, Whale-skin Boot," gave his son plenty of money. As a Lower Boy, Beaumont-Greene had but a sorry time of it. Somebody discovered that he was what Gilbert once described as an "imperfect ablutioner." The Caterpillar made a point of telling new boys the nature of the punishment meted out to the unclean. He had assisted at the "toshing" of Beaumont-Greene.

"A nasty job," the Caterpillar would remark, looking at his own speckless finger-nails; "but it had to be done. We took the Greene person" (the Caterpillar alone refused to defame the fine name of Beaumont by linking it to Greene) "and placed him naked in a large tosh. Into that tosh the house was invited to pour any fluid that could be spared. One forgets things; but, unless I'm mistaken, the particular sheep-wash used was made up of lemonade, syrups, ink—plenty of that—milk (I bought a quart myself), tooth-powder, paraffin, and a cake of Sapolio—Monkey Brand! We scrubbed the Yahoo thoroughly, washed its teeth, ears, hair, and then we dried it. I don't know who smeared marmalade on to the towel, but the drying part was not very successful. Rather tough—eh? Yes, very tough—on *us*, but effective. The Greene person has toshed regularly ever since. At least, so I'm told; I never go near him myself, and he's considerate enough to keep out of my way."

Beaumont-Greene had not, it is true, the appetite for reckless breaking of the law which distinguished Lovell and his particular pals; but Lovell's good qualities cancelled to a certain extent what was vicious. A fine cricketer, a plucky football-player, he might have proved a credit to his house had a master other than Dirty Dick been originally in command of it. Before he was out of the Shell, he had declared war against Authority. Beaumont Greene, on the other hand, detested games, and sneered at those who played them. Pulpy, pimply, gross in mind and body, he stood for that heavy, amorphous resistance to good, which is so difficult to overcome.

During the first half of the winter quarter, John saw but little of Esmé Kinloch. It is one of the characteristics of a Public School, that the boys—as in the greater world for which it is a preparation—are in layers. Some layers overlap; others never touch. Fluff was a fag; his friend John was in the Fifth Form, and a "fez." In a word, an Atlantic rolled between them. John, however, would often give Fluff a "con," and occasionally they would walk together. Fluff was no longer the delicate, girlish child of a year ago. He had bloomed into a very handsome boy, attractive, like all the members of is mother's family, with engaging manners, and he had also shown signs of developing into a cricketer. Fluff could paddle his own canoe, provided, of course, that he kept out of the rapids.

But about the middle of the term John noticed that Fluff was losing colour and spirits, the latter never very exuberant. It was not in John's nature to ask questions which he might answer for himself by taking pains to do so. He watched Fluff closely. Then he demanded bluntly—

"What's up?"

"Nothing."

"That's a cram," said John, severely. "I didn't believe you'd tell me a cram, Esmé."

"You don't care tuppence whether I tell crams or not now."

John weighed the "now" deliberately.

"That's another cram," he said slowly. "Has anybody been rotting you?"

Silence. John repeated the question. Still silence. Then John added—

"You know, Esmé, that I shall stick to you till I find out what's up; so you may as well save time by telling me at once."

"It's Beaumont-Greene," faltered Fluff.

"That fat beast! What's he done?"

"He hasn't done much—yet."

"Tell everything!"

"He came into my room one night and turned me up in my bed. I woke, on my head, in the dark, half-smothered, and couldn't think what had happened; it was simply awful. Then I heard his beastly voice saying, 'If I let you down, will you do what I ask you?' I'd have promised anything to get out of that horrible choking prison, and now he threatens to turn me up every night, and I dream of it——"

"Go on," said John, grimly. "No, you needn't go on. I can guess what this low cad is up to."

"He said he'd be my friend; as if I'd have a beast like that for a friend."

"Did you tell him that?"

"Yes, I did."

"You're a good-plucked 'un, Esmé. And he's made it warm for you ever since?"

"Yes."

"But he hasn't turned you up again?"

"N-no; but he will. I'd almost sooner he'd do it, and have done with it. I can't sleep."

"Now, don't be a silly fool," John commanded. "I'm going to think this out, and I'll bet I make that fat, pimply beast sit up and howl."

"Thanks awfully, John."

But the more John thought of what he had undertaken to do, the less clearly he saw his way to do it. Evidently Beaumont-Greene was too prudent to bully Fluff; he had resorted to the crueller alternative of terrorizing him. Lawrence would have settled this fellow's hash—so John reflected—in a jiffy, but Trieve, "Miss Trieve," was hopelessly incapable. Presently inspiration came. He seized an opportunity when Beaumont-Greene happened to be by himself; then he marched boldly into his room, leaving the door ajar.

"Hullo! what do you want?"

Beaumont-Greene was sitting opposite the fire, reading a novel and leisurely consuming macaroons.

"I want you to leave young Kinloch alone—*please.*"

Beaumont-Greene nearly choked; then he spluttered out—

"Say that again, will you?"

"I want you to leave young Kinloch alone."

"Really? Anything else?"

"Nothing more, thank you."

Beaumont-Greene slowly raised himself out of his chair and glared at John, whose head came to his chin.

"You've plenty of cheek."

"What I have isn't spotty, anyway."

John saw the veins begin to swell in Beaumont Greene's throat. He thought with relief of the door ajar, but it was part of his policy—a carefully devised policy— to provoke, if possible, a scene. Then others would interfere, explanations would be in order, and public opinion would accomplish the rest.

The Hill

"You infernal young jackanapes!"

"You pretty pet!"

"Get out of my room! Hook it!"

"I want to," said John, coolly enough, although his heart was throbbing. "It's horribly fuggy in here, and I've Jambi* to do; but I'm not going till you give me your word that you'll leave young Kinloch alone."

"If you don't walk out I'll chuck you out."

"You must catch me first," said John.

And then a very pretty chase took place. Beaumont Greene, fat, scant of breath, full of macaroons, began to pursue John round and round the table. John skilfully interposed chairs, sofa-cushions, anything he could lay hands on. Passing the washstand, he secured an enormous sponge, which an instant later flew souse into the face of the grampus. An abridged edition of Liddell and Scott's Greek Lexicon followed. This nearly brought the big fellow to grass. In his rage he, too, began to hurl what objects happened to be within reach, but he was a shocking bad shot; he missed, or John dodged every time. John did not miss. Finally, as John had foreseen, a couple of Sixth Form fellows rushed in.

"What's the meaning of this infernal row?" asked one.

"Ask him," said John.

Authority stared at Beaumont-Greene, and then at his wrecked room.

"I told him to hook it, and he wouldn't," spluttered the gasping Greene.

"Why?"

Half a dozen other fellows had come into the room. Amongst them the Duffer and the Caterpillar.

"I wanted to hook it," John explained, "because it's so beastly fuggy; but Beaumont-Greene wouldn't promise me to do something he ought to do."

"This is mysterious."

"The swaggering young blackguard cheeked me,"

---

* Iambi—Iambic verses.

growled Greene.

"I was very polite—at first," pleaded John.

"Hook it now, anyway," said Authority.

"Not till he promises. If you turn me out, I'll come back after you're gone."

"What is it you want him to promise?"

John had achieved his object.

"I want him to leave young Kinloch *alone.*"

The two Sixth Form boys glanced at each other; at John; at the gross, spotted face of Beaumont-Greene. Then the senior said coldly—

"I suppose you have no objection, Beaumont-Greene, to promise Verney or any one else that you will leave young Kinloch alone?"

"I've never laid a finger on the kid," growled the big fellow; but he looked pale and frightened.

"Then you promise—eh?"

"Yes."

"On your word of honour?"

"Yes."

That night John told Fluff with great glee how Beaumont-Greene had been made to "sit up and howl."

Chapter Eight

Verney Boscobel

In honour of all who believe that life was made
for friendship.

THE immediate result of the incident described in the last
chapter was to strengthen the bond between John and
Desmond. Desmond had the epic from Fluff, from the
Caterpillar, and finally from John himself.

"You bearded that poisonous beast in his den,"
exclaimed he; "you plotted and planned for the
scrimmage; you foresaw what would happen. Well, you
are a corker, Jonathan."

"You'd have thought of something much better."

"Not I," Desmond replied.

Scaife, however, made no remarks. Possibly, because
Desmond made too many, singing John's praises behind
his back and to his face, in and out of season. This, of
course, was indiscreet, and led to hard words and harder
feelings. Beaumont-Greene realized that John had tarred
and feathered him. The fags, you may be sure, rubbed the
tar in. If Beaumont-Greene threatened to kick an
impudent Fourth Form boy, that youngster would bid
him be careful.

"If you don't behave yourself," he would say, "I shall
have to send Verney to your room."

Lovell senior remarked that Beaumont-Greene was a
"swine," but that Verney had put on "lift" and must be
snubbed. What? A boy who had not been two years in the
school *dared* to take the law into his own hands! The
matter ought to have been laid before the Head of the
House.

Accordingly, John found himself, much to his dismay,
unpopular with the Olympians. The last month of this
term was, in some ways, the most disagreeable he had yet
spent at Harrow.

The Hill

But the gain of Desmond's friendship far outweighed the loss of popularity. John tingled with pleasure when he reflected that he had achieved his ambition to stand between Scaife and Desmond. At the same time, he was uncomfortably aware that Scaife seemed to have climbed high above Desmond, who had stood still. In moments of depression John told himself that he was a makeshift, that Desmond would leave him and join the Demon whenever that splendid young person chose to whistle him up. Scaife had failed to get his Football Flannels, but he came so near to beating all previous records that the School began to regard him as a "Blood." He was seen arm-in-arm with Lovell, strolling up and down the High Street, and the fags breathlessly repeated what Desmond had predicted a year ago: the Demon was the coming man. And always, when John and Desmond passed him, John thought he could read a derisive triumph upon the Demon's handsome face, an expression which said plainly: "You young fool, don't you know that I'm playing cat and mouse with you?"

The three still met twice daily to prepare work. But the moment that was done, Scaife disappeared, leaving John and Desmond together.

"He's playing bridge in Lovell's room," said Desmond. More facts were gleaned from the Caterpillar, who had joined the bridge-players, but played seldom.

"One draws the line," said he, "at playing for stakes one can't afford to lose. Lovell and the Demon have made it too hot."

"And Warde will make it hotter," said John.

"Not he," replied the Caterpillar. "The Demon is a wonder. Thanks to his brains, detection is impossible. He suggested that Lovell's room should be used. Warde wouldn't dare to burst in upon one of the Sixth. And you ought to see their dodgy arrangements. Lovell has his young brother on guard. I'm hanged if the Demon didn't invent a sort of drill, which they go through with a stopwatch. It's a star performance, I tell you. Young Lovell bolts in. In thirty-five seconds—they have got it down to that—the cards and markers are hidden; and the four of 'em are jawing away about footer."

"All the same," said John, obstinately, "Warde will be too much for 'em."

"Oh, rot!" said the Caterpillar.

The Manor got into the semi-finals of the football matches, and when the School broke up for the Christmas holidays it was generally conceded that the fortunes of the ancient house were mending. In the Manor itself Warde's influence was hardly yet perceptible: only a very few knew that it was diffusing itself, percolating into nooks and crevices, undreamed of: the hearts of the Fourth Form, for instance. In Dirty Dick's time there had been almost universal slackness. In pupil-room, Rutford read a book; boys could work or not as they pleased, provided their tutor was not disturbed. Warde, on the other hand, made it a point of honour to work with his pupils. His indefatigable energies, his good humour, his patience, were never so conspicuous as when he was coaching duffers. In other ways he made the boys realize that he was at the Manor for their advantage, not his own. The gardens and park were kept strictly private by Dirty Dick. Warde threw them open; a favour hardly appreciated in the winter quarter, but the House admitted that it would be awfully jolly in the summer to lie under the trees far from the "crowd." In a word—a "privilege."

Upon the last Saturday, to John's delight, Desmond asked him to spend a week in Eaton Square. John had paid two visits to White Ladies; he was now about to experience something entirely new. White Ladies and Verney Boscobel were typical of the past; they illustrated the history of the families who had inhabited them. The great world went to White Ladies to see the pictures and the gardens, the Gobelin tapestries, the Duchess and her guests; but the same world dined in Eaton Square to see Charles Desmond.

During this visit, our John first learned what miracles one individual may accomplish. At White Ladies, he had dimly perceived, as has been said, the duties and responsibilities imposed upon rank and wealth. In Eaton Square he saw more plainly the duties and responsibilities imposed upon a man of great talents.

The Hill

Both Charles Desmond and the Duke of Trent were hard workers, but the labours of the duke seemed to John (and to other wise persons) drab-coloured. Charles Desmond's work, in contrast, presented all the colours of the spectrum. John left White Ladies, thanking his stars that he was not a duke; he came away from Eaton Square filled with the ambition to be Private Secretary to the great Minister. And when Mr. Desmond said to him with his genial smile, "Well, young John, Harry, I hope, will be my secretary, and the crutch of my declining years. But what would you like to be?" John replied fervently, "Oh, sir, I should like to be Harry's understudy."

"Would you?"

And then John saw the face of his kind host change. The smile faded. Mr. Desmond had taken his answer as John meant it to be taken—seriously. He examined John as if he were already a candidate for office. The piercing eyes probed deep. Then he said slowly, "I should like to have you under me, John. We shall talk of this again, my boy. My own sons——" He paused, sighed, and then laughed, tapping John's cheek with his slender, finely-formed fingers. But he passed on without finishing his sentence. John knew that, of Cæsar's brothers, Hugo, the eldest, was Secretary of Legation at Teheran; Bill "devilled" for a famous barrister; Lionel wore her Majesty's livery. Strange that none had elected to serve his own father! Cæsar explained later.

"You see," he said, "the dear old governor outshines everybody. Hugo and the others felt that under him they would be in eclipse, for ever and ever—eh?"

"I see," said John, gravely. "Yes, there's something in that. He wants you, Cæsar."

"Dear old governor!" the other replied. "Yes—he's keen on that. But I hope to make my own little mark. I'd like to have my name on a brass tablet in Harrow Chapel; that would be something." His eyes began to glow and sparkle.

Next day, at dinner, Rodney's name cropped up.

"Rodney paved the way for Nelson," Mr. Desmond observed. "I look upon him as one of our greatest Harrovians. We ought to have a building to Rodney's memory. I put him before Peel or Byron."

"Oh, I say, father——" Hot protest from Cæsar.

"Act before word, Harry; practice before precept. Rodney was a man of action. I should like to have been Rodney."

"I should like to have been Sheridan," said Cæsar. "I often look at his name on the third panel of the Fourth Form Room."

He glanced at his father, who smiled, knowing that a delicate compliment was intended, for enthusiastic admirers had spoken of Charles Desmond as the Richard Brinsley Sheridan of the modern House of Commons. The father said curtly—

"A sky-rocket, my dear Harry." Then he turned to John. "And of all our famous Harrovians whom would you like to take as a pattern, young John?"

John hesitated. Two or three of the guests present were celebrities. Amongst them was England's greatest critic sitting beside an ambassador. There happened to be a lull in the talk. All looked curiously at John.

"I'd like to be another Lord Shaftesbury," he said slowly.

"Good! Capital!" Mr. Desmond nodded his head. "I knew him well." He poured out anecdote after anecdote illustrating the character and temperament of the statesman-philanthropist: his self-sacrifice, his devotion to an ideal, his curious exclusiveness, his refinement, his faith in an aristocracy never diminished by the indefatigable zeal wherein he laboured to better the condition of the poor. "If every rich man were animated by Shaftesbury's spirit," said Mr. Desmond, in conclusion, "extreme poverty would be wiped out of England, and yet we should retain all that makes life charming and profitable. He was no leveller, save of foul rookeries. First and last he believed in order, particularly his own—a true nobleman. And the inspiration of his great career came to him on the Hill."

"Indeed?" said the Critic.

"John Verney will tell you all about it," said Mr. Desmond, glancing cheerily at our hero. His was ever the habit to draw out the humblest of his guests.

So John recited how young Anthony Ashley, standing

on the Hill, just below the churchyard, chanced to see a pauper's coffin fall to the ground and burst open, revealing the pitiful corpse within, and how he had exclaimed in horror, "Good heavens! Can this be permitted simply because the man was poor and friendless?" And how, then and there, the boy had sworn to devote his powers to the amelioration of poverty-stricken lives.

"Yes," said Mr. Desmond. "He told me that the next fifteen minutes decided his career. Ah, he succeeded greatly. Why, when I was at Harrow we used to cross from Waterloo to Euston through some of the worst slums in the world. You boys can't realize what they looked like. And Shaftesbury's work and example wiped them out of our civilization."*

When John returned to his uncle's house of Verney Boscobel (his home since his father's death), Cæsar Desmond accompanied him. Then it seemed to John that his cup brimmed, that everything he desired had been granted unto him. Verney Boscobel stood in the heart of the great forest, one of the few large manors within that splendid demesne. The boys arrived at Lyndhurst Road Station late in the evening, long after dusk, and were driven in darkness through Bartley and Minstead up to the high-lying moors of Stoneycross. Next morning, early, John woke his friend, and opened the shutters.

"Jolly morning," he said. "Have a look at the Forest, old chap."

Cæsar jumped out of bed, and drew a long breath.

"Ah!" he exclaimed; "it's fairyland."

Frost had silvered all things below. Above, motionless upon the blue heavens, as if still frozen by the icy fingers

---

* There is a tablet on the wall of the Old Schools which bears he following inscription:—Near this spot Anthony Ashley Cooper Afterwards the 7th Earl of Shaftesbury, K.G. While yet a boy in Harrow School Saw with shame and indignation The pauper's funeral Which helped to awaken his lifelong Devotion to the service of the poor And the oppressed.

of a December night, were some aerial transparencies of aqueous vapour, amethystine in colour, with edges of white foam. In the east, obscured, but not concealed, by grey mist, hung the crimson orb of the sun. From it faint rays shot forth, touching the clouds beneath, which, roused, so to speak, out of sleep, drifted lethargically in a southerly direction.

> Underneath the young grey dawn
> A multitude of dense, white, fleecy clouds
> Were wandering in thick flocks, ...
> Shepherded by the slow, unwilling wind.

Desmond drew in his breath, sighing with purest delight. From the lawns encompassing the house his eyes strayed into a glade of bracken, gold gleaming through silver—a glade shadowed by noble oaks and beeches, with one birch tree in the middle of it surpassingly graceful. Upon this each delicate bough and spray were outlined sharply against the sky. Beyond the glade stretched the moor, rugged, bleak, and treeless, sloping sharply upward. Beyond the moor lay the Forest—belts of firs darkly purple; and flanking these the irregular masses of oaks and beeches, varying in tint from palest lavender to rose and brown, some still in shadow, some in ever increasing glow of sunlight; not one the same, and each in itself containing a thousand differing forms, yet all harmonious parts of the resplendent whole.

"I'm so glad you like my home," said John. "Shall we have a gallop before breakfast? It's only a white frost."

So they galloped away into fairyland, returning with mortal appetites to the oak-panelled dining-hall, whence a Verney had ridden forth to join his kinsman, Sir Edmund, in arms for the King upon the distant field of Edge Hill. After breakfast the boys explored the quaint old house; and John showed Cæsar the twenty-bore gun, and promised his guest much rabbit-shooting, and two days' hunting, at least, with the New Forest Hounds, and some pike-fishing, and possibly an encounter with a big grayling—which, later, the boys saw walloping about in the Test above Broadlands—a splendid fish, once hooked by John, and lost—a three-pounder, of course.

O golden age! You will never forget that Christmas—will you, John? If you live to be Prime Minister of England, the memory of those first days alone with your friend will remain green when the colour has been sucked by Time out of everything else. Fifty years hence, maybe, you will see Cæsar's curly head and his blue eyes full of fun and life, and you will hear his joyous laughter—peal upon peal—echoing through the corridors of Verney Boscobel. Your mother took him to her heart—didn't she? And all the servants, from butler to scullery-maid, voted him the jolliest, cheeriest boy that ever came to Hampshire. Why, Mrs. Osman, the cook, with a temper like tinder from too much heat, refused flatly to let Cæsar make toffee in her kitchen. But just then a barrel-organ turned up, and before she could open her mouth, Cæsar was dancing a polka with her; and after that he could make toffee, or hay, or anything else, wherever and whenever he pleased.

When they returned to the Manor, John hoped and prayed that this blessed intimacy would continue. It did—for a time. The three boys got their remove, and found themselves in the Second Fifth, where they proposed to linger till after the summer term. Lovell and Scaife seemed inseparable, and bridge began again, apparently an inexhaustible source of amusement and excitement. Then came the Torpid matches; and John, as Lawrence predicted, was captain of the cock-house Eleven—the first great victory of the Manorites. During the term, Scaife and Desmond won no races, being in age betwixt and between winners of Upper and Lower School races. Scaife refused to train. Desmond took a few runs, but abandoned them for racquets, the chief game in the Easter term, but only played regularly by boys whose purses are well lined. John confined his attention to "Squash." Cæsar played "Harder" with the Demon. The three worked together as of yore. John now perceived that Scaife had joined a clique pledged to fight Reform. It was in the air that something might happen. Warde eyed the big fellows shrewdly, as if measuring weapons. He confounded some by asking them to dine with him. At dessert he would talk of sport, or games, or politics—everything, in fine, except "shop." The more worthy came away from these pleasant evenings with rather a hangdog expression, as if they had been receiving goods under false pretences. John and Desmond were made especially welcome. And, after dinner, John, whose voice had not yet cracked, would sing, to Mrs. Warde's accompaniment, such songs as "O Bay of Dublin, my heart yu're throublin'," or "Think of me sometimes," or Handel's "Where'er you walk." The Caterpillar made no secret of a passion for Iris Warde, and became a dangerous rival of one of the younger masters. He talked to Warde about genealogies and hunting, topics of conversation in which they had a common interest outside Harrow. John guessed that Warde was making an effort to secure Egerton, who, for his part, took the world as he found it, consorting alike with John and his friends, and also with Lovell and Co. From the Caterpillar John learned that Beaumont-Greene had begun to play bridge.

"Scaife and Lovell are skinning the beast," he added confidentially.

"Green he is, and no error."

"Ructions soon," said John.

"I don't believe it," replied the Caterpillar. "Take my word, Warde knows what he's about. He's playing up to the younger members of the house—you, Cæsar, and you, Jonathan—and he's letting the others slide."

"Giving 'em rope," said John, "to hang 'emselves."

"Well, now, there's something in that. That hadn't occurred to me. What? You think that he's eggin' 'em on, eh? Eggin' 'em on!"

"I think that, if I were you, Caterpillar, I'd cut loose from that gang."

"They've made it rather warm for you."

"I don't care a hang about that."

As a matter of fact, John's life had been made very unpleasant by the fast set. Upon the other hand, the Duffer, Fluff, and many Lower School boys reckoned him their leader and adviser. And—such is the irony of Fate—

The Hill

John's popularity with friends caused him more anxiety than unpopularity with enemies. Towards the end of the term, Desmond spoke of applying to Warde for a certain room to be shared by himself and John. John had to decline an arrangement desired passionately, because he had indiscreetly promised not to chuck the Duffer. Cæsar dropped the subject. After this, John noticed a slight coldness. He wondered whether Cæsar were jealous, jealousy being John's own besetting sin. Finally, he came to the conclusion that his friend might be not jealous but unreasonable. In any case, during the last three weeks of the term, John saw less of Cæsar, and more—more, indeed, than he wanted—of the Duffer and Fluff.

And then came the paralysing news that Desmond had promised to spend ten days with Scaife's people, that a Professional had been hired, and that both boys were going to give their undivided energies to cricket.

Afterwards, John often wondered whether Scaife, with truly demoniac insight into Desmond's character, had let him go, so as to seize him with more tenacious grasp when an opportunity presented itself.

As soon as John saw Cæsar after the Easter holidays, he knew that, temporarily, at any rate, he had lost his friend. Cæsar, indeed, was demonstratively glad to see him, and dragged him off next day to walk to a certain bridge where a few short weeks before the boys had carved their names upon the wooden railing, surrounding them with a circle and the Crossed Arrows. But Cæsar could talk of nothing else but Scaife and cricket. They had both "come on" tremendously. Scaife's people had a splendid cricket-ground.

Poor John! If he could have submerged the Scaife cricket-ground and the Scaife family by nodding his head, I fear that he would have nodded it, although he told himself that he was an ungenerous beast and cad not to sympathize with his pal.

And before the boys got back to the Manor, Cæsar said, not without a blush, that he had learned to play bridge.

"I shall teach you, Jonathan."

"No."

"I say—yes."

"You're not going to play with Lovell and that beast Beaumont-Greene?"

"The Demon says no cards this term, when lock-up's late. And look here, Jonathan, I've made the Demon promise to make the peace between Lovell and you. You'll play for the House, of course, and we must all pull together, as Warde says."

John might have smiled at this opportune mention of Warde, but sense of humour was swamped in apprehension. Desmond went on to talk about Scaife.

"He'll make 'em sit up, you see! The 'pro.' we had is the finest cover-point in England. I never saw such a chap. He dashes at the ball. Hit it as hard as you please, he runs in, picks it up, and snaps it back to the wicket-keeper as easy as if he was playing pitch and toss. And, by Jove! the Demon can do it. You wait. I never saw any fellow like him. He's only just sixteen, and he'll get his Flannels. You needn't shake your old head, I know he will. And we must work like blazes to get ours next summer."

John discounted much of this talk, but he soon found out that Cæsar had not overestimated the Demon's activity. The draw at Lord's in the previous summer had been attributed, by such experts as Webbe and Hornby, to bad fielding. The Demon told John, with his hateful, derisive smile, that he had remembered this when he selected a "pro." Not for the first time, John realized Scaife's over-powering ability to achieve his own ends. Who, but Scaife, would have made fielding the principal object of his holiday practice?

Within a fortnight, Scaife was put into the Sixth Form game. Desmond found himself—thanks to Scaife—playing in the First Fifth game; but John was placed in Second Fifth Beta. Fortunately, he found an ally in Warde, who had a private pitch in the small park surrounding the Manor, where he coached the weaker players of his House. John told himself that he ought to get his "cap"; but, as the weeks slipped by, despite several creditable performances, he became aware that the "cap" was withheld, although it had been given to Fluff. There were

The Hill

five vacancies in the House Eleven, but, according to precedent, these need not be filled up till after the last House-match, and possibly not even then. In a word, John might play for the House, and even distinguish himself, without receiving the coveted distinction. How sore John felt!

About the end of May he noticed that something was amiss with Cæsar. Generally they walked together on Sunday, but not always. During these walks, as has been said, Cæsar did most of the talking. Now, of a sudden, he became a half-hearted listener, and to John's repeated question, "What's up?" he would reply irritably, "Oh, don't bother—nothing."

Finally, John heard from the Caterpillar that Cæsar was playing bridge, and losing.

"They don't play often," the Caterpillar added; "but on wet afternoons they make up for lost time. Cæsar is outclassed. I've told him, but he's mad keen about the game."

Later, John learned from the same source that Sunday afternoon was a bridge-fixture with Lovell and Co. At any rate, Cæsar did not play on Sunday. That was something.

Upon the following Saturday, after making an honest fifteen runs and taking three wickets in a closely-contested game, John was running into the Yard just before six Bill, when Lovell stopped him.

"You can get your 'cap,'" he said coldly.

"Oh, thanks; thanks awfully!"

Cæsar received this agreeable news with indifference.

"You ought to have had it before Fluff," he growled.

"To-morrow, we'll walk to John Lyon's farm," said John, eagerly.

"Engaged," Cæsar replied.

"Oh, Cæsar, you're—you're——"

"Well?"

"You're going to play bridge?"

"Yes. What of it? It's only once in a way. I *do* bar cards on Sunday; but there are reasons."

"What reasons?"

"Reasons which—er—I'll keep to myself."

"All right," said John, stiffly, but with a breaking heart.

Next day he asked Fluff to walk with him, but Fluff was walking with some one else. The Duffer had letters to write, and stigmatized walking as a beastly grind. John determined to walk by himself; but as he was leaving the Manor he met the Caterpillar, a tremendous buck, arrayed in his best—patent-leather boots, white waistcoat, a flower in his buttonhole.

"Where are you off to, Jonathan?"

"To Preston. You'd better come, Caterpillar."

"I never walk far in these boots. Peal made 'em."

"Change 'em, can't you?"

"Right."

While he was absent, John seriously considered the propriety of taking Egerton into his confidence. Sincerely attached to Egerton, and valuing his advice, he knew, none the less, that the Caterpillar looked at everybody and everything with the eyes of a colonel in the Guards. To tell Colonel Egerton's son that one's heart was lacerated because Cæsar Desmond was playing bridge on Sunday, seemed to invite jeers. And, besides, that wasn't the real reason. John felt wretched because the Sunday walk had been sacrificed to Moloch. Presently Egerton came downstairs, spick and span, but not quite so smart. The boys walked quickly, talking of cricket.

"The Demon'll get his Flannels," said Egerton. "I'm glad Lovell gave you your cap, Jonathan; you deserved it a month ago. It wasn't my fault you didn't get it at the beginning of the term."

"I'm sure of that," said John, gratefully.

"You don't look particularly bucked-up. A grin improves your face, my dear fellow."

At this John burst into explosive speech. Those beasts had got hold of Cæsar. The Caterpillar stared; he had never heard John let himself go. John's vocabulary surprised him.

"Whew-w-w!" he whistled. "Gad! Jonathan, you do pile on the agony. Cæsar's all right. Don't worry."

"He's not all right. I thought Cæsar had backbone—"

"Hold on," said the Caterpillar, gravely.

The Hill

John thought he was about to be rebuked for disloyalty to a pal, an abominable sin in the Caterpillar's eyes.

"Well?" said John.

"I'm going to tell you something," said Egerton. "But you must swear not to give me away."

"I'll swear."

"You're a good little cove, Jonathan, but sometimes you smell just a little bit of—er—bread and butter. Keep cool. Personally, I would sooner that you, at your age, did smell of bread and butter than whisky. Well, you think that Cæsar is going straight to the bow-wows because he plays bridge. You accuse him in your own little mind of feebleness, and so forth. Yes, just so. And it's doosid unfair to Cæsar, because he's given up his walk to-day entirely on your account.

Ah! I thought that would make you sit up."

"My account?" John repeated blankly.

"Yes; Cæsar would be furious if he knew that I was peaching, but he won't know, and instead of this—er—trifling affair weakening your good opinion of your pal, it will strengthen it."

"Oh, do go on, Caterpillar."

"Yesterday I was in Lovell's room. We were talking of the first House match. Scaife and Cæsar were there. I took it upon myself to say you ought to be given your 'cap'; and then Cæsar burst out, 'Oh yes, Lovell, do give him his "cap." If you knew how he'd slaved to earn it.' But Lovell only laughed. And then Scaife chipped in, 'Look here, Cæsar,' he said, 'do I understand that you put this thing, which after all is none of your business or mine, as a favour which Lovell might do *you*?' And Cæsar answered, 'You can put it that way, if you like, Demon.' And then Scaife laughed. I don't like Scaife's laugh, Jonathan."

"I loathe it," said John.

"Well, when Scaife laughed, Lovell looked first at him and then at Cæsar. It came to me that Lovell was primed to say something. At any rate, he turned to Cæsar, and said slowly, 'Tit for tat. If I do this for you, will you do something for me?' And Cæsar spoke up as usual, without a second's hesitation, 'Of course, I will.' And then Scaife laughed again, just as Lovell said, 'All right, I'll give Verney his "cap" before tea, and you will make a fourth at bridge with us to-morrow afternoon.'"

"Oh, oh!" groaned John.

"Dash it all, don't look so wretched. There's not much more. Cæsar hesitated a moment. Then he said quietly enough, 'Done!' Personally, I don't think Lovell was playing—well—cricket, but I do know that he wanted a fourth at bridge, because I'd just refused to make that fourth myself. They play too high for me."

"It's awfully good of you to have told me this."

"Pray don't mention it! Hullo! What's up now?"

John's face was very red, and his fists were clenched.

"Nothing," he gasped. "Only this—I'd like to kill Scaife. I'd like to cut off his infernal head."

The Caterpillar laughed indulgently. "Jonathan, you're a rum 'un. You think it wicked to play cards on Sunday; but you would like"—he imitated John's trembling, passionate voice—" you would like to cut off Scaife's infernal head."

"Yes—I would," said John.

That same week he had a memorable talk with Warde; recorded because it illustrates Warde's methods, and because, ultimately, it came to be regarded by John as the turning-point of his intellectual life. Since he had taken the Lower Remove, John's energies of mind and body had been concentrated upon improving himself at games. Vaguely aware that some of the School-prizes were within his grasp, he had not deemed them worth the winning. To him, therefore, Warde abruptly began—

"You pride yourself upon being straight—eh, Verney?"

"Why, yes," said John, meeting Warde's blue eyes not without misgiving.

"Well, to me, you're about as straight as a note of interrogation. I never see you without saying to myself, 'Is Verney going to bury his talents in the cricket-ground?'"

"Oh!"

"Some parents, too many of them, send their boys here to make a few nice friends, to play games, to scrape up the School with a remove once a year. That, I take it, is not what Mrs. Verney wants?"

"N—no, sir."

"You ought to be in the Sixth—and you know it. Twice, or oftener, you have deliberately taken things easy, because you wanted a soft time of it during the summer term, and because you wished to remain in the same form with Desmond, who, intellectually, is your—inferior. Is that square dealing with your people?"

John was silent, but red of countenance. Warde went on, more vehemently—"I know all about your co-operative system of work. I have a harder name for it. And I know just what you can do, and I want to see you do it, for your own sake, for the sake of Mrs. Verney, and for the Hill's sake. I've pushed you on at cricket a bit, haven't I? Yes. You owe me something. Pay up by entering for a School-prize, and winning it!"

"A School-prize?"

"Yes; Lord Charles Russell's Shakespeare Medal. The exam. is next October. I'll coach you. Is it a bargain?"

He held out his hand, staring frankly, but piercingly, into John's eyes.

"All right, sir," said John, after a pause. "I'll try."

"And buck up for your remove."

John smiled feebly, and sighed.

Chapter Nine

Black Spots

The Avon bears to endless years
  A magic voice along,
Where Shakespeare strayed in Stratford's shade,
  And waked the world to song.
We heard the music soft and wild,
  We thrilled to pulses new;
The winds that reared the Avon's child
  Were Herga's* nurses too.

THAT evening John told Cæsar what Warde had said to him, and then added, "I mean to have a shot at 'the Swan of Avon.'"

Cæsar looked glum.

"But how about the remove? We'd agreed to stay in the Second Fifth till Christmas. It's the jolliest form in the school."

"If we put our backs—and heads—into Trials,† we can easily get a remove."

"Blow Trials."

John turned aside.

"Look here, Jonathan," said Cæsar, eagerly. "To please me, give up your swatting scheme. We can't spoil the end of this jolly term."

He caught hold of John's arm, squeezing it affectionately. Never had our hero been so sorely tempted.

"We must stick together, you and I," entreated Desmond.

"No," said John.

---

* The Anglo-Saxon form of Harrow.
† The terminal examination.

The Hill

"As you please," Cæsar replied coldly.

A detestable week followed. John tackled his Shakespeare alone, working doggedly. Then, quite suddenly, the giant gripped him. He had always possessed a remarkable memory, and as a child he had learnt by heart many passages out of the plays (a fact well known to the crafty Warde); but these he had swallowed without digesting them. Now he became keen, the keener because he met with violent opposition from the Caterpillar and the Duffer, who were of opinion that Shakespeare was a "back number."

John won the prize, and on the following Speech Day saw his mother's face radiant with pride and happiness, as he received the Medal from the Head Master's hands.

"You look as pleased as if I'd got my Flannels," said John.

"Surely this Medal is a greater thing?"

"Oh, mum, you don't know much about boys."

"Perhaps not, but," her eyes twinkled, "I know something about Shakespeare, and he's a friend that will stand by you when cricketing days are over."

"If you're pleased, so am I," said John.

Scaife got his Flannels; and at Lord's his fielding was mentioned as the finest ever seen in a Public School match. John witnessed the game from the top of the Trent coach, and he stopped at Trent House. But he didn't enjoy his exeat, because he knew that Cæsar was in trouble. Cæsar owed Scaife thirteen pounds, and the fact that this debt could not be paid without confession to his father was driving him distracted. Scaife, it is true, laughed genially at Cæsar's distress.

"Settle when you please," he said; "but, for Heaven's sake, don't peach to your governor! Mine would laugh and pay up; yours will pay up and make you swear not to touch another card while you're at Harrow."

"Just what he *will* do," Cæsar told John.

"And the best thing that could happen," John said bluntly. "If you don't cut loose now, it will be much worse next term."

"Rot," Desmond had replied. "I'm paying the usual bill

for learning a difficult game. That's how the Demon puts it. But I've a turn for bridge, and now I can hold my own. I'm better than Beaumont-Greene, and quite as good as Lovell. The Demon, of course, is in another class."

"And therefore he oughtn't to play with you. It's robbery."

"Now you're talking bosh."

The Eton and Harrow match ended in another draw. Time and Scaife's fielding saved Harrow from defeat. The fact of a draw had significance. A draw spelled compromise. John had indulged in a superstitious fancy common enough to persons older than he. "If Harrow wins," he put it to himself, "Cæsar will triumph; if Eton wins, Cæsar will lose." When the match proved a draw, John drew the conclusion that his pal would "funk" telling the truth; an apprehension presently confirmed.

"I didn't tell the governor," said Cæsar, when John and he met. "My eldest brother, Hugo, is coming home, and I shall screw it out of him. He's a good sort, and he's going to marry a girl who is simply rolling. He'll fork out, I know he will. I feel awfully cheery."

"I don't," said John.

He had good reason to fear that Cæsar and he were drifting apart. Now he worked by himself. And his voice had broken. A small thing this, but John was sensible that his singing voice touched corners in Cæsar's soul to which his speaking voice never penetrated. More, Cæsar and he had agreed to differ upon points of conscience other than card-playing. And every point of conscientious difference increases the distance between true friends in geometrical progression. Poor Jonathan!

But we have his grateful testimony that Warde stood by him. And Warde made him see life at Harrow (and beyond) in a new light. Warde, indeed, decomposed the light into primary colours, a sort of experiment in moral chemistry, and not without fascination for an intelligent boy. Sometimes, it became difficult to follow Warde— members of the Alpine Club said that often it was impossible—because he jumped where others crawled. And he clipped words, phrases, thoughts so uncommonly short.

The Hill

"You're beginning to see, Verney, eh? Scales crumbling away, my boy. And strong sunshine hurts the eyes—at first. Black spots are dancing before you. I know the little devils."

Or again—"This remove will wipe a bit more off the debt, won't it? Ha, ha! I've made you reckon up what you owe Mrs. Verney. But there are others——"

"I'm awfully grateful to you, sir."

"Never mind me."

"What do you mean, sir?"

"New Testament; Matthew; twenty-fifth chapter—I forget verse.* Look it up. Christ answers your question. Make life easier and happier for some of the new boys. Pass on gratitude. Set it a-rolling. See?"

John had appetite for such talk, but Warde never gave much of it—half a dozen sentences, a smile, a nod of the head, a keen look, and a striding off elsewhere. But when John repeated what Warde had said to Cæsar, that young gentleman looked uneasy.

"Warde means well," he said; "and he's doing wonders with the Manor, but I hope he's not going to make a sort of tin parson of you?"

"As if he could!" said John.

"You're miles ahead of me, Jonathan."

"No, no."

"I say—yes."

"Cæsar," said John, in desperation, "perhaps we *are* sliding apart, but it isn't my fault, indeed it isn't. And think what it means to—me. You've heaps of friends, and I never was first, I know that. You can do without me, but I can't do without you."

"Dear old Jonathan." Cæsar held out his hand, smiling.

"I'm a jealous ass, Cæsar. And, as for calling me a parson," he laughed scornfully, "why, I'd sooner walk with

---

* "Inasmuch as ye have done it unto one of the least of these My brethren, ye have done it unto Me."

you, even if you were the worst sinner in the world, than with any saint that ever lived."

The feeling in John's voice drove Cæsar's gay smile from his face.

Did he realize, possibly, for the first time, that if John and he remained friends, he might drag John down? Suddenly his face brightened.

"Jonathan," he said gravely, "to please you, I'll not touch a card again this term, and we'll have such good times this last three weeks that you'll forget the rest of it."

And what delights can equal those
   That stir the spirit's inner deeps,
   When one that loves but knows not reaps
A truth from one that loves and knows?

The Manor played in the cock-house match at cricket, being but barely defeated by Damer's. Everybody admitted that this glorious state of affairs was due to Warde's coaching of the weaker members of the Eleven. Scaife fielded brilliantly, and John, watching him, said to himself that at such times the Demon was irresistible, Warde invited the Eleven to dinner, and spoke of nothing but football, much to every one's amusement.

"He's right," said the Caterpillar; "we're not cock-house at cricket this year, but we may be at footer."

John spent his holidays abroad with his mother, and when the School reassembled, he found himself in the First Fifth *alone*. With satisfaction he reflected that this was Lovell's last term, and Beaumont-Greene's too. Warde said a few words at first lock-up.

"We are going to be cock-house at footer, I hope," he began, "and next term Scaife will show the School what he can do at racquets; but I want more. I'm a glutton. How about work, eh? Lot o' slacking last term. Is it honest? You fellows cost your people a deal of money. And it's well spent, if, *if* you tackle everything in school life as you tackled Mr. Damer's last July. That's all."

"He's giving you what he gave me," said John.

"Good fellow, Warde," observed the Caterpillar; "in his room every night after prayers to mug up his form work."

The Hill

"What?" Murmurs of incredulity.

"Fact, 'pon my word. And he never refuses a 'con' to a fellow who wants it."

"He's paid for it," sneered Scaife.

The other boys nodded; enthusiasm was chilled. Yes, of course Warde was paid for it. John caught Scaife's eye.

"You don't believe that he's in love with his job, as he told us?"

"Skittles—that!"

John looked solemn. He had a bomb to throw.

"Skittles, is it?" he echoed. The other boys turned to listen. "Do you think he'd take a better-paid billet?"

Scaife laughed derisively. "Of course he would, like a shot. But he's not likely to get the chance."

"He has just been offered the Head Mastership of Wellborough. It's worth about four thousand a year."

"Pooh! who told you that?"

"Cæsar's father."

"It's true," said Cæsar.

"And he refused it," said John, triumphantly.

"Then he's a fool," said Scaife, angrily. He marched out of the room, slamming the door. But the Manor, as a corporate body, when it heard of Warde's refusal to accept promotion, was profoundly impressed. Thus the term began with good resolutions upon the part of the better sort.

Very soon, however, with the shortening days, bridge began again. John made no protest, afraid of losing his pal. He called himself coward, and considered the expediency of learning bridge, so as to be in the same boat with Cæsar. Cæsar told him that he had not asked his brother Hugo for the thirteen pounds. Hugo, it seemed, had come back from Teheran with a decoration and the air of an ambassador. He spoke of his "services."

"I knew that Hugo would make me swear not to play again," said Cæsar to John, "and, naturally, I want to get some of the plunder back. I am getting it back. I raked thirty bob out of Beaumont-Greene last night."

John said nothing.

Presently it came to his ears that Cæsar was getting more plunder back. The Caterpillar, an agreeable gossip, because he condemned nothing except dirt and low-breeding, told John that Beaumont-Greene was losing many shekels. And about the middle of October Cæsar said to John—

"What do you think, old Jonathan? I've jolly nearly paid on the Demon. And you wanted me to chuck the thing. Nice sort of counsellor."

"Beaumont-Greene must have lost a pot?"

"You bet," said Cæsar; "but that doesn't keep me awake at night. He has got the *Imperishable Seamless Whaleskin Boot* behind him."

Next time John met Beaumont-Greene he eyed him sharply. The big fellow was pulpier than ever; his complexion the colour of skilly. Yes; he looked much worried. Perhaps the "Imperishable Boot" lasted too long. And, nowadays, so many fellows wore shoes. Thus John to himself.

Beaumont-Greene, indeed, not only looked worried, he was worried, hideously worried, and with excellent reason. He had an absurdly, wickedly, large allowance, but not more than a sovereign of it was left. More, he owed Scaife twenty pounds, and Lovell another ten. Both these young gentlemen had hinted plainly that they wanted to see their money.

"I must have the stuff now," said Lovell, when Beaumont-Greene asked for time. "I'm going to shoot a lot this Christmas, and the governor makes me pay for my cartridges."

"So does mine," said Scaife, grinning. He was quite indifferent to the money, but he liked to see Beaumont-Greene squirm. He continued suavely, "You ought to settle before you leave. Ain't your people in Rome? Yes. And you're going to join 'em. Why, hang it, some Dago may stick a knife into you, and where should we be then—hey? Your governor wouldn't settle a gambling debt, would he?"

This was too true. Scaife grinned diabolically. He knew that Beaumont-Greene's father was endeavouring to establish a credit-account with the Recording Angel. Originally a Nonconformist, he had joined the Church of England after he had made his fortune (cf. *Shavings from*

The Hill

the Workshops of our Merchant Princes, which appeared in the pages of "Prattle"). Then, the famous inventor of the Imperishable Boot had taken to endowing churches; and he published pamphlets denouncing drink and gambling, pamphlets sent to his son at Harrow, who (with an eye to backsheesh) had praised his sire's prose somewhat indiscreetly.

"You shall have your confounded money," said Beaumont-Greene, violently.

"Thanks," said Scaife, sweetly. "When we asked you to join us" (slight emphasis on the "us"), "we knew that we could rely on you to settle promptly."

The Demon grinned for the third time, knowing that he had touched a weak spot; not a difficult thing to do, if you touched the big fellow at all. A young man of spirit would have told his creditors to go to Jericho. Beaumont-Greene might have said, "You have skinned me a bit. I don't whine about that; I mean to pay up; but you'll have to wait till I have the money. I'm stoney now." Scaife and Lovell must have accepted this as an ultimatum. But Beaumont-Greene's wretched pride interfered. He had posed as a sort of Golden Youth. To confess himself pinchbeck seemed an unspeakable humiliation.

Men have been known to take to drink under the impending sword of dishonour. Beaumont-Greene swallowed instead large quantities of food at the Creameries; and then wrote to his father, saying that he would like to have a cheque for thirty pounds by return of post. He was leaving Harrow, he pointed out, and he wished to give his friends some handsome presents. Young Desmond, for instance, the great minister's son, had been kind to him (Beaumont-Greene prided himself upon this touch), and Scaife, too, he was under obligations to Scaife, who would be a power by-and-by, and so forth. ... To confess frankly that he owed thirty pounds gambled away at cards required more cheek than our stout youth possessed. His father refused to play bridge on principle, because he could never remember how many trumps were out.

The father answered by return of post, but enclosed no cheque. He pointed out to his dear Thomas that giving handsome presents with another's money was an objectionable habit. Thomas received a large, possibly too large an allowance. He must exercise self-denial, if he wished to make presents. His quarterly allowance would be paid as usual next Christmas, and not a minute before. There would be time then to reconsider the propriety of giving young Desmond a suitable gift. ...

Common sense told Beaumont-Greene to show this letter to Scaife and Lovell. But he saw the Demon's derisive grin, and recoiled from it.

At this moment temptation seized him relentlessly. Beaumont-Greene never resisted temptation. For fun, so he put it, he would write the sort of letter which his father ought to have written, and which would have put him at his ease. It ran thus—

MY DEAR THOMAS,

No doubt you will want to give some leaving presents, and a spread or two. I should like my son to do the thing handsomely. You know better than I how much this will cost, but I am prepared to send you, say twenty-five or thirty pounds for such a purpose. Or, you can have the bills sent to me.

With love,
Your affectionate father,
GEORGE BEAUMONT-GREENE.

Beaumont-Greene, like the immortal Mr. Toots, rather fancied himself as a letter-writer. The longer he looked at his effusion, the more he liked it. His handwriting was not unlike his father's—modelled, indeed, upon it. With a little careful manipulation of a few letters——!

The day was cold, but Beaumont-Greene suddenly found himself in a perspiration. None the less, it seemed easier to forge a letter than to avow himself penniless. Detection? Impossible! Two or three tradesmen in Harrow would advance the money if he showed them this letter. Next Christmas they would be paid. Within a quarter of an hour he made up his mind to cross the Rubicon, and crossed it with undue haste. He forged the letter, placed it in an envelope which had come from Rome, and went to his tailor's.

Under pretext of looking at patterns, he led the man aside.

"You can do me a favour," he began, in his usual heavy, hesitating manner.

"With pleasure," said the tradesman, smiling. Then, seeing an opportunity, he added, "You are leaving Harrow, Mr. Beaumont-Greene, but I trust, sir, you will not take your custom with you. We have always tried to please you."

Beaumont-Greene, in his turn, saw opportunity.

"Yes, yes," he answered. Then he produced the letter, envelope and all. "I have here a letter from my father, who is in Rome. I'll read it to you. No; you can read it yourself."

The tailor read the letter.

"Very handsome," he replied; "*very* handsome indeed, sir. Your father is a true gentleman."

"It happens," said Beaumont-Greene, more easily, for the thing seemed to be simpler than he had anticipated— "it happens that I *do* want to make some presents, but I'm not going to buy them here. I shall send to the Stores, you know. I have their catalogue."

"Just so, sir. Excellent place the Stores for nearly everything; except, perhaps, my line."

"I should not think of buying clothes there. But at the Stores one must pay cash. I've not got the cash, and my father is in Rome. I should like to have the money to-day, if possible. Will you oblige me?"

The tradesman hesitated. In the past there have been grave scandals connected with lending money to boys. And Harrow tradesmen are at the mercy of the Head Master. If a school-tailor be put out of bounds, he can put up his shutters at once. Still——

"I'll let you have the money," said the man, eying Beaumont-Greene keenly.

"Thanks."

The tailor observed a slight flush and a sudden intake of breath—signs which stirred suspicion.

"Will you take it in notes, sir?"

Here Beaumont-Greene made his first blunder. He

had an ill-defined idea that paper was dangerous stuff.

"In gold, please."

He forgot that gold is not easily sent in a letter. The tailor hesitated, but he had gone too far to back out.

"Very well, sir. I have not twenty-five pounds——"

"Thirty, if you please. I shall want thirty."

"I have not quite that amount here, but I can get it."

When the man came back with a small canvas bag in his hand, Beaumont-Greene had pocketed the letter. He received the money, counted it, thanked the tailor, and turned to go.

"If you please, sir——"

"Yes?"

"I should like to keep your father's letter, sir. As a form of receipt, sir. When you settle I'll return it. If—if anything should happen to—to you, sir, where would I be?"

Beaumont-Greene's temper showed itself.

"You all talk as if I was on my death-bed," he said.

The tailor stared. Others, then, had suggested to this large, unwholesome youth the possibility of premature decease.

"Not at all, sir, but we do live in the valley of shadders. My wife's step-father, as fine and hearty a specimen as you'd wish to see, sir, was taken only last month; at breakfast, too, as he was chipping his third egg."

Beaumont-Greene said loftily, "Blow your wife's step-father and his third egg. Here's the letter."

He flung down the letter and marched out of the shop. The tradesman looked at him, shaking his head. "He'll never come back," he muttered.

"I know his sort too well." Then, business happening to be slack, he re-read the letter before putting it away. Then he whistled softly and read it for the third time, frowning and biting his lips. The "Beaumont-Greene" in the signature and on the envelope did not look to be written by the same hand.

"There's something fishy here," muttered the tradesman. "I must show this to Amelia."

It was his habit to consult his wife in emergencies. The chief cutter and two assistants said that Amelia was the power behind the throne. Amelia read the letter, listened to what her husband had to say, stared hard at the envelope, and delivered herself—

"The hand that wrote the envelope never wrote the letter, that's plain—to me. Now, William, you've got me and the children to think of. This may mean the loss of our business, and worse too. You put on your hat and go straight to the Manor. Mr. Warde's a gentleman, and I don't think he'll let me and the children suffer for your foolishness. Don't you wait another minute."

Nor did he.

After prayers that night, Warde asked Beaumont-Greene to come to his study. Beaumont-Greene obeyed, smiling blandly. Within three weeks he was leaving; doubtless Warde wanted to say something civil. The big fellow was feeling quite himself. He had paid Scaife and Lovell, not without a little pardonable braggadocio.

"You fellows have put me to some inconvenience," he said. "I make it a rule not to run things fine, but after all thirty quid is no great sum.

Here you are."

"We don't want to drive you into the workhouse," said Scaife. "Thanks. Give you your revenge any time. I dare say between now and the end of the term you'll have most of it back."

Warde asked Beaumont-Greene to sit down in a particular chair, which faced the light from a large lamp. Then he took up an envelope. Suddenly cold chills trickled down Beaumont-Greene's spine. He recognized the envelope. That scoundrel had betrayed him. Not for a moment, however, did he suppose that the forgery had been detected.

"On the strength of this letter," said Warde, gravely, "you borrowed thirty pounds from a tradesman?"

Denial being fatuous, Beaumont-Greene said—"Yes, sir."

"You know, I suppose, that Harrow tradesmen are expressly forbidden to lend boys money?"

"I am hardly a boy, sir. And—er—under the circumstances——"

Warde smiled very grimly.

"Ah—under the circumstances. Have you any objection to telling me the exact circumstances?"

"Not at all, sir. I wished to make some presents to my friends. I am going to give a large leaving-breakfast."

"Oh! Still, thirty pounds is a large sum——"

"Not to my father, sir. I—er—thought of coming to you, sir, with that letter."

"Did you?"

Warde took the letter from the envelope, and glanced at it with faint interest, so Beaumont-Greene thought. Then he picked up a magnifying glass and played with it. It was a trick of his to pick up objects on his desk, and turn them in his thin nervous fingers. Beaumont-Greene was not seriously alarmed. He had great faith in a weapon which had served him faithfully, his lying tongue.

"Yes, sir. I thought you would be willing to advance the money for a few days, and then——"

"And then?"

"And then I thought I wouldn't bother you. It never occurred to me that I was getting a tradesman into trouble. I hope you won't be hard on him, sir."

"I shall not be hard on him," said Warde, "because"— for a moment his eyes flashed—"because he came to me and confessed his fault; but I won't deny that I gave him a very uncomfortable quarter of an hour. He sat in your chair."

Beaumont-Greene shuffled uneasily.

"Have you this thirty pounds in your pocket?" asked Warde, casually.

Beaumont-Greene began to regret his haste in settling.

"No, sir."

"Some of it?"

"None of it."

"You sent it to London? To buy these handsome presents?"

"Ye-es, sir."

"You hadn't much time. Lock-up's early, and you received the money in gold. Did you buy Orders?"

Beaumont-Greene's head began to buzz. He found

himself wondering why Warde was speaking in this smooth, quiet voice, so different from his usual curt, incisive tones.

"Yes, sir."

"At the Harrow post-office?"

"Yes, sir."

"Ah."

Again the house-master picked up the letter, but this time he didn't lay down the lens. Instead he used it, very deliberately.

Beaumont-Greene shivered; with difficulty he clenched his teeth, so as to prevent them clicking like castanets. Then Warde held up the sheet of paper to the light of the lamp. Obviously he wished to examine the watermark. The paper was thin notepaper, the kind that is sold everywhere for foreign correspondence. Beaumont-Greene, economical in such matters, had bought a couple of quires when his people went abroad. The paper he had bought did not quite match the Roman envelope. Warde opened a drawer, from which he took some thin paper. This also he held up to the light.

"It's an odd coincidence," he said, tranquilly; "your father in Rome uses the same notepaper that I buy here. But the envelope is Italian?"

He spoke interrogatively, but the wretch opposite had lost the power of speech. He collapsed. Warde rose, throwing aside his quiet manner as if it were a drab-coloured cloak. Now he was himself, alert, on edge, sanguine.

"You fool!" he exclaimed; "you clumsy fool! Why, a child could find you out. And you—you have dared to play with such an edged tool as forgery. Now, do the one thing which is left to you: make a clean breast of it to me—at once."

In imposing this command, a command which he knew would be obeyed, inasmuch as he perceived that he dominated the weak grovelling creature in front of him, Warde overlooked the possibility that this boy's confession might implicate other boys. Already he had formed in his mind a working hypothesis to account for this forged letter. The fellow, no doubt, was in debt to some Harrow townsman.

"For whom did you *steal* this money? To whom did you pay it to-day?

Answer!"

And he was answered.

"I owed the money to Scaife and Lovell."

Then he told the story of the card-playing. At the last word he fell on his knees, blubbering.

"Get up," said Warde, sharply. "Pull yourself together if you can."

The master began to walk up and down the room, frowning and biting his lips. From time to time he glanced at Beaumont-Greene. Seeing his utter collapse, he rang the bell, answered by the ever-discreet Dumbleton.

"Dumbleton, take Mr. Beaumont-Greene to the sick-room. There is no one in it, I believe?"

"No, sir."

"You will fetch what he may require for the night; quietly, you understand."

"Very good, sir."

"Follow Dumbleton," Warde addressed Beaumont-Greene. "You will consider yourself under arrest. Your meals will be brought to you. You will hold no communication with anybody except Dumbleton and me; you will send no messages; you will write no notes. Do you hear?"

"Yes, sir."

"Then go."

Dumbleton opened the door. Young man and servant passed out and into the passage beyond. Warde waited one moment, then he followed them into the passage; but instead of going upstairs, he paused for an instant with his fingers upon the handle of the door which led from the private side to the boys' quarters. He sighed as he passed through.

At this moment Lovell was sitting in his room alone with Scaife. They had no suspicion of what had taken place in the study. In the afternoon there had been a match with an Old Harrovian team, and both Scaife and Lovell had played for the School. But as yet neither had got his Flannels. As Warde passed through the private side door, Scaife was saying angrily—

"I believe Challoner" (Challoner was captain of the football Eleven and a monitor) "has a grudge against us. If we had a chance—and we had—of getting our Flannels last year, why isn't it a cert. this, eh?"

Lovell shrugged his shoulders.

"It is a cert.," he answered; "and you're right. Challoner doesn't like us, and it amuses him to keep us out of our just rights. The monitors know I detest 'em, and they don't think you're called the Demon for nothing. Challoner is more of a monitor than a footer-player. How about a rubber? There's just time."

"I don't mind."

Lovell went to the door and opened it.

"Bo-o-o-o-o-o-y!"

The familiar cry—that imperious call which makes an Harrovian feel himself master of more or less willing slaves—echoed through the house. Immediately the night-fag came running; it was not considered healthy to keep Lovell waiting.

"Ask Beaumont-Greene to come up here and——"

He paused. Warde had just turned the corner, and was approaching. Lovell hesitated. Then he repeated what he had just said, with a slight variation for Warde's benefit. "Tell him I want to ask him a question about the house-subscriptions."

"Right," said the fag, bustling off.

Lovell waited to receive his house-master. He had very good manners.

"Can I do anything for you, sir?" he asked.

"Yes," said Warde, deliberately. He entered Lovell's room and looked at Scaife, who rose at once.

"I wish to speak with you alone, Lovell."

"Certainly, sir. Won't you sit down?"

Warde waited till Scaife had closed the door, then he said quietly—

"Lovell, does Beaumont-Greene owe you money?"

Chapter Ten

Decapitation

*Ferdinand Mendez Pinto was but a type of thee,
thou liar of the first magnitude!*

LOVELL betrayed his astonishment by a slight start;
however, he faced Warde with a smile. Warde, clean
shaven, alert, with youthful figure, looked but little older
than his pupil. For a moment the two stared steadily at
each other; then, very politely, Lovell said—

"No, sir, he does not."

Warde continued curtly, "Then he has paid you what
he did owe you?"

Lovell nodded, shrugging his shoulders. Plainly,
Warde had discovered the fact of the debt. Probably that
fool Beaumont-Greene had applied to his father, and the
father had written to Warde. It was unthinkable that
Warde knew more than this. Having reached this
conclusion, Lovell turned over in his mind two or three
specious lies that might meet the exigency.

"Yes," he replied, with apparent frankness,
"Beaumont-Greene did owe me money, and he has paid
me."

After a slight pause, Warde said quietly, "It is my duty,
as your tutor, to ask you how Beaumont-Greene became
indebted to you?"

"I lent him the money," said Lovell.

"Ah! Please call 'Boy.'"

Lovell went into the passage. Had he an intuition that
he was about to call "Boy" for the last time, or did the
pent-up excitement find an outlet in sound? He had never
called "Boy" so loudly or clearly. The night-fag scurried
up again.

"Tell him to send Scaife here," said Warde.

Lovell's florid face paled. Scaife would introduce
complications. And yet, if it had come to Warde's ears

that Beaumont-Greene was in debt to two of his schoolfellows, and if he had found out the name of one, it was
not surprising that he knew the name of the other also.
As he gave the fag the message, he regretted that Scaife
and he could not have a minute's private conversation
together.

"You lent Beaumont-Greene ten pounds, Lovell?"

"Yes, sir."

Scaife came in, cool, handsomer than usual because
of the sparkle in his eyes.

"Shut the door, Scaife. Look at me, please. Beaumont-
Greene owed you money?"

Scaife glanced at Lovell, whose left eyelid quivered.

"Kindly stand behind Scaife, Lovell. Thank you.
Answer my question, Scaife."

"Yes, sir; he owed me money."

"Have you lent him money too?" said Lovell.

It was admirably done—the hint cleverly conveyed, the
mild amazement. Warde smiled grimly. Scaife understood, and took his cue.

"Yes; I have lent him money," said he, after a slight
pause.

"Twenty pounds?"

"I believe, sir, that is the amount."

"And can you offer me any explanation why
Beaumont-Greene, whose father, to my knowledge, has
always given him a very large allowance, should borrow
thirty pounds of you two?"

"I haven't the smallest idea, have you, Lovell?"

"No," said Lovell. "Unless his younger brother, who is
at Eton, has got into trouble. He's very fond of his
brothers."

"Um! You speak up for your—friend."

Lovell frowned. "A friend, sir—no."

"Of course," said Warde, reflectively, "if it is true that
Beaumont-Greene borrowed this money to help a
brother——"

He paused, staring at Lovell. From the bottom of a big
heart he was praying that Lovell would not lie.

"Beaumont-Greene certainly gave me to understand
that the affair was pressing. Having the money, I hadn't

the heart to refuse."

"But you pressed for repayment?" said Warde, sharply.

"That is true, sir. I'm on an allowance; and I shall have many expenses this holidays."

"You, Scaife, asked for your money?"

"Yes, sir."

"Well, between you, you have driven this unhappy wretch into crime."

"Crime, sir?"

At last their self-possession abandoned them. Crime is a word which looms large in the imaginations of youth. What had Beaumont-Greene done?

"What crime, sir?"

Scaife, the more self-possessed, although fully two years the younger, asked the question.

"Forgery."

"Forgery?" Lovell repeated. He was plainly shocked.

"The idiot!" exclaimed Scaife.

"Yes—forgery. Have you anything to say? It is a time when the truth, all the truth, might be accepted as an extenuating circumstance. I speak to you first, Lovell. You're a Sixth Form boy—remember, I have been one myself—and it is your duty to help me."

"I beg pardon, sir," Lovell replied. "I have never considered it my duty as a Sixth Form boy to play the usher."

"Nor did I; but you ought to work on parallel lines with us. You accepted the privileges of the Sixth."

Lovell's flush deepened.

"More," continued Warde, "you know that we, the masters, have implicit trust in the Sixth Form, a trust but seldom betrayed. For instance, I should not think of entering your room without tapping on the door; under ordinary circumstances I should accept your bare word unhesitatingly. I say emphatically that if you, knowing these things, have accepted the privileges of your order with the deliberate intention of ignoring its duties, you have not acted like a man of honour."

"Sir!"

"Don't bluff! Now, for the last time, will you give me

what I have given you—trust?"

"I have nothing more to say," Lovell answered stiffly.

"And you, Scaife?"

"I am sorry, sir, that Beaumont-Greene has been such a fool. We lent him this money, because he wanted it badly; and he said he would pay us back before the end of the term."

"You stick to that story?"

"Why, yes, sir. Why should we tell you a lie?"

"Ah, why, indeed?" sighed Warde. Then his voice grew hard and sharp.

The persuasiveness, the carefully-framed sentences, gave place to his curtest manner. "This matter," said he, "is out of my hands. The Head Master will deal with it. I must ask you for your keys, Lovell."

"And if I refuse to give them up?"

"Then we must break into your boxes. Thanks." He took the keys.

"Follow me, please."

The pair followed him into the private side, upstairs, and into the sick-room. There were three beds in it; upon one sat Beaumont-Greene. His complexion turned a sickly drab when he saw Lovell and Scaife. He even glanced at the window with a hunted expression. The window was three stories from the ground, and heavily barred ever since a boy in delirium had tried to jump from it.

"Your night-things will be brought to you," said Warde.

He went out slowly. The boys heard the key turn in the massive lock. They were prisoners. Scaife walked up to Beaumont-Greene.

"You told Warde about the bridge?"

"Ye-es; I had to. Scaife, don't look at me like that. Lovell"—his voice broke into a terrified scream—"don't let him hit me. I couldn't help it—I swear I——"

"You cur!" said Scaife. "I wouldn't touch you with a forty-foot pole."

Just what passed between Warde and the Head Master must be surmised.

Carefully hidden in Lovell's boxes were found cards

and markers. Upon the latter remained the results of the last game played, and under the winning column a rough calculation in pounds, shillings, and pence. There were no names.

Next day, during first school, a notice came round to each Form to be in the Speech-room at 8.30. Not a boy knew or guessed the reason of this summons. The Manorites, aware that three of their House were in the sickroom, believed that an infectious disease had broken out. Only Desmond, John, and the Caterpillar experienced heart-breaking fears that a catastrophe had taken place.

When the School assembled at half-past eight, the monitors came in, followed by the Head Master in cap and gown. Then, a moment later, the School Custos entered with Scaife. They sat down upon a small bench near the door. Immediately the whispers, the shuffling of feet, the occasional cough, died down into a thrilling silence. The Head Master stood up.

He was a man of singularly impressive face and figure. And his voice had what may be described as an edge to it—the cutting quality so invaluable to any speaker who desires to make a deep impression upon his audience. He began his address in the clear, cold accents of one who sets forth facts which can neither be controverted nor ignored. Slowly, inexorably, without wasting a word or a second, he told the School what had happened. Then he paused.

As his voice melted away, the boys moved restlessly. Upon their faces shone a curious excitement and relief. Gambling in its many-headed forms is too deeply rooted in human hearts to awaken any great antipathy. So far, then, the sympathy of the audience lay with the culprits; this the Head Master knew.

When he spoke again, his voice had changed, subtly, but unmistakably.

"You were afraid," he said, "that I had something worse—ah, yes, unspeakably worse—to tell you. Thank God, this is not one of those cases from which every clean, manly boy must recoil in disgust. But, on that account, don't blind yourselves to the issues involved.

The Hill

This playing of bridge—a game you have seen your own people playing night after night, perhaps—is harmless enough in itself. I can say more—it is a game, and hence its fascination, which calls into use some of the finest qualities of the brain: judgment, memory, the faculty of making correct deductions, foresight, and patience. It teaches restraint; it makes for pleasant fellowship. It does all this and more, provided that it never degenerates into gambling. The very moment that the game becomes a gamble, if any one of the players is likely to lose a sum greater than he can reasonably afford to pay, greater than he would cheerfully spend upon any other form of entertainment, then bridge becomes cursed. And because you boys have not the experience to determine the difference between a mere game and a gamble, card-playing is forbidden you, and rightly so. Now, let us consider what has happened. A stupid foolish fellow, playing with boys infinitely cleverer than himself, has lost a sum of money which he could not pay. To obtain the means of paying it, he deliberately forged a letter and a signature. And then followed the inevitable lying—lie upon lie. That is always the price of lies—'to lie on still.'

"I would mitigate the punishment, if I could, but I must think of the majority. This sort of malignant disease must be cut out. Two of the three offenders are young men; they were leaving at the end of this term. They will leave, instead—to-day. The third boy is much younger. Because of his youth, I have been persuaded by his house-master to give him a further chance."

Again he paused. Then he exclaimed loudly, "Scaife!"

Scaife stood up, very pale. "Here, sir!"

"Scaife, you will go into the Fourth Form Room,* and prepare to receive the punishment which no member of the Eleven should ever deserve."

John sat with his Form while the Head Master was

---

* The place of execution.

H. A. Vachell

addressing the School. Not far off was the Caterpillar, less
cool than usual, so John remarked. His collar, for
instance, seemed to be too tight; and he moved restlessly
upon his chair. Many very brave men become nervous
when a great danger has passed them by. Egerton said
afterwards, "I felt like getting down a hole, and pulling the
hole after me. Not my own. Some Yankee's, you know."
Still, he displayed remarkable self-possession under
trying circumstances. Two of Lovell's particular friends
were seen to turn the colour of Cheddar cheese. But
Desmond, so John noticed, grew red rather than yellow.
Nor did he tremble, but his fists were clenched, and his
eyes kindled.

As Scaife left the Speech-room, followed by Titchener
(the provider of birches, whose duty it is to see that boys
about to be swished are properly prepared to receive
punishment), the boys began to shuffle in their places.
But the Head Master held up his hand. It was then that
Lovell's two particular friends, who had partially
recovered, felt that the earth was once more slipping from
under them.

"It takes four to play bridge." The Caterpillar's fingers
went to his collar again. "In this case there must have
been a fourth, possibly a fifth and a sixth. Not more, I
think, because the secret was too well kept. We are
confronted with the disagreeable fact that three boys are
going to receive the most severe punishments I can inflict,
and that another escapes scot-free. *For I do not know
the—name—of—the—fourth.*"

The Head Master waited to let each deliberate word
soak in. Perhaps he had calculated the effect of his voice
upon a boy of sensibility and imagination. That Scaife, his
friend, should suffer the indignity of a swishing, and that
he should escape scot-free, seemed to Cæsar Desmond
not a bit of rare good fortune—as it appeared to the
others—but an incredible miscarriage of justice. To
submit tamely to such a burden was unthinkable. He
sprang to his feet, ardent, impetuous, afire with the spirit
which makes men accept death rather than dishonour;
and then, in a voice that rang through the room, thrilling
the coldest and most callous heart, he exclaimed—

"I was the fourth."

A curious sound escaped from the audience—a gasp of surprise, of admiration, and of dismay, at least, so the Head Master interpreted it. And looking at the faces about him, he read approval or disapproval, according as each boy betrayed the feeling in his heart.

"You, Desmond?"

"Yes, sir."

The Caterpillar rose slowly. He was cool enough now.

"I was the fifth."

But Lovell's two particular friends sat tight, as they put it. Let us not blame them.

"You, Egerton?"

"Yes, sir."

For a moment the Head Master hesitated. Into his mind there flashed the image of two notable figures—the fathers whom he had entreated to send sons to the Manor. If—if by so doing he had compassed the boys' ruin, could he ever have forgiven himself? But now, the boys themselves had justified his action; they had proved worthy of their breeding and the traditions of the Hill.

"Come here," he said.

When they stood opposite to him, he continued—

"You give yourselves up to receive the punishment I am about to inflict upon Scaife?"

The boys did not answer, save with their eyes. The silence in the great room was so profound that John made sure that the beating of his heart must be heard by everybody.

"I shall not punish you. This voluntary confession has done much to redeem your fault. Meet me in my study at nine this evening, and I will talk to you. When I came here I hardly hoped to find saints, but I did expect to find—gentlemen. And I have not been disappointed."

He addressed the others. "You will return to your boarding-houses, and quietly, if you please."

The immediate and most noticeable effect of Lovell's expulsion was the loss of the next House match. Damer's defeated the Manor easily. Some of the fags whispered to each other that the injuries inflicted by the Head Master on Scaife had been so severe as to incapacitate the star-player of the House. Two boys had concealed themselves in the Armoury (which is just below the Fourth Form Room) upon the morning when Scaife was flogged. But they reported—nothing. However severe the punishment might have been, Scaife received it without a whimper.

In truth, Scaife received but one cut, and that a light one. The Head Master wished to lay stripes upon the boy's heart, not his body. When he saw him prepared to receive punishment, he said gravely—

"I have never flogged a member of the Eleven. And now, at the last moment, I offer you the choice between a flogging and expulsion."

"I prefer to be flogged."

And then—one cut.

But Scaife never forgot the walk from the Yard to the Manor, after execution. He was too proud to run, too proud not to face the boys he happened to meet. They turned aside their eyes from his furious glare. But he met no members of his own House. They had the delicacy to leave the coast clear. When he reached his room, he found Desmond alone. Desmond said nervously—

"I asked Warde if we could have breakfast here this morning, instead of going into Hall. I've got some ripping salmon."

Scaife had faced everything with a brazen indifference, but the sympathy in his friend's voice overpowered him. He flung himself upon the sofa by the window and wept, not as a boy weeps, but with the cruel, grinding sobs of a man. He wept for his stained pride, for his vain-glory, not because he had sinned and caused others to sin. The boy watching him, seeing the hero self-abased, hearing his heartbreaking sobs, interpreted very differently those sounds. Infinitely distressed, turning over and over in his mind some soothing phrases, some word of comfort and encouragement, Desmond waited till the first paroxysm had passed. What he said then shall not be set down in cold print. You may be sure he proved that friendship between two strong vigorous boys is no frail thread, but a golden chain which adversity strengthens and refines.

Scaife rose up with his heart softened, not by his own tears, but by the tears he saw in Desmond's eyes.

"I'm all right now," he said. Then, with frowning brows, he added thoughtfully, "I deserve what I got for being a fool. I ought to have foreseen that such a swine as Beaumont-Greene would be sure to betray us sooner or later. I shall be wiser next time."

"Next—time?" The dismay in Desmond's voice made Scaife smile.

"Don't worry, Cæsar. No more bridge for me; but," he laughed harshly, "the leopard can't change his spots, and he won't give up hunting because he has fallen into a trap, and got out of it. Come, let's tackle the salmon."

The winter term came to an end, and the School broke up. Upon the evening of the last Sunday, Warde said a few words to John.

"I propose to make some changes in the house," he said abruptly.

"Would you like to share No. 7 with Desmond?"

No. 7 was the jolliest two-room at the Manor. It overlooked the gardens, and was larger than some three-rooms. Then John remembered Scaife and the Duffer.

"Desmond has been with Scaife ever since he came to the house, sir."

"True. But I'm going to give Scaife a room to himself. He's entitled to it as the future Captain of the Eleven. That is—settled. You and Duff must part. He's two forms below you in the school, and never likely to soar much higher than the Second Fifth. Next term you will be in the Sixth, and by the summer I hope Desmond will have joined you.

You will find together.* Of course Scaife can find with you, if you wish. I've spoken to him and Desmond."

And so, John's fondest hope was realized. When he came back to the Manor, Desmond and he spent much

---

* "Finding" is the privilege, accorded to the Sixth Form, of having breakfast and tea served in their own rooms instead of in Hall.

time and rather more money than they could afford in making No. 7 the cosiest room in the house. Consciences were salved thus:—John bought for Desmond some picture or other decorative object which cost more money than he felt justified in spending on himself; then Desmond made John a similar present. It was whipping the devil round the stump, John said, but oh! the delight of giving his friend something he coveted, and receiving presents from him in return.

During this term, Scaife became one of the school racquet-players. In many ways he was admittedly the most remarkable boy at Harrow, the Admirable Crichton who appears now and again in every decade. He won the high jump and the hurdle-race. These triumphs kept him out of mischief, and occupied every minute of his time. He associated with the "Bloods," and one day Desmond told John that he considered himself to have been "dropped" by this tremendous swell. John discreetly held his tongue; but in his own mind, as before, he was convinced that Scaife and Desmond would come together again. The inexorable circumstance of Scaife's superiority at games had separated the boys, but only for a brief season. Desmond would become a "Blood" soon, and then it would be John's turn to be "dropped." Being a philosopher, our hero did not worry too much over the future, but made the most of the present, with a grateful and joyous heart. In his humility, he was unable to measure his influence on Desmond. In athletic pursuits an inferior, in all intellectual attainments he was pulling far ahead of his friend. The artful Warde had a word to say, which gave John food for thought.

"You can never equal your friend at cricket or footer, Verney. If you wish to score, it is time to play your own game."

Shortly after this, John realized that Warde had read Cæsar aright. Charles Desmond's son, as has been said, acclaimed quality wherever he met it. John's intellectual advance amazed and then fascinated him. When John discovered this, he worked harder. Warde smiled. John ran second for the Prize Poem. He had genuine feeling for Nature, but he lacked as yet the technical ability to display it. A more practised versifier won the prize; but John's taste for history and literature secured him the Bourchier, not without a struggle which whetted to keenness every faculty he possessed. More, to his delight, he realized that his enthusiasm was contagious. Cæsar entered eagerly into his friend's competitions; struggle and strife appealed to the Irishman. He talked over John's themes, read his verses, and predicted triumphs. Warde told John that Cæsar Desmond might have stuck in the First Fifth, had it not been for this quickening of the clay. The days succeeded each other swiftly and smoothly. Warde was seen to smile more than ever during this term. Certain big fellows who opposed him were leaving or had already left. Bohun, now Head of the House, was a sturdy, straightforward monitor, not a famous athlete, but able to hold his own in any field of endeavour. Just before the Christmas holidays, Warde discovered, to his horror, that the drainage at the Manor was out of order. At great expense a new and perfect system was laid down. At last Warde told himself his house might be pronounced sanitary within and without.

When the summer term came, Desmond joined John in the Sixth Form. They were entitled to single rooms, but they asked and obtained permission to remain in No. 7. Desmond was invested with the right to fag, and the right to "find." How blessed a privilege the right to find is, boys who have enjoyed it will attest. The cosy meals in one's own room, the pleasant talk, the sense of intimacy, the freedom from restraint. Custom stales all good things, but how delicious they taste at first!

The privilege of fagging is not, however, unadulterated bliss. When Warde said to Cæsar, "Well, Desmond, how do you like ordering about your slave?" Desmond replied, ruefully, "Well, sir, little Duff has broken my inkstand, spilt the ink on our new carpet, and let Verney's bullfinch escape. I think, on the whole, I'd as soon wait on myself."

Early in June it became plain that unless the unforeseen occurred, Harrow would have a strong Eleven, and that Desmond would be a member of it. John and Fluff were playing in the Sixth Form game; but John had no chance of his Flannels, although he had improved in batting and bowling, thanks to Warde's indefatigable coaching. Scaife hardly ever spoke to John now, but occasionally he came into No. 7 to talk to Desmond. Upon these rare occasions John would generally find an excuse for leaving the room. Always, when he returned, Desmond seemed to be restless and perplexed. His admiration for Scaife had waxed rather than waned. Indeed, John himself, detesting Scaife—for it had come to that—fearing him on Desmond's account, admired him notwithstanding: captivated by his amazing grace, good looks, and audacity. His recklessness held even the "Bloods" spellbound. A coach ran through Harrow in the afternoons of that season. Scaife made a bet that he would drive this coach from one end of the High Street to the other, under the very nose of Authority. The rules of the school set forth rigorously that no boy is to drive in or on any vehicle whatever. Only the Cycle Corps are allowed to use bicycles. Scaife's bet, you may be sure, excited extraordinary interest. He won it easily, disguised as the coachman—a make-up clever enough to deceive even those who were in the secret. His friends knew that he kept two polo-ponies at Wembley. One afternoon he dared to play in a match against the Nondescripts. Warde's daughter, just out of the schoolroom, happened to be present, and she rubbed her lovely eyes when she saw Scaife careering over the field. Scaife laughed when he saw her; but before she left the ground a note had reached her.

DEAR MISS WARDE,

I am sure that you have too much sporting blood in your veins to tell your father that you have seen me playing polo.

Yours very sincerely,

REGINALD SCAIFE.

To run such risks seemed to John madness; to Desmond it indicated genius.

"There never was such a fellow," said Cæsar to John.

The Hill

When Cæsar spoke in that tone John knew that Scaife had but to hold up a finger, and that Cæsar would come to him even as a bird drops into the jaws of a snake. Cæsar was strong, but the Demon was stronger.

After the Zingari Match, Desmond got his Flannels. He was cheered at six Bill. Everybody liked him; everybody was proud of him, proud of his father, proud of the long line of Desmonds, all distinguished, good-looking, and with charming manners. The School roared its satisfaction. John stood a little back, by the cloisters. Cæsar ran past him, down the steps and into the street, hat in hand, blushing like a girl. John felt a lump in his throat. He thrilled because glory shone about his friend; but the poignant reflection came, that Cæsar was running swiftly, out of the Yard and out of his own life. And before lock-up he saw, what he had seen in fancy a thousand times, Cæsar arm-in-arm with Scaife and the Captain of the Eleven, Cæsar in his new straw,* looking happier than John had ever seen him, Cæsar, the "Blood," rolling triumphantly down the High Street, the envied of all beholders, the hero of the hour.

John called himself a selfish beast, because he had wished for one terrible moment, wished with heart and soul, that Cæsar was unpopular and obscure.

---

* The black-and-white straw hat only worn by members of the School Cricket Eleven.

Chapter Eleven

Self-Questioning

Friend, of my infinite dreams
  Little enough endures;
Little howe'er it seems,
  It is yours, all yours.
Fame hath a fleeting breath,
  Hope may be frail or fond;
But Love shall be Love till death,
  And perhaps beyond.

UNTIL the Metropolitan Railway joined Harrow to Baker Street, the Hill stood in the midst of genuine and unspoilt country, separated by five miles of grass from the nearest point of the metropolis, and encompassed by isolated dwellings, ranging in rank and scale from villas to country houses.* Most of the latter have fallen victims to the speculative builder, and have been cut up into alleys of brick and stucco. But one or two still remain among their hayfields and rhododendrons.

John Verney had an eager curiosity, not common in schoolboys, to know something about the countryside in which he dwelt. As a Lower Boy, whenever released from "Compulsory" and House-games, he used to wander with alert eyes and ears up and down the green lanes of Roxeth and Harrow Weald, enjoying fresh glimpses of the far-seen Spire, making friends with cottagers, picking up traditions of an older and more lawless† epoch, and, with

---

* Of these, the Park, now a boarding-house, was a characteristic specimen. It belonged to Lord Northwick, Lord of the Manor of Harrow.
† In the thirties Harrow boys played "Jack o' Lantern," or nocturnal hare and hounds. They used to attend Kingsbury Races and Sudbury Fair. Lord Alexander Russell when he was a boy at the Grove, kept a pack of beagles at the foot of the Hill.

The Hill

these, an ever-increasing love and loyalty to Harrow. So Byron had wandered a hundred years before.

These solitary rambles, however, were regarded with disfavour by schoolfellows who lacked John's imaginative temperament. The Caterpillar, for instance, protested, "Did I see you hobnobbing with a chaw the other day? I thought so; and you looked like a confounded bug-hunter." The Duffer's notions of topography were bounded by the cricket-ground on the one side of the Hill, and the footer-fields on the other; and his traditions held nothing much more romantic than A. J. Webbe's scores at Lord's. Fluff, as has been said, was too far removed from John to make him more than an occasional companion. And so, for several terms, John, for the most part, walked alone. By the time Desmond joined him, he had gleaned a knowledge which fascinated a friend of like sensibility and imagination. Together they revisited the old and explored the new. One never-to-be-forgotten day the boys discovered a deserted house of some pretensions about a mile from the Hill. Its grounds, covering several acres, were enclosed by a high oak paling, within which stood a thick belt of trees, effectually concealing what lay beyond. Grim iron gates, always locked, frowned upon the wayfarer; but John, flattening an inquisitive nose against the ironwork, could discern a carriage-drive overgrown with grass and weeds, and at the end of it a white stone portico. After this the place became to both boys a sort of Enchanted Castle. A dozen times they peered through the gates. No one went in or out of the grass-grown drive. The gatekeeper's lodge was uninhabited; there were no adjacent cottages where information might be sought. The boys called it "The Haunted House," and peopled it with ghosts; gorgeous bucks of the Regency, languishing beauties such as Lawrence painted, fiery politicians, duellists, mysterious black-a-vized foreigners. John connected it in fancy with the days when the gorgeous Duke of Chandos (who had Handel for his chapel-organist and was a Governor of Harrow and guardian of Lord Rodney) kept court at Cannons. He told Cæsar anecdotes of Dr. Parr, with his preposterous wig, his clouds of tobacco, his sesquipedalian quotations, coming down from Stanmore; and also of the great Lord Abercorn, another Governor of the school, who used to go out shooting in the blue riband of the Garter, and who entertained Pitt and Sir Walter Scott at Bentley Priory.

"What a lot you know!" said Cæsar. "And you have a memory like my father's. I'm beginning to think, Jonathan, that you'll be a swell like him some day—in the Cabinet, perhaps."

"Ah," said John, with shining eyes.

"I hope I shall live to see it," Desmond added, with feeling.

"Thanks, old chap. A crust or a triumph shared with a pal tastes twice as good."

One soft afternoon in spring, after four Bill, Desmond and John were approaching the iron gates of the Haunted House. They had not taken this particular walk since the day when Desmond got his Flannels. During the winter term, Scaife and Desmond became members of the Football Eleven. During this term Scaife won the hundred yards and quarter-mile; Desmond won the half-mile and mile. In a word, they had done, from the athletic point of view, nearly all that could be done. A glorious victory at Lord's seemed assured. Scaife, Captain and epitome of the brains and muscles of the Eleven, had grown into a powerful man, with the mind, the tastes, the passions of manhood. Desmond, on the other hand, while nearly as tall (and much handsomer in John's eyes), still retained the look of youth. Indeed, he looked younger than John, although a year his senior; and John knew himself to be the elder and wiser, knew that Desmond leaned upon him whenever a crutch was wanted.

The chief difficulty which besets a school friendship between two boys is that of being alone together. In Form, in the playing-fields, in the boarding-house, life is public. Even in the most secluded lane, a Harrow boy is not secure against the unwelcome salutations of heated athletes who have been taking a cross-country run, or leaping over, or into, the Pinner brook. To John the need of sanctuary had become pressing.

Upon this blessed spring afternoon—ever afterwards recalled with special affection—a retreat was suddenly

The Hill

provided. As the boys jumped over the last stile into the lane which led to the Haunted House, Desmond exclaimed—

"By Jove, the gates are open!"

Then they saw that a man, a sort of caretaker, was in the act of shutting them.

"May we go in?" John asked civilly.

The man hesitated, eying the boys. Desmond's smile melted him, as it would have melted a mummy.

"There's nothing to see," he said.

Then, in answer to a few eager questions, he told the story of the Haunted House; haunted, indeed, by the ghosts of what might have been. A city magnate owned the place. He had bought it because he wished to educate his only son at Harrow as a "Home-Boarder," or day-boy. A few weeks before the boy should have joined the school, he fell ill with diphtheria, and died. The mother, who nursed him, caught the disease and died also. The father, left alone, turned his back upon a place he loathed, resolving to hold it till building-values increased, but never to set eyes on it again. The caretaker and his wife occupied a couple of rooms in the house.

The boys glanced at the house, a common-place mansion, and began to explore the gardens. To their delight they found in the shrubberies, now a wilderness of laurel and rhododendron, a tower—what our forefathers called a "Gazebo," and their neighbours a "Folly." The top of it commanded a wide, unbroken view—

> Of all the lowland western lea,
>   The Uxbridge flats and meadows,
> To where the Ruislip waters see
>   The Oxhey lights and shadows.

"There's the Spire," said John.

The man, who had joined them, nodded. "Yes," said he, "and my mistress and her boy are buried underneath it. She wanted him to be there—at the school, I mean and there he is."

"We're very much obliged to you," said Desmond. He slipped a shilling into the man's hand, and added, "May

168

we stay here for a bit? And perhaps we might come again—eh?"

"Thank you, sir," the man replied, touching his hat. "Come whenever you like, sir. The gates ain't really locked. I'll show you the trick of opening 'em when you come down."

He descended the steep flight of steps after the boys had thanked him.

"Sad story," said John, staring at the distant Spire.

Desmond hesitated. At times he revealed (to John alone) a curious melancholy.

"Sad," he repeated. "I don't know about that. Sad for the father, of course, but perhaps the son is well out of it. Don't look so amazed, Jonathan. Most fellows seem to make awful muddles of their lives. You won't, of course. I see you on pinnacles, but I——" He broke off with a mirthless laugh.

John waited. The air about them was soft and moist after a recent shower. The south-west wind stirred the pulses. Earth was once more tumid, about to bring forth. Already the hedges were green under the brown; bulbs were pushing delicate spears through the sweet-smelling soil; the buds upon a clump of fine beeches had begun to open. In this solitude, alone with teeming nature, John tried to interpret his friend's mood; but the spirit of melancholy eluded him, as if it were a will-o'-the-wisp dancing over an impassable marsh. Suddenly, there came to him, as there had come to the quicker imagination of his friend, the overpowering mystery of Spring, the sense of inevitable change, the impossibility of arresting it. At the moment all things seemed unsubstantial. Even the familiar Spire, powdered with gold by the slanting rays of the sun, appeared thinly transparent against the rosy mists behind it. The Hill, the solid Hill, rose out of the valley, a lavender-coloured shade upon the horizon.

"He came here," continued Desmond, dreamily—John guessed that he was speaking of the father—" a rich, prosperous man. I dare say he worked like a slave in the city. And he wanted peace and quiet after the Stock Exchange. Who wouldn't? And he planted out these gardens, thinking that every plant would grow up and thrive, and his son with them. And then the boy died; and the wife followed; and the enchanted castle became a place of horror; and now it is a wilderness. Haunted? I should think it was—haunted! I wish we'd never set foot in it. There's a curse on it."

"Let's go," said John.

"Too late. We'll stay now, and we'll come again, every Sunday. Wild and desolate as things look, they will be lovely when we get back in summer. Don't talk. I'm going to light a pipe."

Through the circling cloud of tobacco-smoke John stared at the face which had illumined nearly every hour of his school-life. Its peculiar vividness always amazed John, the vitality of It, and yet the perfect delicacy. Scaife's handsome features were full of vitality also, but coarseness underlay their bold lines and peered out of the keen, flashing eyes. When the Caterpillar left Harrow he had said to John—

"Good-bye, Jonathan. Awful rot your going to such a hole as Oxford! One has had quite enough schooling after five years here. It's settled I'm going into the Guards. My father tells me that old Scaife tried to get the Demon down on the Duke's list. But we don't fancy the Scaife brand."

Often and often John wondered whether Desmond saw the brand as plainly as the Caterpillar and he did. Sometimes he felt almost sure that a word, a look, a gesture betraying the bounder, had revolted Desmond; but a few hours later the bounder bounded into favour again, captivating eye and heart by some brilliant feat. And then his brains! He was so diabolically clever. John could always recall his face as he lay back in the chair in No. 15, sick, bruised, befuddled, and yet even in that moment of extreme prostration able to "play the game," as he put it, to defeat house-master and doctor by sheer strength of will and intellect. It was Scaife who had persuaded Desmond to smoke. ...

Cæsar's voice broke in upon these meditations.

"I say—what are you frowning about?"

John, very red, replied nervously, "Now that you're in the Sixth, you ought to chuck smoking."

"What rot!" said Cæsar. "And here, in this tower, where one couldn't possibly be nailed——"

"That's it," said John. "It's just because you can't possibly be nailed that it seems to me not quite square."

Cæsar burst out laughing. "Jonathan, you are a rum 'un. Anyway—heregoes!"

As he spoke he flung the pipe into the bushes below.

"Thanks," said John, quietly.

"We'll come here again. I like this old tower."

"You won't come here without me?"

"Oh, ho! I'm not to let the Demon into our paradise—eh? What a jealous old bird you are! Well, I like you to be jealous." And he laughed again.

"I am jealous," said John, slowly.

The School broke up on the following Tuesday, and Desmond went home with John.

This happened to be the first time that the friends had spent Easter together. John wondered whether Cæsar would take the Sacrament with his mother and him. He and Cæsar had been confirmed side by side in the Chapel at Harrow. He felt sure that Desmond would not refuse if he were asked. On Easter Eve, Mrs. Verney said, in her quiet, persuasive voice—

"You will join us to-morrow morning, Harry?"

Desmond flushed, and said, "Yes."

Not remembering his own mother, who had died when he was a child, he often told John that he felt like a son to Mrs. Verney. Upon Easter morning, the three met in the hall, and Desmond asked for a Prayer-book.

"I've lost mine," he murmured.

That afternoon, when they were alone upon the splendid moor above Stoneycross, Desmond said suddenly—

"Religion means a lot to you, Jonathan, doesn't it?"

"Yes."

"But you never talk about it."

"No."

"Why not?"

"I don't know how to begin."

"There's such sickening hypocrisy in this world."

The Hill

John nodded.

"But your religion is a help to you, eh? Keeps you straight?"

John nodded again. Then Desmond said with an air of finality—

"I wish I'd some of your faith. I want it badly."

"If you want it badly, you will get it."

A long silence succeeded. Then Desmond exclaimed "Hullo! By Jove, there's a fox, a splendid fellow! He's come up here amongst the rabbits for a Sunday dinner. Gone awa-a-a-ay!"

He put his hand to his mouth and halloaed. A minute later he was talking of hunting. Religion was not mentioned till they were approaching the house for tea. On the threshold, Desmond said with a nervous laugh—

"I'd like your mother to give me a Prayer-book—a small one, nothing expensive."

During the following week they hunted with fox hounds or stag-hounds every day, except Wednesday. In the New Forest the Easter hunting is unique. Tremendous fellows come down from the shires—masters of famous packs, thrusters, keen to see May foxes killed. And the Forest entertains them handsomely, you may be sure. Big hampers are unpacked under the oaks which may have been saplings when William Rufus ruled in England; there are dinners, and, of course, a hunt-ball in the ancient village of Lyndhurst. But as each pleasant day passed, John told himself that the end was drawing near. This was almost the last holidays Cæsar and he would spend together; and, afterwards, would this friendship, so romantic a passion with one at least of them—would it wither away, or would it endure to the end?

At the end of a fortnight, Desmond returned to Eaton Square. Upon the eve of departure, Mrs. Verney gave him a small Prayer-book.

"I have written something in it," she said; "but don't open it now."

He looked at the fly-leaf as the train rolled out of Lyndhurst Station. Upon it, in Mrs. Verney's delicate handwriting, were a few lines. First his name and the date. Below, a text—"Unto whomsoever much is given, of him shall be much required." And, below that again, a verse—

Not thankful when it pleaseth me,
As if Thy blessings had spare days:
But such a heart whose pulse may be—
  Thy praise.

Desmond stared at the graceful writing long after the train had passed Totton. "Am I ungrateful?" he asked himself. "Not to them," he muttered; "surely not to them." He recalled what Warde had said about ingratitude being the unpardonable sin. Ah! it was loathsome, ingratitude! And much had been given to him. How much? For the first time he made, so to speak, an inventory of what he had received—his innumerable blessings. *What had he given in return?* And now the fine handwriting seemed blurred; he saw it through tears which he ought to have shed. "Oh, my God," he murmured, "am I ungrateful?" The question bit deeper into his mind, sinking from there into his soul.

When the School reassembled, a curious incident occurred. John happened to be going up the fine flight of steps that leads to the Old Schools. He was carrying some books and papers. Scaife, running down the steps, charged into him. By great good fortune, no damage was done except to a nicely-bound Sophocles. John, however, felt assured that Scaife had deliberately intended to knock him down, seized, possibly, by an ecstasy of blind rage not uncommon with him. Scaife smiled derisively, and said—

"A thousand apologies, Verney."

"*One* is enough," John replied, "if it is sincere."

They eyed each other steadily. John read a furious challenge in Scaife's bold eyes—more, a menace, the threatening frown of power thwarted. Scaife seemed to expand, to fill the horizon, to blot out the glad sunshine. Once again the curious certainty gripped the younger that Scaife was indeed the personification of evil, the more malefic because it stalked abroad masked. For Scaife had outlived his reputation as a breaker of the law. Since that terrible experience in the Fourth Form Room, he had paid tithe of mint and cummin. As a Sixth Form boy he upheld authority, laughing the while in his sleeve. He knew, of course, that one mistake, one slip, would be fatal. And he prided himself on not making mistakes. He gambled, but not with boys; he drank, not with boys; he denied his body nothing it craved; but he never forgot that expulsion from Harrow meant the loss of a commission in a smart cavalry regiment. When it was intimated to him that the Guards did not want his father's son, he laughed bitterly, and swore to himself that he would show the stuck-up snobs what a soldier they had turned away. A soldier he fully intended to be—a dashing cavalry leader, if the Fates were kind. His luck would stand by him; if not—why— what was life without luck? He had never been a reader, but he read now the lives of soldiers. Murat, Uxbridge, Cardigan, Hodson, were his heroes. Talking of their achievements, he inflamed his own mind and Desmond's.

The pleasant summer days passed. May melted into June. And each Sunday John and Desmond walked to the Haunted House, ascended the tower, and talked. Scaife was leaving at the end of the summer. Desmond was staying on for the winter term; then John would have him entirely to himself. This thought illumined dark hours, when he saw his friend whirled away by Scaife, transported, as it were, by the irresistible power of the man of action. That nothing should be wanting to that trebly-fortunate youth, he had helped to win the Public Schools' Racquets Championship. The Manor was now the crack house—cock-house at racquets and football, certain to be cock-house at cricket. And Scaife got most of the credit, not Warde, who smiled more than ever, and talked continually of Balliol Scholarships. He never bragged of victories past.

Meantime, John was devoting all energies to the competition for the Prize Essay. The Head Master had propounded as theme: "The History and Influence of Parliamentary Oratory." Bit by bit, John read or declaimed it to Desmond. Then, according to custom, Desmond copied it out for his friend. Signed "*Spero*

Infestis," with a sealed envelope containing John's name inside and the motto outside, the MS. was placed in the Head Master's letter-box. John, cooling rapidly after the fever of composition, condemned his stuff as hopelessly bad; Cæsar went about telling everybody that Jonathan would win easily, "with a bit to spare." John did win, but that proved to be the least part of his triumph. The Essay had to be declaimed upon Speech Day. Once more John experienced the pangs that had twisted him at the concert, long ago, when he had sung to the Nation's hero. And as before, he began weakly. Then, the fire seizing him, self-consciousness was exorcised by feeling, and forgetful of the hundreds of faces about him, he burst into genuine oratory. Thrilled himself, he thrilled others. His voice faltered again, but with an emotion that found an echo in the hearts of his audience; his hand shook, feeling the pulse of old and young in front of him. Dominated, swept away by his theme, he dominated others. When he finished, in the silence that preceded the roar of applause, he knew that he had triumphed, for he saw Desmond's glowing countenance, radiant with pleasure, transfigured by amazement and admiration. Next day a great newspaper hailed the Harrow boy as one destined to delight and to lead, perhaps, an all-conquering party in the House of Commons. And yet, warmed to the core by this praise, John counted it as nothing compared with his mother's smile and Desmond's fervent grip.

Fortune, however, comes to no man—or boy—with both hands full. Immediately after Speech Day, John's bubble of pride and happiness was pricked by Scaife. Midsummer madness seized the Demon. One may conceive that the innate recklessness of his nature, suppressed by an iron will, and smouldering throughout many months, burst at last into flame. Desmond told John that the Demon had spent a riotous night in town. He had slipped out of the Manor after prayers, had driven up to a certain club in Regent Street, returned in time for first school, fresh as paint—so Desmond said—and then, not content with such an achievement, must needs brag of it to Desmond.

The Hill

"And if he's nailed, Eton wins," concluded Desmond. "I've told you, because together we must put a stop to such larks."

John slightly raised his thick eyebrows. It was curious that Cæsar always chose to ignore the hatred which he must have known to exist between his two friends. Or did be fatuously believe that, because John exercised an influence over himself, the same influence would or could be exercised over Scaife?

"We?" said John.

"I've tried and failed. But together, I say——"

"I shan't interfere, Cæsar."

"Jonathan, you must."

"It would be a fool's errand."

"We three have gone up the School together. You have never been fair to Scaife. I tell you he's sound at core. Why, after he was swished——"

Desmond told John what had passed; John shook his head. He could understand better than any one else why Scaife had broken down.

"He has splendid ambitions," pursued Desmond. "He's going to be a great soldier, you see. He thinks of nothing else. You never have liked him, but because of that I thought you would do what you could."

The disappointment and chagrin in his voice shook John's resolution.

"To please you, I'll try."

And accordingly the absurd experiment was made. Afterwards, John asked himself a thousand times why he had not foreseen the inevitable result. But the explanation is almost too simple to be recorded: he wished to convince a friend that he would attempt anything to prove his friendship.

That night they went together to Scaife's room. The second-best room in the Manor, situated upon the first floor, it overlooked the back of the garden, where there was a tangled thicket of laurustinus and rhododendron. Scaife had spent much money in making this room as comfortable as possible. It had the appearance of a man's room, and presented all the characteristics of the man who lived in it. Everything connected with Scaife's triumphal march through the School was preserved. On the walls were his caps, fezes, and cups. You could hardly see the paper for the framed photographs of Scaife and his fellow "bloods." Scaife as cricketer, Scaife as football-player, Scaife as racquet-player and athlete, stared boldly and triumphantly at you. He had a fine desk covered with massive silver ornaments. Upon this, as upon everything else in the room, was the hall-mark of the successful man of business. The papers, the pens and pencils, the filed bills and letters, the books of reference, spoke eloquently of a mind that used order as a means to a definite end. All his books were well bound. His boots were on trees. His racquets were in their press. Had you opened his chest of drawers, you would have found his clothes in perfect condition. Obviously, to an observant eye, the owner of this room gave his mind to details, because he realized that on details hang great and successful enterprises.

Scaife stared at John, but welcomed him civilly enough. Cricket, of course, explained this unexpected visit. As Desmond blurted out what was in his mind, Scaife frowned; then he laughed unpleasantly.

"And so I told Jonathan," concluded Desmond.

"So you told Jonathan," repeated Scaife. "Are you in the habit of telling Jonathan,"—the derisive inflection as he pronounced the name warned John at least that he had much better have stayed away—"things which concern others and which don't concern him?"

"If you're going to take it like that——"

"Keep cool, Cæsar. I'll admit that you mean well. I should like to hear what Verney has to say."

At that John spoke—haltingly. Fluent speech upon any subject very dear to him had always been difficult. He could talk glibly enough about ordinary topics; his sense of humour, his retentive memory, made him welcome even in the critical society of Eaton Square, but you know him as a creature of unplumbed reserves. The matter in hand was so vital that he could not touch it with firm hands or voice. He spoke at his worst, and he knew it; concluding an incoherent and slightly inarticulate recital of the reasons which ought to keep Scaife in his house at night with a lame "Two heads ought to prevail against one."

Scaife showed his fine teeth. "You think that? Your head and Cæsar's against mine?"

The challenge revealed itself in the derisive, sneering tone.

John shrugged his shoulders and rose. "I have blundered; I am sorry."

"Hold hard," said Scaife. He read censure upon Desmond's ingenuous countenance. Then his temper whipped him to a furious resentment against John, as an enemy who had turned the tables with good breeding; who had gained, indeed, a victory against odds. Scaife drew in his breath; his brows met in a frown. "You have not blundered; and you are not sorry," he said deliberately. "I'm not a fool, Verney; but perhaps I have underrated your ability. You're as clever as they make 'em. You knew well enough that you were the last person in the world to lead me in a string; you knew that, I say, and yet you come here to pose as the righteous youth, doing his duty—eh?—against odds, and accepting credit for the same from Cæsar. Why, it's plain to me as the nose upon your face that in your heart you would like me to be sacked."

Desmond interrupted. "You are mad, Demon. Take that back; take it back!"

"Ask him," said Scaife. "He hates me, and common decency ought to have kept him out of this room. But he's not a liar. Ask him. Put it your own way. Soften it, make pap of it, if you like, but get an answer."

"Jonathan, it is not true, is it? You don't like Scaife; but you would be sorry, very sorry, to see him—sacked."

"I'm glad you've not funked it," said Scaife. "You've put it squarely.

Let him answer it as squarely."

John was white to the lips, white and trembling; despicable in his own eyes, how much more despicable, therefore, in the eyes of his friend, whose passionate faith in him was about to be scorched and shrivelled.

Scaife began to laugh.

"For God's sake, don't laugh!" said Desmond.

"Jonathan, I know you are too proud to defend yourself against such an abominable charge."

"He's not a liar," said Scaife.

"It's true," said John, in a strangled voice.

"You have wished that he might be sacked?"

"Yes."

John met Desmond's indignant eyes with an expression which the other was too impetuous, too inexperienced, to interpret. Into that look of passionate reproach he flung all that must be left unsaid, all that Scaife could read as easily as if it were scored in letters of flame. Because, in his modesty and humility, he had ever reckoned that Scaife would prevail against himself— because, with unerring instinct, he had apprehended, as few boys could apprehend, the issues involved, he had desired, fervently desired, that Scaife should be swept from Cæsar's path. But this he could not plead as an excuse to his friend; and Scaife had known that, and had used his knowledge with fiendish success. John lowered his eyes and walked from the room.

When he met Desmond again, nothing was said on either side. John told himself that he would speak, if Desmond spoke first. But evidently Desmond had determined already the nature of their future relations. They no longer shared No. 7, John being in the Upper Sixth with a room to himself, but they still "found" together. To separate would mean a public scandal from which each shrank in horror. No; let them meet at meals as before till the end of the term. Indeed, so little change was made in their previous intercourse, that John began to hope that Cæsar would walk with him as usual upon the following Sunday. And if he did—if he did, John felt that he would speak. On the top of the tower, looking towards the Spire, alone with his friend, exalted above the thorns and brambles or the wilderness, words would come to him.

But on the following Sunday Desmond walked with Scaife.

Chapter Twelve

Lords

There we sat in the circle vast,
  Hard by the tents, from noon,
And looked as the day went slowly past
  And the runs came all too soon;
And never, I think, in the years gone by,
  Since cricketer first went in,
Did the dying so refuse to die,
  Or the winning so hardly win.

"MY dear Jonathan, I'm delighted to see you. You know my father, I think?" It was the Caterpillar that spoke.

John shook hands with Colonel Egerton.

The three were standing in the Members' Enclosure at Lord's. The Caterpillar, gorgeous in frock-coat, with three corn-flowers* in the lapel of it, was about as great a buck as his sire, quite as conspicuous, and, seemingly, as cool. It happened to be a blazing hot day, but heat seldom affected Colonel Egerton.

"By Jove," he said to John, "I'm told it's a certainty this year, and I've come early, too early for me, to see a glorious victory. There's civil war raging on the top of the Trent coach, I give you my word."

"We've won the toss," said John.

"Ah, there's Charles Desmond, an early bird too."

He bustled away, leaving John and the Caterpillar together. The great ground in front of them was being cleared. One could see, through the few people scattered here and there, the wickets pitched in the middle of that vast expanse of lawn, and the umpires in their long white

---

* The blue of the Harrow colours.

coats. Upon the top of the steps, in the middle of the pavilion, the Eton captain was collecting his Eleven. The Duffer, who had got his Flannels at the last moment, came up and joined John and the Caterpillar.

"The Manor's well to the front," said the Caterpillar.

"By Jove! I never thought to see Fluff in the Eleven."

"Fluff came on tremendously this term," the Duffer replied.

"Of course the Kinlochs are a cricketing family."

"Good joke the brothers playing against each other," said John.

"Warde," the Duffer nodded in the direction of Warde, who was talking with Charles Desmond and Colonel Egerton, "has worked like a slave. He made a cricketer out of Fluff and a scholar out of Jonathan. He's so mad keen to see us win, that he's given me the jumps."

"You must keep cool," the Caterpillar murmured. "I've just come from the Trent coach. Fluff has it from the brother who is playing that the Eton bowling is weak. But Strathpeffer, the eldest son, tells me the batsmen are stronger than last year. He seemed anxious to bet; so we have a fiver about it. They're taking the field."

The Eton Eleven walked towards the wicket, loudly cheered. Cæsar came up in his pads, carrying his bat and gloves. He shook hands with the Caterpillar, and said, with a groan, that he had to take the first ball.

"Keep cool," said the Caterpillar. "The bowling's weak; I have it from Cosmo Kinloch. They're in a precious funk."

"So am I," said the Duffer.

"But you're a bowler," said Desmond. "If I get out first ball, I shall cut my throat."

But Cæsar looked alert, cool, and neither under-nor over-confident.

"You'll cut the ball, not your throat," said the Duffer. Cutting was Cæsar's strong point.

The Caterpillar nodded, and spoke oracularly—

"My governor says he never shoots at a snipe without muttering to himself, 'Snipe on toast.' It steadies his nerves. When you see the ball leave the bowler's band, you say to yourself, 'Eton on toast.'"

"Your own, Caterpillar?"

"My own," said the Caterpillar, modestly. "I don't often make a joke, but that's mine. Pass it on."

The other Harrovian about to go in beckoned to Desmond.

"Cæsar won't be bowled first ball," said the Caterpillar. "He's the sort that rises to an emergency. Can't we find a seat?"

They sat down and watched the Eton captain placing his field. Desmond and his companion were walking slowly towards the wickets amid Harrow cheers. The cheering was lukewarm as yet. It would have fire enough in it presently. The Caterpillar pointed out some of the swells.

"That's old Lyburn. Hasn't missed a match since '64. Was brought here once with a broken leg! Carried in a litter, by Jove! That fellow with the long white beard is Lord Fawley. He made 78 *not out* in the days of Charlemagne."

"It was in '53," said the Duffer, who never joked on really serious subjects; "and he made 68, not 78. He's pulling his beard. I believe he's as nervous as I am."

Presently the innumerable voices about them were hushed; all eyes turned in one direction. Desmond was about to take the first ball. It was delivered moderately fast, with a slight break. Desmond played forward.

"Well played, sir! Well pla-a-ayed!"

The shout rumbled round the huge circle. The beginning and the end of a great match are always thrilling. The second and third balls were played like the first. John could hear Mr. Desmond saying to Warde, "He has Hugo's style and way of standing—eh?" And Warde replied, "Yes; but he's a finer batsman. Ah-h-h!"

The first real cheer burst like a bomb. Desmond had cut the sixth ball to the boundary.

Over! The new bowler was a tall, thin boy with flaxen hair.

"That's Cosmo Kinloch, Fluff's brother," said John.

"I wonder they can't do better than that. Even I knocked him all over the shop at White Ladies last summer."

"He's come on, they tell me," said the Caterpillar.

The Hill

"Good Lord, he nearly had him first ball."

Fluff's brother bowled slows of a good length, with an awkward break from the off to the leg.

"Teasers," said the Caterpillar, critically. "Hullo! No, my young friend, that may do well enough in Shropshire, not here."

A ball breaking sharply from the off had struck the batsman's pad; he had stepped in front of his wicket to cut it. Country umpires are often beguiled by bowlers into giving wrong decisions in such cases, not so your London expert. Cosmo Kinloch appealed—in vain.

"He'll send a short one down now," said John. "You see."

And, sure enough, a long hop came to the off, curling inwards after it pitched. The Eton captain had nearly all his men on the off side. The Harrovian pulled the ball right round to the boundary.

"Well hit!"

"Well pulled!"

"Two 4's; that's a good beginning," said the Duffer.

A couple of singles followed, and then the first "10" went up amid cheers.

"Here's my governor," said the Duffer. "He was three years in the Eleven and Captain his last term."

"You've told us that a thousand times," said the Caterpillar.

The Rev. Septimus Duff greeted the boys warmly. His eyes sparkled out of a cheery, bearded face. Look at him well. An Harrovian of the Harrovians this. His grandfathers on the maternal and paternal side had been friends at Harrow in Byron's time. The Rev. Septimus wore rather a shabby coat and a terrible hat, but the consummate Caterpillar, who respected pedigrees, regarded him with pride and veneration. He came up from his obscure West Country vicarage to town just once a year—to see the match. If you asked him, he would tell you quite simply that he would sooner see the match and his old friends than go to Palestine; and the Rev. Septimus has yearned to visit Palestine ever since he left Cambridge; and it is not likely that this great wish will ever be gratified. He is the father of three sons, but the

Duffer is the first to get into the Eleven. Charles Desmond joins them. At the moment, Charles Desmond is supposed to be one of the most harried men in the Empire. Times are troublous. A war-cloud, as large as Kruger's hand, has just risen in the South, and is spreading itself over the whole world. But to-day the great Minister has left the cares of office in Downing Street. He hails the Rev. Septimus with a genial laugh and a hearty grasp of the hand.

"Ah, Sep, upon your word of honour, now—would you sooner be here to see the Duffer take half a dozen wickets, or be down in Somerset, bishop of Bath and Wells?"

"When *you* offer me the bishopric," replied the Rev. Septimus, with a twinkle, "I'll answer that question, my dear Charles, and not before."

"You old humbug! You're so puffed up with sinful pride that you've stuck your topper on to your head the wrong way about."

"Bless my soul," said the Duffer's father, "so I have."

"That topper of the governor's," the Duffer remarked solemnly, "has seen twenty-five matches at least."

John looked at no hats; his eyes were on the pitch. Another round of cheers proclaimed that "20" had gone up. Both boys are batting steadily; no more boundary hits; a snick here, a snack there—and then—merciful Heavens!—Cæsar has cut a curling ball "bang" into short slip's hands.

Short slip—wretched youth—muffs it! Derisive remarks from the Rev. Septimus.

"Well caught! Well held! Tha-a-nks!"

The Caterpillar would pronounce this sort of chaff bad form in a contemporary. He removes his hat.

"By Jove!" says he. "It's very warm."

Cæsar times the next ball beautifully. It glides past point and under the ropes.

Early as it is, the ground seems to be packed with people. Glorious weather has allured everybody. Stand after stand is filled up. The colour becomes kaleidoscopic. The Rev. Septimus, during the brief interval of an over, allows his eyes to stray round the huge circle. Upon the ground are the youth, the beauty, the rank and fashion of the kingdom, and, best of all, his old friends. The Rev. Septimus has a weakness, being, of course, human to the finger-tips. He calls himself a *laudator temporis acti*. In his day, the match was less of a function. The boys sat round upon the grass; behind them were the carriages and coaches—you could drive on to the ground then!— and here and there, only here and there, a tent or a small stand. *Consule Planco*—the parson loves a Latin tag—the match was an immense picnic for Harrovians and Etonians. And, my word, you ought to have heard the chaff when an unlucky fielder put the ball on the floor. Or, when a batsman interposed a pad where a bat ought to have been. Or, if a player was bowled first ball. Or, if he swaggered as he walked, the cynosure of all eyes, from the pavilion to the pitch. Upon this subject the Rev. Septimus will preach a longer (and a more interesting) sermon than any you will hear from his pulpit in Blackford-Orcas Church.

Loud cheers put an end to the parson's reminiscences. Desmond's companion has been clean bowled for a useful fifteen runs. He walks towards the pavilion slowly. Then, as he hears the Harrow cheers, he blushes like a nymph of sixteen, for he counts himself a failure. Last year he made a "duck" in his first innings, and five in the second. No cheers then. This is his first taste of the honey mortals call success. He has faced the great world, and captured its applause.

"When does Scaife go in?" the Rev. Septimus asks.

"Second wicket down."

More cheers as the second man in strolls down the steps. A careful cove, so the Duffer tells his father—one who will try to break the back of the bowling.

"They're taking off Fluff's brother," the Caterpillar observes.

A thick-set young man holds the ball. He makes some slight alteration in the field. The wicket-keeper stands back; the slips and point retreat a few yards. The ball that took the first wicket was the last of an over. Desmond has to receive the attack of the new bowler.

The thick-set Etonian, having arranged the off side to

his satisfaction, prepares to take a long run. He holds the ball in the left hand, runs sideways at great speed, changes the ball from the left hand to the right at the last moment, and seems to hurl both it and himself at the batsman.

"Greased lightning!" says John.

A dry summer has made the pitch rather fiery. The ball, short-pitched, whizzes just over Cæsar's head. A second and a third seem to graze his cap. Murmurs are heard. Is the Eton bowler trying to kill or maim his antagonist? Is he deliberately endeavouring to establish a paralysing "funk"?

But the fourth ball is a "fizzer"—the right length, a bailer, terrifically fast, but just off the wicket. Desmond snicks it between short slip and third man; it goes to the boundary.

"That's what Cæsar likes," says the Duffer. "He can cut behind the wicket till the cows come home."

"Cut—and come again," says the Caterpillar.

The fifth ball is played forward for a risky single. The Rev. Septimus forgets that times have changed. And if they have, what of it? He hasn't. His deep vibrant voice rolls across the lawn right up to the batsman—

"Steady there! Steady!"

And now the new-comer has to take the last ball of the over—his first. Alas and alack! The sixth ball is dead on to the middle stump. The Harrovian plays forward. Man alive, you ought to have played back at that! The ball grazes the top edge of the bat's blade and flies straight into the welcoming hands of the wicket-keeper.

Two wickets for 33.

Breathless suspense, broken by tumultuous cheers as Scaife strides on to the ground. His bat is under his arm; he is drawing on his gloves. Thousands of men and as many women are staring at his splendid face and figure.

"What a mover!" murmurs the Rev. Septimus.

Scaife strides on. Upon his face is the expression John knows so well and fears so much—the consciousness of power, the stern determination to be first, to shatter previous records. John can predict—and does so with absolute certainty—what will happen. For six overs the

The Hill

Demon will treat every ball—good, bad, and indifferent—with the most distinguished consideration. And then, when his "eye" is in, he will give the Etonians such leather-hunting as they never had before.

After a long stand made by Scaife and Desmond, Cæsar is caught at cover-point, but Scaife remains. It is a Colossus batting, not a Harrow boy. The balls come down the pitch; the Demon's shoulders and chest widen; the great knotted arms go up—crash! First singles; then twos; then threes; and then boundary after boundary. To John—and to how many others?—Scaife has been transformed into a tremendous human machine, inexorably cutting and slicing, pulling and drawing—the embodied symbol of force, ruthlessly applied, indefatigable, omnipotent.

The Eton captain, hopeful against odds, puts on a cunning and cool dealer in "lobs." Fluff is in, playing steadily, holding up his wicket, letting the giant make the runs. The Etonian delivers his first ball. Scaife leaves the crease. Fluff sees the ball slowly spinning—harmless enough till it pitches, and then deadly as a writhing serpent. Scaife will not let it pitch. The ball curves slightly from the leg to the off. Scaife is facing the pavilion——

A stupendous roar bursts from the crowd. The ball, hit with terrific force, sails away over the green sward, over the ropes, over the heads of the spectators, and slap on to the top of the pavilion.

Only four; but one of the finest swipes ever seen at Lord's. Shade of Mynn, come forth from the tomb to applaud that mighty stroke!

But the dealer in lobs knows that the man who leaves his citadel, leaves it, sooner or later, not to return. In the hope that Scaife, intoxicated with triumph, will run out again, he pitches the next lob too much up—a half-volley. Scaife smiles.

John's prediction has been fulfilled. A record has been established. Never before in an Eton and Harrow match have two balls been hit over the ropes in succession. The crowds have lost their self-possession. Men, women, and children are becoming delirious. The Rev. Septimus throws his ancient topper into the air; the Caterpillar splits a brand-new pair of delicate grey gloves. Upon the tops of the coaches, mothers, sisters, aunts, and cousins are cheering like Fourth-Form boys.

The Harrow first innings closed with 289 runs, Scaife carrying out his bat for an almost flawless 126. Desmond made 72; Fluff was in for twenty-seven minutes—a great performance for him—and was caught in the slips after compiling a useful 17.

But the remarkable feature of the innings was the short time in which so many runs were made—exactly three hours. The elevens went in to lunch, as the crowd poured over the ground, laughing and chattering. This is a delightful hour to the Rev. Septimus. He will walk to the wickets, and wait there for his innumerable friends. It will be, "Hullo, Sep!" "By Jove, here's dear old Sep!" "Sep, you unfriendly beast, why do you never come to see us?" "Sep, when are you going to send that awful tile of yours to the British Museum?" And so on.

Twenty men, at least—some of them with names known wherever the Union Jack waves—will ask the Rev. Sep to lunch with them; but the Rev. Sep will say, as he has said these thirty years, that he doesn't come to Lord's to "gorge." A sandwich presently, and a glass of "fizz," if you please; but time is precious. A tall bishop strolls up one of the pillars of the Church, an eloquent preacher, and an autocrat in his diocese. Most people regard him with awe. The Rev. Sep greets him with a scandalous slap on the back, and addresses him, the apostolic one, as— Lamper.* And the Lord Bishop of Dudley says, like the others—

"Hullo, Sep! We used to think you a slogger, but you never came anywhere near that smite of Scaife's."

"I thought his smite was coming too near me," says

---

* Lamper, *i.e.* lamp-post.

the Rev. Sep, with a shrewd glance at the pavilion. "Lamper, old chap, I *am* glad to see your 'phiz' again."

And so they stroll off together, mighty prelate and humble country parson, once again happy Harrow boys.

And now, before Eton goes in, we must climb on to the Trent coach. Fluff and his brother Cosmo, the Eton bowler, are lunching in other company, but we shall find Colonel Egerton and the Caterpillar and Warde; so the Hill slightly outnumbers the Plain, as the duke puts it. Next to the duchess sits Mrs. Verney. The duke is torn nearly in two between his desire that Fluff should make runs and that Cosmo, the Etonian, should take wickets. His Eton sons regard him as a traitor, a "rat" and Colonel Egerton gravely offers him the corn-flowers out of his coat.

"You can laugh," the duke says seriously, "but when I see what Harrow has done for Esmé, I'm almost sorry"—he looks at his youngest son (nearly, but not quite, as delicate-looking as Fluff used to be)—"I'm almost sorry that I didn't send Alastair there also."

Alastair smiles contemptuously. "If you had," he says, "I should have never spoken to you again. Esmé is a forgiving chap, but you've wrecked his life. At least, that's my opinion."

After luncheon, the crowd on the lawn thickens. The ladies want to see the pitch, and, shall we add, to display their wonderful frocks. The enclosure at Ascot on Cup Day is not so gay and pretty a scene as this. The Caterpillar, sly dog, has secured Iris Warde, and looks uncommonly pleased with himself and his companion; a smart pair, but smart pairs are common as gooseberries. It is the year of picture hats and Gainsborough dresses.

"England at its best," says Miss Iris.

"And in its best," the Caterpillar replies solemnly.

Iris Warde is as keen as her father's daughter ought to be. She tells the Caterpillar that when she was a small girl with only threepence a week pocket-money, she used to save a penny a week for twelve weeks preceding the match, so as to be able to put a shilling into the plate on Sunday *if Harrow won.*

"And I dare say you'll marry an Etonian and wear light

blue after all," growls the Caterpillar.

"Never!" says Miss Iris.

Now, amongst the black coats in the pavilion you see a white figure or two. The Elevens have finished lunch, and are mixing with the crowd. Scaife is talking with a famous Old Carthusian, one of the finest living exponents of cricket, sometime an "International" at football, and a D.S.O. The great man is very cordial, for he sees in Scaife an All-England player. Scaife listens, smiling. Obviously, he is impatient to begin again. As soon as possible he collects his men, and leads them into the field. One can hear the policemen saying in loud, firm voices, "Pass along, please; pass along!" As if by magic the crowds on the lawn melt away. In a few minutes the Etonians come out of the pavilion. The sun shines upon their pale-blue caps and sashes, and upon faces slightly pale also, but not yet blue. For Eton has a strong batting team, and Scaife and Desmond have proved that it is a batsman's wicket.

And now the connoisseurs, the really great players, settle themselves down comfortably to watch Scaife field. That, to them, is the great attraction, apart from the contest between the rival schools. Some of these Olympians have been heard to say that Scaife's innings against weak bowling was no very meritorious performance, although the two "swipes," they admit, were parlous knocks. Still, Public School cricket is kindergarten cricket, and if you've not been at Eton or Harrow, and if you loathe a fashionable crowd, and if you think first-class fielding is worth coming to Lord's to see, why, then, my dear fellow, look at Scaife!

Scaife stands at cover-point. If you put up your binoculars, you will see that he is almost on his toes. His heels are not touching the ground. And he bends slightly, not quite as low as a sprinter, but so low that he can start with amazing speed. For two overs not a ball worth fielding rolls his way. Ah! that will be punished. A long hop comes down the pitch. The Etonian squares his shoulders. His eye, to be sure, is on the ball, but in his mind's eye is the boundary; in his ear the first burst of applause. Bat meets ball with a smack which echoes from the Tennis-Court to the stands across the ground. Now watch Scaife! He dashes at top speed for the only point where his hands may intercept that hard-hit ball. And, by Heaven! he stops it, and flicks it up to the wicket-keeper, who chips off the bails.

"How's that?"

"Not out!"

"Well fielded; well fielded, sir!"

"A very close squeak," says the Caterpillar. "They won't steal many runs from the Demon."

"Sometimes," says Miss Iris, "I really think that he is a demon."

The Caterpillar nods. "You're more than half right, Miss Warde."

Presently, the first wicket falls; then the second soon after. And the score is under twenty. The Rev. Septimus is beaming; the Bishop seated beside him looks as if he were about to pronounce a benediction; Charles Desmond is scintillating with wit and good humour. Visions of a single innings victory engross the minds of these three. They are in the front row of the pavilion, and they mean to see every ball of the game.

But soon it becomes evident that a determined stand is being made. Runs come slowly, but they come; the score creeps up—thirty, forty, fifty. Fluff goes on to bowl. On his day Fluff is tricky, but this, apparently, is not his day. The runs come more quickly. The Rev. Septimus removes his hat, wipes his forehead, and replaces his hat. It is on the back of his head, but he is unaware of that. The Bishop appears now as if he were reading a new commination—to wit, "Cursed is he that smiteth his neighbour; cursed is he that bowleth half volleys." The Minister is frowning; things may look black in South Africa, but they're looking blacker in St. John's Wood.

One hundred runs for two wickets.

The Eton cheers are becoming exasperating. A few seats away Warde is twiddling his thumbs and biting his lips. Old Lord Fawley has slipped into the pavilion for a brandy and soda.

At last!

Scaife takes off Fluff and puts on a fast bowler,

changing his own place in the field to short slip. The ball, a first ball and very fast, puzzles the batsman, accustomed to slows. He mistimes it; it grazes the edge of his bat, and whizzes off far to the right of Scaife, but the Demon has it. Somehow or other, ask of the spirits of the air—not of the writer—somehow his wonderful right hand has met and held the ball.

"Well caught, sir; well caught!"

"That boy ought to be knighted on the spot," says Charles Desmond. Then the three generously applaud the retiring batsman. He has played a brilliant innings, and restored the confidence of all Etonians.

The Eton captain descends the steps; a veteran this, not a dashing player, but sure, patient, and full of grit. He asks the umpire to give him middle and leg; then he notes the positions of the field.

"Whew-w-w-w!"

"D——n it!" ejaculates Charles Desmond. Bishop and parson regard him with gratitude. There are times when an honest oath becomes expedient. The Eton captain has cut the first ball into Fluff's hands, and Fluff has dropped it! Alastair Kinloch, from the top of the Trent coach, screams out, "Jolly well muffed!" The great Minister silently thanks Heaven that point is the Duke's son and not his.

And, of course, the Eton captain never gives another chance till he is dismissed with half a century to his credit. Meantime five more wickets have fallen. Seven down for 191! Eton leaves the field with a score of 226 against Harrow's 289. Harrow goes in without delay, and one wicket is taken for 13 runs before the stumps are drawn. Charles Desmond looks at the sky.

"Looks like rain to-night," he says anxiously.

And so ends Friday's play.

The morrow dawned grey, obscured by mist rising from ground soaked by two hours' heavy rain. You may be sure that all our friends were early at Lord's, and that the pitch was examined by thousands of anxious eyes. The Eton fast bowler was seen to smile. Upon a similar wicket had he not done the famous hat-trick only three

The Hill

weeks before? The rain, however, was over, and soon the sun would drive away the filmy mists. No man alive could foretell what condition the pitch would be in after a few hours of blazing sunshine. The Rev. Septimus told Charles Desmond that he considered the situation to be critical, and, although he had read the morning paper, he was not alluding even indirectly to South African affairs. Charles Desmond said that, other things being equal, the Hill would triumph; but he admitted that other things were very far from equal. It looked as if Harrow would have to bat upon a treacherous wicket, and Eton on a sound one.

At half-past ten punctually the men were in the field. Scaife issued last instructions. "Block the bowling; don't try to score till you see what tricks the ground will play. A minute saved now may mean a quarter of an hour to us later." Cæsar nodded cheerfully. The fact that the luck had changed stimulated every fibre of his being. And he said that he felt in his bones that this was going to be a famous match, like that of '85—something never to be forgotten.

Charles Desmond spoke few words while his son was batting. It was a tradition among the Desmonds that they rose superior to emergency. The Minister wondered whether his Harry would rise or fall. The fast bowler delivered the first ball. It bumped horribly. The Rev. Septimus shuddered and closed his eyes. Cæsar got well over it. The third ball was cut for three. The fourth whizzed down—a wide. The fast bowler dipped the ball into the sawdust.

"It isn't all jam for him," whispered the Rev. Septimus.

"Well bowled—well bowled!"

Alas! the middle stump was knocked clean out of the ground. Cæsar's partner, a steady, careful player, had been bowled by his first ball.

Two wickets for 17.

The crowd were expecting the hero, but Fluff was walking towards the wickets, wondering whether he should reach them alive. Never had his heart beat as at this moment. Scaife had come up to him as soon as he had examined the pitch.

"Fluff, I am putting you in early because you are a fellow I can trust. My first and last word is, hit at nothing that isn't wide of the wicket. The ground will probably improve fast."

Fluff nodded. A hive of bees seemed to have lodged in his head, and an active automatic hammer in his heart; but he didn't dare tell the Demon that funk, abject funk, possessed him, body and soul.

The second bowler began his first over. He bowled slows. Desmond played the six balls back along the ground. A maiden over.

And then that thick-set, muscular beast, for so Fluff regarded him, stared fixedly at Fluff's middle stump. Fluff glanced round. The wicket-keeper had a grim smile on his lips, for his billet was no easy one. Cosmo Kinloch at short slip looked as if it were a foregone conclusion that Fluff would put the ball into his hands. Then Fluff faced the bowler. Now for it!

The first ball was half a foot off the wicket, but Fluff let it go by. The second came true enough. Fluff blocked it. The third flew past Fluff's leg, but he just snicked it. Desmond started to run, and then stopped, holding up his hand. Cheers rippled round the ring for the first hit to the boundary. That was a bit of sheer luck, Fluff reflected.

After this both boys played steadily for some ten minutes. Then, very slowly, Cæsar began to score. He had made about fifteen when he drove a ball hard to the on, Fluff backing up. Desmond, watching the travelling ball, called to him to run. It seemed to Desmond almost certain that the ball would go to the boundary. Too late he realized that it had been magnificently fielded. Desmond strained every nerve, but his bat had not reached the crease when the bails flew to right and left.

Out! And run out!

Three wickets for 41!

A quarter of an hour later Fluff was bowled with a yorker. He had made eleven runs, and kept up his wicket during a crisis. Harrow cheered him loudly.

And then came the terrible moment of the morning. Scaife went in when Fluff's wicket fell. The ground had improved, but it was still treacherous. The fast bowler sent down a straight one. It shot under Scaife's bat and spread-eagled his stumps.

The wicket-keeper knows what the Harrow captain said, but it does not bear repeating. Every eye was on his scowling, furious face as he returned to the pavilion; and the Rev. Septimus scowled also, because he had always maintained that any Harrovian could accept defeat like a gentleman. Upon the other side of the ground the Caterpillar was saying to his father, "I always said he was hairy at the heel."

It was admitted afterwards that the Duffer's performance was the one really bright spot in Harrow's second innings. Being a bowler, he went in last but one. It happened that Fluff's brother was in possession of the ball. It will never be known why the Duffer chose to treat Cosmo Kinloch's balls with utter scorn and contempt. The Duffer was tall, strong, and a terrific slogger. Nobody expected him to make a run, but he made twenty in one over—all boundary hits. When he left the wickets he had added thirty-eight to the score, and wouldn't have changed places with an emperor. The Rev. Septimus followed him into the room where the players change.

"My dear boy," he said, "I've never been able to give you a gold watch, but you must take mine; here it is, and—and God bless you!"

But the Duffer swore stoutly that he preferred his own Waterbury.

Eton went in to make 211 runs in four hours, upon a wicket almost as sound as it had been upon the Friday. Scaife put the Duffer on to bowl. The Demon had belief in luck.

"It's your day, Duffer," he said. "Pitch 'em up."

The Duffer, to his sire's exuberant satisfaction, "pitched 'em up" so successfully that he took four wickets for 33. Four out of five! The other bowlers, however, being not so successful, Eton accumulated a hundred runs. The captains had agreed to draw stumps at 7.30. To win, therefore, the Plain must make another hundred in two hours; and three of their crack batsmen were out.

After tea an amazing change took place in the temper of the spectators. Conviction seized them that the finish was likely to be close and thrilling; that the one thing worth undivided attention was taking place in the middle of the ground. As the minutes passed, a curious silence fell upon the crowd, broken only by the cheers of the rival schools. The boys, old and young alike, were watching every ball, every stroke. The Eton captain was still in, playing steadily, not brilliantly; the Harrow bowling was getting slack.

In the pavilion, the Rev. Septimus, Warde, and Charles Desmond were sitting together. Not far from them was Scaife's father, a big, burly man with a square head and heavy, strongly-marked features. He had never been a cricketer, but this game gripped him. He sat next to a world-famous financier of the great house of Neuchatel, whose sons had been sent to the Hill. Run after run, run after run was added to the score. Scaife's father turned to Neuchatel.

"I'd write a cheque for ten thousand pounds," he said, "if we could win."

Lionel Neuchatel nodded. "Yes," he muttered; "I have not felt so excited since Sir Bevis won the Derby."

In the deep field Desmond was standing, miserable because he had nothing to do. No balls came his way; for the Eton captain had made up his mind to win this match with singles and twos. Very carefully he placed his balls between the fielders; very carefully his partner followed his chief's example. No stealing of runs, no scoring off straight balls, no gallery play—till victory was assured.

Poor Lord Fawley retired at this point into an inner room, pulling savagely at his white beard. Old Lyburn, who had been sitting beside him, gurgling and gasping, staggered after him. The Rev. Septimus kept wiping his forehead.

"I can't stand this much longer," said Warde, in a hoarse whisper.

"Well hit, sir! Well hit!"

The Eton cheering became frantic. After nearly an

hour's pawky, uninteresting play, the Eton captain suddenly changed his tactics. His "eye" was in; now or never let him score. A half-volley came down from the pavilion end—a half-volley and off the wicket. The Etonian put all the strength and power he had suppressed so manfully into a tremendous swipe, and hit the ball clean over the ropes.

"Do you want to double that bet?" said Strathpeffer to the Caterpillar. They were standing on the top of the Trent coach.

"No, thanks."

"Give you two to one, Egerton?"

"Done—in fivers."

The unhappy bowler sent down another half-volley. Once more the Etonian smote, and smote hard; but this ball was not quite the same as the first, although it appeared identical. The ball soared up and up. Would it fall over the ropes? Thousands of eyes watched its flight. Desmond started to run. Golconda to a sixpence on the fall! It is falling, falling, falling.

"He'll never get there in time," says Charles Desmond.

"Yes he will," Warde answers savagely.

"He has!" screamed the Rev. Septimus. "He—*has!*"

Pandemonium broke loose. Grey-headed men threw their hats into the air; M.P.'s danced; lovely women shrieked; every Harrovian on the ground howled. For Cæsar held the ball fast in his lean brown hands.

The Eton captain walks slowly towards the pavilion. He has to pass Cæsar on his way, and passing him he pauses.

"That was a glorious catch," he says, with the smile of a gallant gentleman.

And as Harrow, as cordially as Eton, cheers the retiring chieftain, the Caterpillar whispers to Mrs. Verney—

"Did you see that? Did you see him stop to congratulate Cæsar?"

"Yes," says Mrs. Verney.

"I hope Scaife saw it too," the Caterpillar replies coolly. "That Eton captain is cut out of whole cloth; no shoddy there, by Jove!"

And Desmond. How does Desmond feel? It is futile to ask him, because he could not tell you, if he tried. But we can answer the question. If the country that he wishes to serve crowns him with all the honours bestowed upon a favoured son, never, *never* will Cæsar Desmond know again a moment of such exquisite, unadulterated joy as this.

Six wickets down and 39 runs to get in less than half an hour!

Every ball now, every stroke, is a matter for cheers, derisive or otherwise. The Rev. Septimus need not prate of golden days gone by. Boys at heart never change. And the atmosphere is so charged with electricity that a spark sets the firmament ablaze.

Seven wickets for 192.

Eight wickets for 197.

Signs of demoralization show themselves on both sides. The bowling has become deplorably feeble, the batting even more so. Four more singles are recorded. Only ten runs remain to be made, with two wickets to fall.

And twelve minutes to play!

Scaife puts on the Duffer again. The lips of the Rev. Sep are seen to move inaudibly. Is he praying, or cursing, because three singles are scored off his son's first three balls?

"Well bowled—well bowled!"

A ball of fair length, easy enough to play under all ordinary circumstances, but a "teaser" when tremendous issues are at stake, has defeated one of the Etonians. The last man runs towards the pitch through a perfect hurricane of howls. Warde rises.

"I can't stand it," he says, and his voice shakes oddly. "You fellows will find me behind the Pavvy after the match."

"I'd go with you," says the Rev. Septimus, in a choked tone, "but if I tried to walk I should tumble down."

Charles Desmond says nothing. But, pray note the expression so faithfully recorded in *Punch*—the compressed lips, the stern frowning brows, the protruded jaw. The famous debater sees all fights to a finish, and fights himself till he drops.

The Hill

Seven runs to make, one wicket to fall, and five minutes to play!!!

Evidently the last man in has received strenuous instructions from his chief. The bowling has degenerated into that of anaemic girls—and two whacks to the boundary mean—Victory. The new-comer is the square, thick-set fast bowler, the worst bat in the Eleven, but a fellow of determination, a slogger and a run-getter against village teams.

He obeys instructions to the letter. The Duffer's fifth ball goes to the boundary.

Three runs to make and two and a half minutes to play!

The Duffer sends down the last ball. The Rev. Septimus covers his eyes. O wretched Duffer! O thou whose knees are as wax, and whose arms are as chopsticks in the hands of a Griffin! O egregious Duff! O degenerate son of a noble sire, dost thou dare at such a moment as this to attack thine enemy with a—long hop?

The square, thick-set bowler shows his teeth as the ball pitches short. Then he smites and runs. Runs, because he has smitten so hard that no hand, surely, can stop the whirling sphere. Runs—ay—and so does the Demon at cover point. This is the Demon's amazing conjuring-trick—what else can you call it? And he has practised it so often, that he reckons failure to be almost impossible. To those watching he seems to spring like a tiger at the ball. By Heaven! he has stopped it—he's snapped it up! But if he despatches it to the wicket-keeper, it will arrive too late. The other Etonian is already within a couple of yards of the crease. Scaife does not hesitate. He aims at the bowler's wicket towards which the burly one is running as fast as legs a thought too short can carry him.

He aims and shies—instantaneously. He shatters the wicket.

"How's that?"

The appeal comes from every part of the ground.

And then, clearly and unmistakably, the umpire's fiat is spoken—

"Out!"

The Rev. Sep rises and rushes off, upsetting chairs, treading on toes, bent only upon being the first to tell Warde that Harrow has won.

"*Io! Io! Io!*"

Chapter Thirteen

"If I Perish, I Perish"

Since we deserved the name of friends,
  And thine effect so lives in me,
  A part of mine may live in thee
And move thee on to noble ends.

THE cheering at Bill upon the following Tuesday must be recorded, inasmuch as it has, indirectly, bearing upon our story. It will be guessed that the enthusiasm, the uproar, the tumultuous excitement were even greater than on a similar occasion some fifteen years before. But, to his amazement, Desmond, not Scaife, was made the particular hero of the hour. Scaife's display of temper festered in the hearts of boys who can forgive anything sooner than low breeding. The Hill had seen the Etonian stop to speak his cheery word of congratulation to Cæsar, and not the Caterpillar alone, but urchins of thirteen had made comparisons.

Scaife, however, could not complain of his reception upon that memorable Tuesday afternoon; the cheering must have been heard a mile away. But Desmond was acclaimed differently. The cheers were no louder—that was impossible—but afterwards, when the excitement had simmered down, Cæsar became the object of a special demonstration by the Monitors and Sixth Form. Nearly every boy of note in the Upper School insisted upon shaking his hand or patting him on the back. Scaife came up with the others, but he left the Yard almost immediately and retired to his room. He had won the great match; Desmond had saved it; and the School apprehended the subtle difference. More, Scaife knew that John had gone up to Desmond with outstretched hands after the match at Lord's. He could hear John's eager voice, see the flame of admiration in his eyes, as he said, "Oh, Cæsar, I am glad it was you who made that catch!" And with those generous words, with that warm clasp of the hand, Scaife had seen the barrier which he had built between the friends dissolve like ice in the dog-days.

The attention of the Manor was now fixed upon the house-matches. It seemed probable that with four members of the School Eleven in the team, the ancient house must prove invincible. But to John's surprise, as this delightful probability ripened into conviction, Warde betrayed unwonted anxiety and even irritability. Miss Iris confided to Desmond, who paid her much court, that she couldn't imagine what was the matter with papa. And mamma, it transpired (from the same source), really feared that the strain at Lord's had been too much, that her indefatigable husband was about to break down. Finally, John made up his mind to ask a question. He was second in command; he had a right to ask the chief if anything were seriously amiss. Accordingly, he waited upon Warde after prayers.

But when he put his question, and expressed, modestly enough, his anxiety and desire to help if he could, Warde bit his lips. Then he burst out violently—

"I am miserable, Verney."

John said nothing. His tutor rose and began to pace up and down the study; then, halting, facing John, he spoke quickly, with restless gestures indicating volcanic disturbance.

"I'm between the devil and the deep sea," he said, "as many a better man has been before me. I thought I'd wiped out the grosser evils in the Manor, but I haven't—I haven't. Do you know that a fellow in this house, perhaps two of 'em, but one at any rate, is getting out at night and going up to town? You needn't answer, Verney. If you do know it, you are powerless to prevent it, or it wouldn't occur."

"Thank you, sir."

"I can only guess who it is. I am not certain. And to make certain, I must play the spy, creep and crawl, do what I loathe to do—suspect the innocent together with the guilty. It's almost breaking my heart."

204

"I can understand that, sir, after what you have done for us."

Warde smiled grimly. "I don't think you do quite understand," he said slowly. "At this moment I am tempted, tempted as I never have been tempted, to let things slide, to shut both eyes and ears, till this term is over. Next term"—he laughed harshly—" I shan't stand in such an awkward place. The deep sea will always be near me, but the devil—the devil will be elsewhere."

John nodded. His serious face expressed neither approval nor disapproval to the man keenly watching it. Afterwards Warde remembered this impassivity.

"If I do not act"—Warde's voice trembled—" I am damned as a traitor in my own eyes."

John had never doubted that his house-master would act. As for creeping and crawling, can peaks be scaled without creeping and crawling? Never——

"You are not to speak a word of warning," Warde continued vehemently.

"If you know what I don't know yet, still you cannot speak to me, because the sinner in this case is a Sixth-Form boy. You cannot speak to me; and you will not speak to him, on your honour?"

There was interrogation in the last sentence. John replied almost inaudibly—

"I shall not speak—on my honour!"

"It is hard, hard indeed, that I should have to foul my own nest, but it must be so. Good night."

John went back to his room, calm without, terribly agitated within. What ruthless spirit had driven him to Warde's study? Yes; at last, inexorably, discovery, disgrace, the ineffaceable brand of expulsion, impended over the head of his enemy, to whom he was pledged to utter no word of warning. Like Warde, he did not know absolutely, but he guessed that Scaife had spent another riotous night to town since the match. He had read it in the eyes glittering with excitement, in the derisive smile of conscious power, in the magnetic audacity of Scaife's glance. And then he remembered Lawrence's parting words—

"It will be a fight to a finish, and, mark me, Warde will

The Hill

win!"

Two wretched days and nights passed. More than once John spurred himself to the point of going to Warde and saying, "Think what you like of me, I am going to warn the boy I loathe that you are at his heels." Still, always at the last moment he did not go. Some power seemed to restrain him. But when he tried to analyse his feelings, he confessed himself muddled. He had obtained, nay, invited, Warde's confidence; and he dared not abuse it. It was a time of anguish. He was unable to concentrate his mind upon work or play, deprived of sleep, haunted by the conviction that if Desmond knew all, he would turn from him for ever. Then, at the most difficult moment of his life, the way of escape was opened.

Since the match, John and Cæsar had resumed the former unrestrained and continual intimacy and intercourse. John was in and out of Desmond's room, Desmond was in and out of John's room, at all hours. They "found" together, of course, but it is not, fortunately, at meals that boys or men discuss the things nearest to their hearts. But at night, just before lights were turned out, or just after, when an Olympian is privileged to work a little longer by the light of the useful "tolly," Cæsar and Jonathan would talk freely of past, present, and future. It was during these much-valued minutes, or on Sunday afternoons, that John would read to his friend the essays or verses which always fired Desmond's admiration and enthusiasm. To John's intellectual activities Cæsar played, so to speak, gallery; even as John upon many an afternoon had sat stewing in the covered racquet-court, applauding Desmond's service into the corner, or his hot returns just above the line. At home, in the holidays, the boys had always met upon the same plane. Of the two, John was the better rider and shot. Both were members of the Philathletic Club* of Harrow, and the fact that

---

* The Philathletic Club deals primarily with all matters which concern Harrow games; it is also a social club. Distinguished athletes,

... cont'd ...

Desmond was incomparably his superior as an athlete was counterbalanced by John's fine intellectual attainments. If John, at times, wished that he could cut behind the wicket in Cæsar's faultless style, Desmond, on the other hand, spoke enviously of the Medal, or the Essay, or some other of John's successes. John spoke often and well in the Debating Society, getting up his subjects with intelligence and care. So it was give-and-take between them, and this adjusted the balance of their friendship, and without this no friendship can be pronounced perfect.

None the less, free and delightful as this resumption of the old intimacy had been, John knew Cæsar too well not to perceive that between them lay an unmentionable five weeks, during which something had occurred. From signs only too well interpreted before, John guessed that Cæsar was once more in debt to the Demon. And finally, Cæsar confessed that he had been betting, that he had won, following Scaife's advice, and then had lost. The loss was greater than the gain, and the difference, some five and twenty pounds, had been sent to Scaife's bookmaker by Scaife. As before, Scaife ridiculed the possibility of such a debt causing his pal any uneasiness, but it chafed Desmond consumedly.

Upon the Saturday of the semi-final house match, in which the Manor had won a great victory by an innings and twenty-three runs, John went to Desmond's room after prayers. He noticed at once that his friend was unusually excited. John, however, attributed this to Cæsar's big score. Success always inflamed Cæsar, just as it seemed to tranquillize John. John began to talk, but he noticed that Cæsar was abstracted, answered in monosyllables, and twice looked at his watch.

"Have you an appointment, Cæsar?"

"No. What were you saying, Jonathan?"

---

monitors, and so forth, are eligible for membership. The Head of the School is *ex officio* President.

The Hill

"You look rather queer to-night."

"Do I?" He laughed nervously.

"You're not bothering over that debt?"

This time Cæsar laughed naturally.

"Rather not. Why, that debt——" He stopped.

"Is it paid?" said John.

"It will be. Don't worry!"

But John looked worried. He perceived that Cæsar's finely-formed hands were trembling, whenever they were still.

"Harry," said he—he never called Desmond Harry except when they were at home—" Harry, what's wrong?"

"Why, nothing—nothing, that is, which amounts to anything."

"Harry, you are the worst liar in England. Something is wrong. Can't you tell me? You must. I'm hanged if I leave you till you do tell me."

He looked steadily at Desmond. In his clear grey eyes were tiny dancing flecks of golden brown, which Desmond had seen once or twice before,--which came whenever John was profoundly moved. The dancing flecks transformed themselves in Desmond's fancy into sprites, the airy creatures of John's will, imposing John's wishes and commands.

"Scaife said I might tell you, if I liked."

"Scaife?" John drew in his breath. "Then Scaife wanted you to tell me; I am sure of that." He felt his way by the dim light of smouldering suspicion. If Scaife wanted John to know anything, it was because such knowledge must prove pain, not pleasure. John did not say this. Then, very abruptly, Desmond continued, "You swear that what I'm about to tell you will be regarded as sacred?"

"Yes."

"It is a matter which concerns Scaife and me, not you. You won't interfere?"

"No."

"I'm going to London."

"*What?*"

"Don't look at me like that, you silly old ass! It's not—not what you think," he laughed nervously. "I have bet

Scaife twenty-five pounds, the amount of my debt in fact, that the bill-of-fare of to-night's supper at the Carlton Hotel will be handed to him after Chapel to-morrow morning. I bike up to town, and bike back. If I don't go this Saturday, I have one more chance before the term is over. That's all."

"That's all," repeated John, stupefied.

"If you can show me an easier way to make a 'pony,' I'll be obliged to you."

"Scaife egged you on to this piece of folly?"

"No, he didn't."

"You may as well make a clean breast of it."

Bit by bit John extracted the facts. Behind them, of course, stood Scaife, loving evil for evil's sake, planting evil, gleaning evil, deliberately setting about the devil's work. Desmond, it appeared, had persuaded Scaife not to go to town till the Lord's match was over. Since the match Scaife had spent two nights in London, whetting an inordinate appetite for forbidden fruit; exciting in Desmond also, not an appetite for the fruit itself, but for the mad excitement of a perilous adventure. Then, when the thoughtless "I'd like a lark of that sort" had been spoken, came the derisive answer, "You haven't the nerve for it." And then again the subtle leading of an ardent and self-willed nature into the morass, Scaife pretending to dissuade a friend, entreating him to consider the risk, urging him to go to bed, as if he were a headstrong child. And finally Desmond's challenge, "Bet you I have the nerve," and its acceptance, protestingly, by the other, and permission given that John should be told.

"And it's to-night?"

"I mean to have that bill-of-fare. Do you think I'd back out now?"

In his mind's eye, our poor John was gazing down a long lane with no turning at the end of it. Could he make his friend believe that Scaife had brought this thing to pass from no other motive than wishing to hurt mortally an enemy by the hand of a friend? No, never would such an ingenuous youth as Cæsar accept, or even listen to, such an abominable explanation.

"Good night," said John.

The Hill

"I see you're rather sick with me, Jonathan. Remember, you made me speak. To-morrow morning we'll have a good laugh over it. We'll walk to the Haunted House, and I'll tell my tale. I shall be on my way in less than an hour."

John went back to his room. The necessity for silence and thought had become imperative. What could he do? It was certain that Warde was waiting and watching. He had inexhaustible patience. Desmond, not the Demon, would be caught and expelled. John returned to Desmond's room.

"You've told me so much," he said; "tell me a little more. How are you going to do it?"

"To do what?"

"Get out of the house? Get a bike—and all that?"

"Easy. Lovell went out that way, and others. You jump from the sill of the first landing window into the horse-chestnut. One must be able to jump, of course; but I can jump. Then you shin down the tree, nip through the shrubbery, and over the locked wicket-gate."

"Yes," John said slowly, "over the gate."

"I borrowed a bike from one of the Cycle Corps, and have hidden it in the garden, in a bush to the right of the gate."

John nodded.

"It's moonlight after ten; I shall enjoy the ride immensely."

"You will try to get back into the house at night?"

"Too dangerous. Lovell did it; but the Demon marches in boldly just before Chapel. He may have slipped out on half a dozen errands as soon as the door is opened in the morning. I shall sleep under a stack. It's a lovely night. Now, old Jonathan, I hope you're satisfied that I'm not either the fool or the sinner you took me to be.

"Look here, Harry. If I appeal to you in the name of our friendship; if I ask you for my sake and for my mother's sake not to do this thing——"

"Jonathan, I must go. Don't make it harder than it is."

"Then it is hard?"

"I won't whine about that. I courted this adventure, and, by Jove! I'm going to see it through. The odds are a hundred to one against my being nailed."

"All right; I'll say no more. Good night."

"Good night, old Jonathan."

John went back to his room, waited three minutes, and then, in despair, made up his mind to seek Scaife. He felt certain that the Demon's extraordinary luck was about to stand between him and expulsion. Desmond would be caught red-handed, but not he. John ground his teeth with rage at the thought. He found Scaife alone—at work on cricketing accounts.

"Hullo, Verney!"

"Cæsar tells me that he is going up to London to-night."

"Oh, he told you that, did he?"

"Yes; you wished him to tell me?"

"Perhaps." Scaife laughed louder.

"You want to prove to me," said John, slowly, "that you are the stronger?"

"Perhaps." Scaife laughed.

"Well, if I surrender, if I admit that you are the stronger, that you have defeated me, won't that be enough?"

"Eh? I don't quite take you."

"You are the stronger." John's voice was very miserable. "I have tried to dissuade him, as you knew I should try, and I have failed. Isn't that enough? You have your triumph. But now be generous. Turn round and use your strength the other way. Make him give up this folly. You don't want to see your own pal—sacked?"

"Precious little chance of that!"

"There is the chance."

Scaife hesitated. Did some worthier impulse stir within him? Who can tell? His keen eye softened, and then hardened again.

"No," he said quickly. "If I agree to what you propose, it is, after all, you who triumph, not I. And I doubt if I could stop him now, even if I tried." He laughed again, for the third time, savagely. "You are hoist with your own petard, Verney. You wanted to see me sacked; and now that there is a chance in a thousand that Cæsar will be sacked, you squirm. I swore to get my knife into you, and, by God, I've done it."

John went out, very pale. He passed through into the private side, and tapped at Warde's study door. Mrs. Warde's voice bade him enter. She looked at John's face. Afterwards she testified that he looked singularly cool and self-possessed.

"I wish to see Mr. Warde," he said.

"He's dining at the Head Master's."

"Will he be in soon?"

"I—er—don't know. Perhaps not. I wouldn't wait for him, Verney, if I were you."

"Thank you," said John. "Good night."

He went back to his room. Mrs. Warde's eyes had read—what? Excitement? Apprehension? Suddenly, conviction came to him that this dinner at the Head Master's was a blind. Why, during that very afternoon, Warde had mentioned casually to Scaife that he was dining out. He had deliberately informed the Demon that the Coast was dear. And at this moment, probably, Warde lay concealed near the chestnut tree, waiting, watching, about to pounce upon the—wrong man!

The temptation to cry *"Cave!"* tore at his vitals. Till this moment the tyranny of honour had never oppressed John. Having resolved to tell Warde that he meant to break his word, it may seem inexplicable that he shouldn't go a step further and break his word without warning the house-master. Upon such nice points of conscience hang issues of world-wide importance. To John, at any rate, the difference between the two paths out of a tangled wood was greater than it might appear to some of us. Warde had trusted him implicitly: could he bring himself to violate Warde's confidence without giving the man notice?

However, what he might have done under pressure must remain a matter of surmise. At this moment a third path became visible. And down it John rushed, without consideration as to where it might lead. The one thing plain at this crisis was the certainty that he had discovered a plan of action which would save two things he valued supremely—his friendship for Cæsar and his word of honour.

Here we are at liberty to speculate what John would have done had he considered dispassionately the consequences of an action to be accomplished at once or not at all. But he had not time to consider anything except the fact that action would put to rout some very tormenting thoughts.

He crumpled his bed, disarranged his room, and put on a cap and a thin overcoat, as all lights in the boys' side of the Mandi were extinguished. Then he stole out of his room, and crept to the window at the end of the passage. A moment later, he had squeezed through it, and was standing upon the sill outside, gazing fearfully at the void beneath, and the distance between the sill and the branch in front of him. Afterwards, he confessed that this moment was the most difficult. He was an active boy, but he had never jumped such a chasm. If he missed the bough——

To hesitate meant shameful retreat. John felt the sweat break upon him; craven fear clutched his heart-strings, and set them a-jangling.

He jumped.

The ease with which he caught the branch was such a physical relief that he almost forgot his errand. He slid quietly down the tree, pausing as he reached the bottom of it. The moon was just rising above the horizon, but under the trees the darkness was Stygian. John pushed quietly through the shrubberies, treading as lightly as possible. Every moment he expected to see the flash of a lantern, to hear Warde's voice, to feel an arresting hand upon the shoulder. It was quite impossible to guess with any reasonable accuracy what part of the garden Warde had selected for a hiding-place. Very soon he reached the edge of the shrubbery, and gazed keenly into the moonlit, park-like meadow below him. Peer as he might, he could see no trace of Warde. A dozen trees might conceal him. Perhaps with the omniscience of the house-master, he had divined that the wicket-gate was the ultimate place of egress. Perhaps the wicket had been used for a similar purpose when Warde himself was a boy at the Manor. It was vital to John's plan that Warde should see him without recognizing him, and give chase. The chase would end in capture at some point as reasonably far from the Manor as possible. Warde might ask for explanations, but none would be forthcoming till the morrow. Meantime, the coast would be clear for Desmond. John, in fine, was playing the part of a pilot-engine.

But where was Warde?

The question answered itself within a minute, and after a fashion absolutely unforeseen. As John was crossing from the shrubbery to the wicket he looked back. To his horror, he saw lights in the boys' side, light in the window of Scaife's room. Instantly John divined what had come to pass, and cursed himself for a fool. Warde, from some coign of vantage, had seen a boy leave his house. Why should he try to arrest the boy? why should he risk the humiliation of running after him, and, perhaps, failing to capture him? No, no; men forty were not likely to work in that boyish fashion. Warde had adopted an infinitely better plan. Assured that a boy had left the house, he had nothing to do but walk round the rooms and find out which one was absent. He had begun with Scaife. Next to Scaife was the room belonging to the Head of the House; then came John's room, and then Cæsar's. Long before Warde reached Cæsar's room, Cæsar would have heard him. Cæsar, at any rate, was saved. John crept back under cover of the shrubberies. He saw the light flicker out of Scaife's window, and shine more steadily in the next room. The window of this room was open, and John could hear the voice of Warde and the Head of the House. John waited. And then the light shone in Desmond's room. John crouched against the wall, trembling. If Cæsar had not heard the voices, if he were fully dressed, if——Suddenly he caught Warde's reassuring words: "Ah, Desmond, sorry to disturb you. Good night."

John waited. Very soon Scaife would come to Desmond's room. Ah! Just so. The night was so still that he could hear quite plainly the boys' muffled voices.

"What's up?"

"Warde is going his rounds. Perhaps he smells a rat."

And then whispers! John strained his ears. Only a word or two more reached him. "Verney——D—d interfering sneak! Let's see!" It was Scaife who was speaking.

John heard his own door opened and shut. Scaife, then, had discovered his absence, and naturally leaped to the conclusion that he had warned Warde. Let him think so! The boys were still whispering together. "Not to-night," Scaife said decisively. "No, no," Desmond replied.

John wondered what remained to be done. Warde, of course, would satisfy himself that no boy in his house was missing except John, before he pronounced him the absentee. Poor Warde! This would be a hard knock for him. John's thoughts were jostling each other freely, when he recalled Desmond's words: "I have one more chance before the term is over." He had wished to clear the way for his friend, not to block it. Then he remembered the terms of the bet, and laughed.

He ran back to the wicket, found the bicycle, lit the lamp, and hoisted the machine over the gate. Then he laughed again. After all, this escaping from bondage, this midnight adventure beneath the impending sword of expulsion, thrilled him to the marrow.

When John returned on Sunday to the Manor, shortly after the doors were unlocked in the morning, he found Dumbleton awaiting him. Dumber's face expressed such amazement and consternation that John nearly laughed in spite of himself.

"It's all hup, sir," said the butler. Only in moments of intense excitement did Dumber misplace or leave out the aspirate. "You're to come with me at once to Mr. Warde's study."

John followed the butler into the familiar room. Warde was not down yet, but evidently Dumber had instructions not to leave the prisoner. John stared at the writing-desk. Then he turned to Dumbleton, and said carelessly—

"This means the sack, eh, Dumber?"

"Yes, sir. 'Ow could you do it, sir? Such a well-be'aved gentleman too!"

"Thank you, Dumber." John took an envelope from the desk, and wrote Scaife's name upon it.

"Dumber, please give Mr. Scaife this—with my compliments. It is, as you see, a bill of fare."

"Very good, sir."

John placed the card into the envelope and handed both to Dumbleton.

"With my compliments!"

"Certainly, sir."

"And *after* Chapel."

"Yes, sir."

A moment later Warde came in. Dumbleton went out immediately with a sorrowful, backward glance at John. The good fellow looked terribly bewildered. For John's face, John's deportment, had amazed him. John was quite unaware of it, but he looked astonishingly well. Excitement had flushed his cheek and lent a sparkle to his grey eyes. He had enjoyed his ride to town and back; he had slept soundly under the lee of a haystack; and he had washed his face and hands in the horse-trough at the foot of Sudbury Hill. And the certainty that Desmond was safe, that in the end he, John, had triumphed over Scaife, filled his soul with joy. Warde, on the other hand, looked wretched; he had passed a sleepless night; he was pale, haggard, gaunt.

"What have you to say, Verney?"

"Nothing, sir."

"Nothing." Warde clenched his hands, and burst into speech, letting all that he had suffered and suppressed escape in tumultuous words and gestures. "Nothing. You dare to stand there and say—nothing. That you should have done this thing? Why, it's incredible! And I who trusted you. And you listened to me with a face like brass, laughing in your sleeve, no doubt, at the fool who betrayed himself. And you came here, so my wife tells me, to see if I was out of the way, if the coast was clear. And you were cool as a cucumber. Oh, you hypocrite, you damnable hypocrite! I have to see you now, but never again will I look willingly upon your face, never! Well, this wretched business must be ended. You got out of my house last night. You heard I was dining with the Head Master. I returned early, and I saw you jump from the passage window. You don't deny that you went up to London, I suppose?"

"No, sir; I don't deny it."

At the moment John, quite unconsciously, looked as if he were glorying in what he had done. Warde could have struck his clean, clear face, unblushingly meeting his furious glance. In disgust, he turned his back and walked to the window. John felt rather than saw that his tutor was profoundly moved. When he turned, two tears were trickling down his cheeks. The sight of them nearly undid John. When Warde spoke again, his voice was choked by his emotion.

"Verney," he said, "I spoke just now in an unrestrained manner, because you—you"—his voice trembled—" have shaken my faith in all I hold most dear. I say to you—I say to you that I believed in you as I believe in my wife. Even now I feel that somehow there is a mistake—that you are not what you confess yourself to be—a brazen-faced humbug. You have worked as I have worked for this House, and in one moment you undo that work. Have you paused to think, what effect this will have upon the others?"

"Not yet, sir."

John looked respectfully sympathetic. Poor Warde! This was rough indeed upon him.

Suddenly the door was flung open, and Desmond burst into the room, with a complete disregard of the customary proprieties, and rushed up to Warde.

"Sir," he said vehemently, "Verney did this to save— *me!*"

Warde saw the slow smile break upon John's face. And, seeing it, he came as near hysterical laughter as a man of his character and temperament can come. He perceived that John, for some amazing reason, had played the scape-goat; that, in fact, he was innocent—not a humbug, not a hypocrite, not a brazen-faced sinner. And the relief was so stupendous that the tutor flung himself back into a chair, gasping. Desmond spoke quietly.

"I was going to town, sir. For the first time, I swear. And only to win a bet, and for the excitement of jumping out of a window. John tried to dissuade me. When he exhausted every argument, he went himself."

"The Lord be praised!" said Warde. He had divined

everything; but he let Desmond tell the story in detail. Scaife's name was left out of the narrative.

Then Warde said slowly, "I shall not refer this business to the Head Master; I shall deal with it myself. For your own sake, Desmond, for the sake of your father, and, above all else, for the sake of this House, I shall do no more than ask you to promise that, for the rest of your time at Harrow, you will endeavour to atone for what has been."

All boys worth their salt are creatures of reserves; let us respect them. It is easy to surmise what passed between the friends—the gratitude, the self-reproach, the humiliation on one side; the sympathy, the encouragement and shy, restrained affection on the other. A bitter-sweet moment for John this, revealing, without disguise, the weakness of Desmond's character, but illuminating the triumph over Scaife, the all-powerful. John had been inhuman if this knowledge had not been as spikenard to him.

Chapel over, the boys came pouring back into the house. In a minute the fags would be hurrying up with the tea and the jam-pots, asking for orders; in a minute Scaife would rush in with questions hot upon his lips. John chuckled to himself as he heard Scaife's step.

"Hullo, Cæsar! Why did you cut Chapel? And——"

John saw that the Carlton supper-card was in his hand. He chuckled again.

"Dumber has just given me—*this*. Did you go, after all?" he asked Cæsar. They had not met since Warde's visit of the night before.

"I didn't go," said Cæsar.

"Dumber gave it to me, with Verney's compliments."

"You've lost your bet," said John.

"But how?"

"Jonathan went to town instead of me," said Desmond. "We thought he was with Warde—he wasn't. This morning, early, I found out that he hadn't slept in his bed. I saw him come back, and I saw Dumber waiting for him. When Dumber came out of Warde's room, he told me that Jonathan had been up to town, and was going to be—sacked."

He blurted out the rest of the story, to which Scaife listened attentively. When Desmond finished, there was a pause.

"You're devilish clever," said Scaife to John.

"I shall pay up the pony," said Desmond.

"No, you won't," said Scaife. "As for the money, I never cared a hang about that. I'm glad—and you ought to know it—that you've won the bet. All the same, Verney isn't entitled to all the glory that you give him."

"He is, he is—and more, too."

Scaife laughed. John felt rather uncomfortable. Always Scaife exhibited his amazing resource at unexpected moments.

"Never mind," Scaife continued, "I won't burst the pretty bubble. And I admit, remember, Verney's cleverness."

He was turning to go, but Desmond clutched his sleeve. When he spoke his fair face was scarlet.

"You sneer at the wrong man and at the wrong time," he said angrily, "and you talk as though I was a fool. Well, I am a fool, perhaps, and I blow bubbles. Prick this one, if you can. I challenge you to do it."

Scaife shrugged his shoulders. "It's so obvious," he said coolly, "that your kind friend ran no risks other than a sprained ankle or a cold."

"What do you mean?"

"He was certain that you would come forward. He forced your hand. There was never the smallest chance of his being sacked, and he knew it."

"Yes," said John, calmly, "I knew it."

"Just so," said Scaife. He went out whistling.

Desmond had time to whisper to John before the fags called them to breakfast in John's room—

"I say, Jonathan, I'm glad you knew that I wouldn't fail you. As the Demon says, you are clever; you are a sight cleverer than he is."

John shook his head. "I'm slow," he said. "As a matter of fact, the thought that you would come to the rescue never occurred to me till I was hiking back from town."

"Anyway, you saved me from being sacked, and as

The Hill

long as I live I——"

"Come on to breakfast," said John.

Chapter Fourteen

Good Night

Good night! Sleep, and so may ever
    Lights half seen across a murky lea,
Child of hope, and courage, and endeavour,
    Gleam a voiceless benison on thee!
        Youth be bearer
            Soon of hardihood;
        Life be fairer,
            Loyaller to good;
Till the far lamps vanish into light,
Rest in the dreamtime. Good night! Good night!

THE last Saturday of the summer term saw the Manor cock-house at cricket: almost a foregone conclusion, and therefore not particularly interesting to outsiders. During the morning Scaife gave his farewell "brekker"* at the Creameries; a banquet of the Olympians to which John received an invitation. He accepted because Desmond made a point of his so doing; but he was quite aware that beneath the veneer of the Demon's genial smile lay implacable hatred and resentment. The breakfast in itself struck John as ostentatious. Scaife's father sent quails, à la Lucullus, and other delicacies. Throughout the meal the talk was of the coming war. At that time most of the Conservative papers poohpoohed the possibility of an appeal to arms, but Scaife's father, admittedly a great authority on South African affairs, had told his son a fight was inevitable. More, he and his friends were already preparing to raise a regiment of mounted infantry. At breakfast Scaife announced this piece of news, and added that in the event of hostilities he would

---

* Brekker, *i.e.* breakfast.

join this regiment, and not try to pass into Sandhurst. And he added that any of his friends who were present, and over eighteen years of age, were cordially invited to send in their names, and that he personally would do all that was possible to secure them billets. The words were hardly out of his mouth, when Cæsar Desmond was on his feet, with an eager—

"Put me down, Demon; put me down first!"

And then Scaife glanced at John, as he answered— "Right you are, Cæsar, and if things go well with us, I fancy that we shall get our commissions in regular regiments soon enough. The governor has had a hint to that effect. Let's drink success to 'Scaife's Horse.'"

The toast was drunk with enthusiasm.

During the holidays, John saw nothing of Desmond, although they wrote to each other once a week. John was reading hard with an eye to a possible Scholarship at Oxford; Desmond was playing cricket with Scaife. Later, Desmond went to the Scaife moor in Scotland. John noted that his friend's letters were full of two things only: sport, and the ever-increasing probability of war. At the end of August John Verney, the explorer, returning to Verney Boscobel after an absence of nearly four years, began to write his now famous book on the Far East. Then John learned from his mother that his uncle had borne all the charges of his education. When he thanked him, the uncle said warmly—

"You have more than repaid me, my dear boy; not another word, please, about that. Warde tells me they expect great things of you at Oxford."

Uncle and nephew were alone, after dinner. John had noticed that the hardships endured in Manchuria and Tibet had left scars upon the traveller. His hair was white, he looked an old man; one whose wanderings in wild places must perforce come soon to an end.

"Uncle," said John. "I want to chuck Oxford."

"Eh?"

"I should like to go into the Army."

"Bless my soul!"

The explorer eyed his nephew with wrinkled brow. John gave reasons; we can guess what they were. The prospect of war had set all ardent souls afire.

"I must think this over, my boy," the uncle replied presently. "I must sleep on it. Have you told your mother?"

"No; I counted upon you to persuade her."

"Um. Now tell me about Lord's! Ah! I'm sorry I missed that match."

Next day, his uncle said nothing of what lay next to John's heart, but the pair rode together over the estate. During that ride it became plain to the young man that his uncle had no intention of settling down. Once or twice, in the driest, most matter-of-fact tone, the elder spoke as if his heir were likely to inherit soon. Finally, John blurted out a protest—

"But, uncle, you are a strong man. Why do you talk as if—as if——" the boy couldn't finish the phrase.

"Tut, tut," said the uncle. "I know what I know;" and he fell into silence.

Not till the evening, after Mrs. Verney had gone to bed, did the man of many wanderings speak freely.

"John," said he, quietly, "I have a story to tell you. Years ago, your father and I fell in love with the same girl. She married the better man." He paused to fill a pipe: John saw that his uncle's fingers trembled slightly; but his voice was cool, measured, almost monotonous. "I made my first expedition to Patagonia. When I came back you were just born; and I asked that I might be your godfather. I went to Africa after the christening. And six years later your father died. I think he had the purest and most unselfish love of the poor and helpless that I have ever known. He wore away his life in the service of the outcast and forlorn. And before he died, he expressed a wish that you should work as he did, for others, but not in precisely the same way. He knew, none better, the limitations imposed upon a parson. He prayed that you might labour in a field larger than one parish. And I promised him that I would do what I could when the time came. It has come—to-night. In my opinion, in Warde's opinion, in your dear mother's opinion, Parliament is the place for you. You will be sufficiently well off. Take all Oxford can give you, and then try for the House of

Commons. Charles Desmond will make you one of his Private Secretaries. I have spoken to him. You have a great career before you."

"But if war breaks out, uncle——"

"War *will* break out. Don't misunderstand me! If you are wanted out there, and the thing is going to be very serious, if you are wanted, you must go; but decidedly you are not wanted yet. And you are an only son; all your mother has. John, you must think of her, and you will think of her, I know."

The conviction in his quiet voice communicated itself to his nephew. There was a pause of nearly a minute; and then John answered, in a voice curiously like his uncle's—

"All right."

Verney senior held out his hand. "I knew you would say that," he murmured.

On the 18th of September, when John returned to the Hill, the country had just learned that the proposals of the Imperial Government to accept the note of August 19 (provided it were not encumbered by conditions which would nullify the intention to give substantial representation to the Uitlanders) had not been accepted. That this meant war, none, least of all a schoolboy, doubted. Desmond could talk of nothing else. He told John that his father had promised to let him leave Harrow before the end of the term, if war were declared. The Demon, so John was informed, had made already preparations. He was taking out his three polo ponies, and had hopes of being appointed Galloper to a certain General. Scaife's Horse was being organized, but in any case would not take the field before several months had elapsed; the Demon intended to be on the spot when the first shot was fired.

To all this gunpowder-talk John listened with envious ears and a curious sinking of the heart. He had looked forward to having Desmond to himself; and lo! his friend was seven thousand miles away—on the veldt, not on the Hill.

"You are not keen," said Desmond.

On the day of the Goose Match, Saturday, September 30th, Scaife came down to Harrow to take leave of his friends. Already, John noted an extraordinary difference in his manner and appearance. He treated John to a slightly patronizing smile, called him Jonathan, asked if he could be of service to him, and posed most successfully as a sort of sucking Alexander.

That he absorbed Desmond's eyes and mind was indisputable. Everything outside South Africa, and in particular the Hill and all things thereon, dwindled into insignificance. Scaife made Desmond a present of the very best maps obtainable, and nailed them on the wall above the mantelpiece, pulling down a fine engraving which John had given to Desmond about a year before. Desmond uttered no protest. The engraving was bundled out of sight behind a sofa.

And after Scaife's departure, Desmond talked of him continually, and always with enthusiasm. Warde added a note or two to the chorus.

"This is an opportunity for Scaife," he told John. "He may distinguish himself very greatly, and the discipline of the camp will transmute the bad metal into gold. War is an alchemist."

Upon the 11th of October war was declared.

After that, Desmond became as one possessed. He went about saying that he pitied his father profoundly because he was a civilian and a non-combatant. Warde wrote to Charles Desmond; "If you mean to send Harry out, send him at once. He's fretting himself to fiddlestrings, doing no work, and causing others to do no work also."

Sir William Symons' victory and death followed, and then the mortifying retreat of General Yule. Upon the 30th day of the month eight hundred and fifty officers and men were isolated and captured. Who does not remember the wave of passionate incredulity that swept across the kingdom when the evil tidings flashed overseas? But Buller and his staff were on the *Dunottar Castle*, and all Harrovians believed devoutly that within a month of landing the Commander-in-Chief would drive the invaders back and conquer the Transvaal.

The Hill

Day after day, Desmond importuned his father. The "fun" would be over, he pointed out, before he got there—and so on. At last word came. A billet had been obtained. Desmond received a long envelope from the War Office. He showed it to all his friends, old and young. Duff junior—Cæsar's fag—became so excited that he asked Warde for permission to enlist as a drummer-boy. The School cheered Cæsar at four Bill.

And then came the parting.

Cæsar was to join the Headquarters' Staff as soon as possible. He spent the last hours with John, but his mind, naturally enough, was concentrated upon his kit. He chattered endlessly of saddlery, revolvers, sleeping bags, and Zeiss' glasses. John packed his portmanteau. And on the morrow the friends parted at the station without a word beyond—

"Good-bye, old Jonathan. Wish you were coming."

"Good-bye, Cæsar. Good luck!"

And then the shrill whistle, the inexorable rolling of the wheels, the bright eager face leaning far out of the window, the waved handkerchief, the last words; "So long!" and John's reply, "So long!"

John saw the face fade; the wheels of the vanishing train seemed to have rolled over his heart; the scream of the engine was the scream of anguish from himself. He left the station and ran to the Tower. There, after the first indescribable moments, some kindly spirit touched him. He became whole. But he had ceased to be a boy. Alone upon the tower he prayed for his friend, prayed fervently that it might be well with him, now and for ever—Amen.

When he returned to the Manor, however, peace seemed to forsake him. The horrible gap, ever-widening, between himself and Desmond, might indeed be bridged by prayer, but not by the shouts of boys and the turmoil of a Public School.

During the rest of the term he worked furiously. Desmond was now on the high seas, whither John followed him at night and on Sundays. Warde, guessing, perhaps, what was passing in John's heart, talked much of Desmond, always hopefully. From Warde, John learned that Charles Desmond had tried to dissuade his favourite son from becoming a soldier.

"He wanted him to go into Parliament," said Warde.

John nodded.

"It was a disappointment. Yes; a great disappointment. Harry would have made a debater. Yes; yes; a nimble wit, an engaging manner, and the gift of the gab. And the father would have had him under his own eye."

"But he wanted to go to South Africa from the beginning."

"You wanted to go," said Warde; "your uncle told me so. It was a greater thing for you, John, to stand aside."

And then John put a question. "Do you think that Harry ought to have stood aside too?"

Warde, however, unwilling to commit himself, spoke of Harry's ardour and patriotism. But at the end he let fall a straw which indicated the true current of his thoughts—

"Mr. Desmond is very lonely."

John swooped on this.

"Then you think, you do think, that Harry should have stayed behind?"

"Perhaps. One hesitates to accuse the boy of anything more than thoughtlessness."

"If he wished to serve his country," began John, warmly.

Warde smiled. "Yes, yes," he assented. "Let us believe that, John; but there has been too much cheap excitement."

Dark days followed. Who will ever forget Stormberg and Magersfontein? A pall seemed to hang over the kingdom. Ladysmith remained in the grip of the invader; the Boers were not yet driven out of Natal. Meantime Cæsar had reached Sir Redvers Buller. A letter to his father, describing the few incidents of the voyage out, and his arrival in South Africa, was sent on to John and received by him on the 1st of February. "John will understand," said Cæsar, in a postscript, "that I have little time for writing." But John did not understand. He wrote regularly to Desmond; no answer came in return

At the end of the Christmas holidays John returned to Harrow. He was now Head of his House, and very nearly

The Hill

Head of the School. The weeks went by slowly. Soon, he and a few others would travel to Oxford for their examination; there would be the strenuous excitement of competition, and the final announcement of success or failure. To all this John told himself that he was lukewarm. Nothing seemed to matter since he had lost sight of Cæsar's face, since the train whirled his friend out of his life. But he worked hard, so hard that the Head Master bade him beware of a breakdown.

The hour of triumph came. John had gratified his own and Warde's ambition; he was a Scholar of Christ Church. And this well-earned success seemed to thaw something in his heart. The congratulations, the warm hand-clasps, the generous joy of schoolfellows not as fortunate, restored his moral circulation. A whole holiday was granted in honour of his success at Oxford. He told himself that now he would take things easy and enjoy himself. The clouds in South Africa were lifting, everybody said the glorious end was in sight. And so far Desmond had escaped wounds and sickness. He had received a commission in Beauregard's Irregular Horse; in the five days' action about Spion Kop he behaved with conspicuous gallantry. Scaife, having obtained his billet of Galloper, was with a General under Lord Methuen.

On the last Monday but one in the term, John was entering the Manor just before lock-up, when a Sixth Form boy from another house passed him, running.

"Have you heard about poor Scaife?" he called out.

"No—what?"

"Warde will tell you; he knows." The boy ran on, not wishing to be late.

John ran too with his heart thumping against his side. He felt certain, from the expression upon the boy's face, that Scaife was dead. And John recalled with intense bitterness and humiliation moments in past years when he had wished that Scaife would die. Charles Desmond had told him only three weeks before that his Harry hoped to join the smart cavalry regiment in which a commission had been promised to Scaife. At that moment John was sensible of an inordinate desire for anything that might come between this wish and its fulfilment. And now, Scaife might be lying dead.

He found Warde in his study staring at a telegram. He looked up as John entered, and in silence handed him the message.

"Demon dead. Died gloriously."

The telegram came from an Harrovian, an old Manorite at the War Office.

John sat down, stunned by the news; Warde regarded him gravely. John met his glance and could not interpret it. Presently, Warde said nervously—

"Why did the fellow write 'Demon' instead of 'Scaife'? I don't like that." He looked sharply at John, who did not understand. Then he added, "I've wired for confirmation. There may be a—mistake."

"What mistake?" said John. Warde's manner confused him, frightened him. "What mistake, sir?"

Warde, twisting the paper, answered miserably—

"There has been an action, but not in Scaife's part of Africa. Beauregard's Horse were engaged and suffered severely. And would anyone say 'Demon' in such a serious context?"

"Oh, my God!" said John, pale and trembling. At last he understood. Add two letters to "Demon" and you have "Desmond." How easily such a mistake could be made!— "Desmond," ill-written, handed to an old Manorite to copy and despatch.

"It's Scaife—it's Scaife," John cried.

Warde said nothing, staring at the thin slip of paper as if he were trying to wrest from it its secret.

"Everybody called him 'Demon,'" said John.

"Still, one ought to be prepared."

For many hideous minutes they sat there, silent, waiting for the second telegram. Dumbleton brought it in, and lingered, anxiously expectant; but Warde dismissed him with a gesture. As the door closed, Warde stood up.

"If our fears are well founded," he said solemnly, "may God give you strength, John Verney, to bear the blow."

Then he tore open the envelope and read the truth—

The Hill

"Henry Desmond killed in action."

"No," said John, fiercely. "It is Scaife, Scaife!"

Warde shook his head, holding John's hand tight between his sinewy fingers. John's face appalled him. He had known, he had guessed, the strength of John's feeling for Desmond, but he had not known the strength of John's hatred of Scaife. And Desmond had been taken—and Scaife left. The irony of it tore the soul.

"Don't speak," commanded Warde.

John closed his lips with instinctive obedience. When he opened them again his face had softened; the words fell upon the silence with a heartrending inflection of misery.

"And now I shall never know—I shall never know."

He broke down piteously. Warde let the first passion of grief spend itself; then he asked John to explain. The good fellow saw that if John could give his trouble words it would be lightened enormously. He divined what had been suppressed.

"What is it that you will never know, John?"

At that John spoke, laying bare his heart. He gave details of the never-ending struggle between Scaife and himself for the soul of his friend; gave them with a clearness of expression which proved beyond all else how his thoughts had crystallized in his mind. Warde listened, holding John's hand, gripping it with sympathy and affection.

The romance of this friendship stirred him profoundly; the romance of the struggle for good and evil; a struggle of which the issues remained still in doubt; a romance which Death had cruelly left unfinished—this had poignant significance for the house-master.

"I shall never know now," John repeated, in conclusion.

"But you have faith in your friend."

"He never wrote to me," said John.

At last it was out, the thorn in his side which had tormented him.

"If he had written," John continued, "if only he had written once. When we parted it was good-bye—just that, nothing more; but I thought he would write, and that everything would be cleared up. And now, silence."

The week wore itself away. A few details were forthcoming: enough to prove that a glorious deed had been done at the cost of a gallant life. England was thrilled because the hero happened to be the son of a popular Minister. The name of Desmond rang through the Empire. John bought every paper and devoured the meagre lines which left so much between them. It seemed that a certain position had to be taken—a small hill. For the hundredth time in this campaign too few men were detailed for the task. The reek of that awful slaughter on Spion Kop was still strong in men's nostrils. Beauregard and his soldiers halted at the foot of the hill, halted in the teeth of a storm of bullets. Then the word was given to attack. But the fire from invisible foes simply exterminated the leading files. The moment came when those behind wavered and recoiled. And then Desmond darted forward—alone, cheering on his fellows. They were all afoot. The men rallied and followed. But they could not overtake the gallant figure pressing on in front. He ran— so the Special Correspondent reported—as if he were racing for a goal. The men staggered after him, aflame with his ardour. They reached the top, captured the guns, drove down the enemy, and returned to the highest point to find their leader—shot through the heart, and dead, and smiling at death. Of all the men who passed through that blizzard of bullets he was the youngest by two years.

Warde told John that the Head Master would preach upon the last Sunday evening of the term, with special reference to Harry Desmond. Could John bear it? John nodded. Since the first breakdown in Warde's study, his heart seemed to have turned to ice. His religious sense, hitherto strong and vital, failed him entirely. He abandoned prayer.

Evensong was over in Harrow Chapel. The Head Master, stately in surplice and scarlet hood, entered the pulpit, and, in his clear, calm tones, announced his text, taken from the 17th verse of the first Chapter of the Book

The Hill

of Ruth—

"The Lord do so to me, and more also, If aught
but death part thee and me."

The subject of the sermon was 'Friendship': the
heart's blood of a Public School: Friendship with its
delights, its perils, its peculiar graces and benedictions.

"To-night," concluded the preacher, amid the breathless silence of the congregation, "this thought of
Friendship has for us a special solemnity. It is
consecrated by the memory of one whom we have just
lost. You, who are leaving the school, have been the
friends and contemporaries of Henry Julius Desmond; his
features are fresh in your memories, and will remain
fresh as long as you live.

Tall, eager, a face to remember,
  A flush that could change as the day;
A spirit that knew not December,
  That brightened the sunshine of May.

"Those lines, as you know, were written of another
Harrovian, who died here on this Hill. Henry Desmond
died on another hill, and died so gloriously that the
shadow of our loss, dark as it seemed to us at first, is
already melting in the radiance of his gain. To die young,
clean, ardent; to die swiftly, in perfect health; to die
saving others from death, or worse—disgrace—to die
scaling heights; to die and to carry with you into the fuller
ampler life beyond, untainted hopes and aspirations,
unembittered memories, all the freshness and gladness of
May—is not that cause for joy rather than sorrow? I say—
yes. Henry Desmond is one stage ahead of us upon a
journey which we all must take, and I entreat you to
consider that, if we have faith in a future life, we must
believe also that we carry hence not only the record of our
acts, whether good or evil, but the memory of them; and
that memory, undimmed by falsehood or self-deception,
will create for us Heaven or Hell. I do not say—God
forbid!—that you should desire death because you are

232

still young, and, comparatively speaking, unspotted from the world; but I say I would sooner see any of you struck down in the flower of his youth than living on to lose, long before death comes, all that makes life worth the living. Better death, a thousand times, than gradual decay of mind and spirit; better death than faithlessness, indifference, and uncleanness. To you who are leaving Harrow, poised for flight into the great world of which this school is the microcosm, I commend the memory of Henry Desmond. It stands in our records for all we venerate and strive for: loyalty, honour, purity, strenuousness, faithfulness in friendship. When temptation assails you, think of that gallant boy running swiftly uphill, leaving craven fear behind, and drawing with him the others who, led by him to the heights, made victory possible. You cannot all be leaders, but you can follow leaders; only see to it that they lead you, as Henry Desmond led the men of Beauregard's Horse, onward and upward."

The preacher ended, and then followed the familiar hymn, always sung upon the last Sunday evening of the term:—

Let Thy father-hand be shielding
  All who here shall meet no more;
May their seed-time past be yielding
  Year by year a richer store;
    Those returning,
  Make more faithful than before.

The last blessing was pronounced, and with glistening eyes the boys streamed out of Chapel; some of them for the last time.

Upon the next Tuesday, John travelled down into the New Forest. April was abroad in Hampshire; the larches already were bright green against the Scotch firs; the beech buds were bursting; only the oaks retained their drab winter's-livery.

During the few days preceding Easter Sunday, John rode or walked to every part of the forest which he had visited in company with his dead friend. At Beaulieu, standing in the ruins of the Abbey, he could hear

The Hill

Desmond's delightful laugh as he recited the misadventures of Hordle John; at Stoneycross he sat upon the bank overlooking the moor, whence they had seen the fox steal into the woods about Rufus's Stone; at the Bell tavern at Brook they had lunched; at Hinton Admiral they had played cricket.

To his mother's and his uncle's silent sympathy John responded but churlishly. His friend had departed without a word, without a sign; that ate into John's heart and consumed it. For the first time since he had been confirmed, he refused to receive the Sacrament. He went to church as a matter of form; but he dared not approach the altar in his present rebellious mood.

Again and again he accused himself of having yielded to a craven fear of offending Desmond by speech too plain. Always he had been so terribly afraid of losing his friend; and now he had lost him indeed. This poignancy of grief may be accounted for in part by the previous long-continued strain of overwork. And it is ever the habit of those who do much to think that they might have done more.

At the beginning of May, John came back to the Hill, for his last term. Out of the future rose the "dreaming spires" of Oxford; beyond them, vague and shadowy, the great Clock-tower of Westminster, keeping watch and ward over the destinies of our Empire.

In a long letter from Charles Desmond, the Minister had spoken of the secretaryship to be kept warm for him, of the pleasure and solace the writer would take in seeing his son's best friend in the place where that son might have stood.

His best friend? Was that true?

The question tormented John. Because Cæsar had been so much to him, he desired, more passionately than he had desired anything in his life, the assurance that he had been something—not everything, only something—to Cæsar.

One day, about the middle of the month, John had been playing cricket, the game of all games which brought Cæsar most vividly to his mind. Then, just before six Bill, he strolled up the Hill and into the Vaughan Library,

234

where go many relics dear to Harrovians are enshrined. Sitting in the splendid window which faces distant Hampstead, John told himself that he must put aside the miseries and perplexities of the past month. Had he been loyal to his friend's memory? Would not a more ardent faith have burned away doubt?

John gazed across the familiar fields to the huge city on the horizon. Soon night would fall, darkness would encompass all things. And then, out of the mirk, would shine the lamps of London.

Warde's voice put his thoughts to instant flight. Some intuition told John that something had happened. Warde said quietly—

"A letter has come for you in Harry Desmond's handwriting."

John, unable to speak, stretched out his hand.

"Take it," said Warde, "to some quiet spot where you cannot be disturbed."

John nodded.

"I have seen how it was with you," Warde continued, with deep emotion, "and you have had my acute sympathy, the more acute, perhaps, because long ago a friend went out of my life without a sign." Warde paused. "Now, unless my whole experience is at fault, you hold in your hand what you want—and what you deserve."

Warde left the library; John put the letter into his pocket. Where should he go? One place beckoned him. Upon the tower, looking towards the Hill, he would read the last letter of his friend.

Within half an hour he was passing through the iron gates. He had not visited the garden since that forlorn winter's afternoon, when he came here, alone, after bidding Desmond good-bye. He could recall the desolation of the scene: bleak Winter dripping tears upon the tomb of Summer. With what disgust he had perceived the decaying masses of vegetation, the sodden turf, the soot upon the bare trunks of the trees. He had rushed away, fancying that he heard Desmond's voice.

"There is a curse on the place."

Now, May had touched what had seemed dead and hideous, and, lo! a miracle. The hawthorns shone white

235

The Hill

against the brilliant green of the laurels; the horse-chestnuts had—to use a fanciful expression of Cæsar's—"lit their lamps." Out of the waving grass glimmered and sparkled a thousand wild flowers. John heard the glad *Frühlingslied* of bees and birds. Then, opening his lungs, he inhaled the life-renewing odours of earth renascent; opening his heart he felt a spiritual essence pervading every fibre of his being. Once more the chilled sap in his veins flowed generously. It was well with him and well with his friend. This conviction possessed him, remember, before he opened the letter.

He ascended the tower, and broke the seal.

"I have been meaning to write to you, dear old chap, ever since we parted; but, somehow, I couldn't bring myself to tackle it in earnest till to-night. To-morrow, we have a thundering big job ahead of us; the last job, perhaps, for me. Old Jonathan, you have been the best friend a man ever had, the only one I love as much as my own brothers—*and even more*. It was from knowing you that I came to see what good-for-nothing fools some fellows are. You were always so unselfish and *straight*; and you made me feel that I was the contrary, and that you knew it, and that I should lose your friendship if I didn't improve a bit. So, if we don't meet again in this jolly old world, it may be a little comfort to you to remember that what you have done for a very worthless pal was not thrown away."

"Good night, Jonathan. I'm going to turn in; we shall be astir before daybreak. Over the veldt the stars are shining. It's so light, that I can just make out the hill upon which, I hope, our flag will be waving within a few hours. The sight of this hill brings back our Hill. If I shut my eyes, I can see it plainly, as we used to see it from the tower, with the Spire rising out of the heart of the old school. I have the absurd conviction strong in me that, to-morrow, I shall get up the hill here faster and easier than the other fellows because you and I have so often run up our Hill together—God bless it—and you! Good night."

THE END

236

Printed in Great Britain
by Amazon.co.uk, Ltd.,
Marston Gate.